T0150064

FIGHTING
THE DEVIL IN DIXIE

ALSO BY WAYNE GREENHAW

NONFICTION

A Generous Life: W. James Samford (2009)

The Thunder of Angels: The Montgomery Bus Boycott and the People Who Broke the Back of Jim Crow with Donnie Williams (2006)

My Heart Is in the Earth: True Stories of Alabama and Mexico (2001)

Alabama: A State of Mind (2000)

Beyond the Night: A Remembrance (1999)

Alabama: Portrait of a State (1998)

Montgomery: The Biography of a City (1993)

Montgomery: Center Stage in the South with Kathy Holland (1990)

Alabama on My Mind (1987)

Flying High: Inside Big-Time Drug Smuggling (1984)

Elephants in the Cottonfields: Ronald Reagan and the New Republican South (1981)

Watch Out for George Wallace (1976)

The Making of a Hero: Lt. William Calley and the My Lai Massacre (1971)

NOVELS

The Long Journey (2002)

King of Country (1994; revised edition 2004)

Hard Travelin' (1972)

The Golfer (1968)

SHORT FICTION

The Spider's Web: A Novella and Stories (2003)

Tombigbee and Other Stories (1992)

POETRY

Ghosts on the Road: Poems of Alabama, Mexico and Beyond (2007)

DRAMA

The Spirit Tree: F. Scott & Zelda Fitzgerald in Montgomery

Rose: A Southern Lady

FIGHTING
THE DEVIL IN DIXIE

HOW CIVIL RIGHTS ACTIVISTS
TOOK ON THE KU KLUX KLAN IN ALABAMA

★

WAYNE GREENHAW

Lawrence Hill Books

Library of Congress Cataloging-in-Publication Data

Greenhaw, Wayne, 1940-
  Fighting the devil in Dixie : how civil rights activists took on the Ku Klux
Klan in Alabama / Wayne Greenhaw.
    p. cm.
  Includes bibliographical references and index.
  ISBN 978-1-56976-345-2 (hardcover)
  1. African Americans—Civil rights—Alabama—History—20th century.
2. Alabama—Race relations—History—20th century. 3. Ku Klux Klan
(1915–)—Alabama—History. I. Title.
  E185.615.G687 2011
  323.1196'0730761—dc22

                                                      2010030114

Interior design: Jonathan Hahn

Published by Lawrence Hill Books
An imprint of Chicago Review Press, Incorporated
814 North Franklin Street
Chicago, Illinois 60610
ISBN 978-1-56976-345-2
Printed in the United States of America
5 4 3 2 1

In memory of our friends

IRMA FEGAS, STAN RICHMAN,
TOM CORK, AND CLAUDE DUNCAN

Ain't nobody gonna turn me 'round,
I'll keep a-walkin', I'll keep a-talkin',
Marching up to freedom land.

—"Marching up to Freedom Land"

O, deep in my heart,
I do believe,
We shall overcome some day.

—"We Shall Overcome" by Reverend Charles
Tindley with Guy Carawan and Pete Seeger

CONTENTS

AUTHOR'S NOTE

I look back on a world suffering from racial schizophrenia.

In the aftermath of the federal court's ruling that ended legal segregated public education, most white adults in my home state of Alabama were silent while a small minority rode nightly, terrorizing black people, bombing houses and churches, castrating and killing. The silent whites simply demanded that their children go to school, come home, and stay out of trouble.

But there was another reaction to the violence. That story is a long and twisting road through emotional hills and hollows. As it moves around curves and through unseen pitfalls, we see the number of black attorneys in Alabama increase from four to five, six to seven, and more. As the roads become bumpy and dangerous, a few Southern white attorneys blossom in Alabama and fight the good fight next to their African American brothers and sisters.

Fighting the Devil in Dixie is the story of these people and their struggle.

PREFACE

DEATH ON THE HIGHWAY: A RECOLLECTION

My own parents never condoned violence and admonished their children to be good, law-abiding citizens. Still, we grew up in a segregated world decorated with WHITE ONLY and COLORED ONLY signs in places of public convenience.

As a boy, I watched my own kin march in a parade in their Ku Klux Klan gowns and pointed hoods. I listened to racist stories told around a midnight campfire. I recorded many of those gruesome tales in memory.

Several days before my sixteenth birthday I saw an angry mob screaming and shouting in protest when a young woman attempted to become the first black student at the University of Alabama.

For more than ten years, from the summer of 1965 until the spring of 1976, I covered politics and civil rights for the *Alabama Journal*, Montgomery's afternoon newspaper. I also wrote columns for the Sunday *Advertiser-Journal*, a combination of the morning and afternoon newspapers owned by the same company. During that time I was also a stringer for the *New York Times*, *Time* magazine, and numerous other publications.

Beginning in the summer of my twenty-fifth year, I covered marches in Montgomery and throughout central Alabama. One afternoon in

Prattville, about fifteen miles northwest of Montgomery, I got out of my car on a downtown street where African American marchers were gathered. For the first time, I carried my new camera. As I headed down the sidewalk, a petite elderly white woman approached me. As she neared, she snarled, "You a Yankee photographer, down here causing trouble." Suddenly she began beating me with a very large purse. A policeman stepped between us and told the woman to leave. Never again did I carry my camera to a demonstration. After that incident I had much more respect for the photographers who covered civil rights in the South.

About a year after I started reporting for the *Journal*, I received a telephone call early on a Sunday morning. The caller would not identify himself. "There's been a killing up here in Elmore County. This killing took place a few hours ago on the side of Highway 231. A white deputy sheriff hit a black man over the head. I saw it. Blood spurted everywhere. They took him to the Elmore County jail, but he was already dead when they got him there."

On Monday morning I repeated the conversation to my editor. When I finished, he asked two or three pertinent questions. I had no answers but made notes. After several preliminary calls I discovered that a black man on leave from the U.S. Army had died early Sunday. Authorities in the sheriff's department said that James Earl Motley, who had been arrested by deputy sheriff Harvey Connor and charged with public intoxication and resisting arrest, died after sustaining lacerations to the head in a fall from the second-deck bunk in the county jail.

I soon interviewed family members and others who had been riding in the car that had been stopped on U.S. 231 about ten miles northeast of Montgomery and several miles southwest of Wetumpka. The arrest occurred a few minutes after 1:00 A.M. Sunday. A girlfriend and another rider said that the deputy hit Motley over the head with a billy club. Motley fell to his knees next to the deputy's car. Then the deputy and a state trooper shoved Motley into the backseat.

Later on Monday, my friend Norman Lumpkin, a young black reporter with radio station WRMA, reported the bare facts. A dedicated and hardworking journalist, Lumpkin had come to Montgomery from

Atlanta. He had learned broadcast journalism from a correspondence course and put it to work using street smarts and long hours. That afternoon we decided to share whatever we found. We compared notes.

When bullyboy whites in positions of authority attempted to push him around, Lumpkin would appear backward and untrained. He was anything but; he was a savvy journalist. When a white lawman snapped at him, he would stumble over words I had heard him pronounce easily and perfectly only moments earlier. One evening that week, as we were driving to a black district outside Wetumpka, I asked him about his performance when a deputy had questioned him harshly. He grinned. "They like to think we're stupid," he said. "If they think it, they know I don't know anything they don't know. Then they talk a lot more. And my tape recorder is always on."

On Tuesday I wrote a story from our interviews with Motley's family and friends. It told about a young black man born and raised in Elmore County. He went to school in segregated institutions and worked for local businesses before he joined the army. Home on leave after a tour of duty in Vietnam, he had been having a good time with friends at a jazz joint north of Montgomery before the car in which he was riding was pulled over on the highway. He ended up in the Elmore County jail, where he was found dead on the floor on Sunday morning.

By Thursday I had been up two nights in a row, interviewing a number of people including three men who agreed to meet in a honky-tonk. One was my original source. He delivered the *Alabama Journal* and the *Montgomery Advertiser* to subscribers in Wetumpka and rural Elmore County. The other two had been keeping him company that Sunday morning while he was waiting for the newspapers at an all-night service station on the side of the highway near the Tallapoosa River bridge. All three told me they had seen the deputy strike Motley, witnessed him and a trooper shove a bleeding Motley into Connor's car, and followed the law enforcement officers back to the jail, where all three watched from a nearby hillside as the deputy and the trooper carried Motley into the jail. "The black man looked as limp as a dishrag," one of the men said.

On Thursday morning I wrote, "Three white men told the *Journal* they saw a white Elmore County deputy sheriff beat a black man over the head with a club, that the black man began bleeding, and they saw the deputy carry the man's body into the Elmore County jail less than an hour later. 'He looked like he was dead,' one witness said."

It was important that the witnesses, although unnamed, were identified as white. Prior to this story, all witnesses quoted had been black. During this time of racial tension, with demonstrations almost daily and nightly in downtown Montgomery, it appeared to many that the death was a black-versus-white issue. Now there were white witnesses.

By the end of the day, white readers across Montgomery were quoting the article and nodding their heads.

On Friday I was handed a subpoena requiring that I appear before an Elmore County coroner's inquest on Saturday morning in a veterinarian's office northeast of Wetumpka.

As I walked into the room on Saturday morning, sheriff Lester Holley, a stone-faced veteran law enforcement officer who had been "the law" in Elmore County for more than thirty years, gazed at me with steely eyes. Next to him sat the rotund deputy, Harvey Connor, who had been accused by my unnamed witnesses of hitting Motley. And behind a desk sat the coroner. As I looked at each of them, my stomach knotted.

"Have a seat, boy, and answer some questions for me," Holley growled.

I said that I could not tell them the names of the persons I had quoted in my article.

Holley looked around the room and then back at me. "Now, boy, there ain't nobody else in here but us four folks, so it don't matter none what you tell us. You tell, and we won't tell anybody you told." He grinned. "You know what I mean?"

With my hands shaking, I shook my head and read aloud the Alabama law that stated a reporter's source is sacred and secret.

"Aw, now, boy, we don't need all that. You just nod if I mention the name of the fellow who told you." He called out several names.

I looked into his face without moving.

"I know you want to cooperate with us," Sheriff Holley said. "You look like a good citizen. All we want is to get at the bottom of all this foolishness. There's a bunch of niggers lying to beat the band, and my deputy here is getting hurt by all this stuff. I've been sheriff a long time, and I'm not going to run again. I just don't need all this stuff."

I said nothing.

They didn't arrest me.

As I was leaving, Sheriff Holley followed. Outside, he said, "I just want you to know that I know who the sons of bitches are." He chuckled, turned, and walked back into the office.

Lumpkin interviewed me for his radio newscast. Now, because I had been questioned behind closed doors, I was a part of the story.

Back in Montgomery, I sat at my desk alone on Saturday afternoon and wrote a first-person story about the coroner's inquest for Sunday's *Advertiser-Journal*.

During the following week, after district attorney Upshaw G. Jones presented the case to the Elmore County grand jury, the eighteen all-white, all-male jurors brought a no bill, failing to indict Connor for a crime. However, the same afternoon, a federal grand jury in Montgomery brought charges against the deputy for violating the civil rights of James Earl Motley under color of the law, that is, while Connor was acting as a law enforcement officer.

Several months later, the deputy was tried. Witness after witness testified against the defendant. The state trooper who had answered his radio that night told about the deputy's hitting Motley. "When he hit the man, what did you do?" the lawyer asked. The trooper's eyes watered. "What did you do?" the lawyer asked again.

"I turned away," he answered, his voice quivering.

Deputy Sheriff Connor took the stand and testified almost word for word what the three white witnesses had told me earlier.

Standing in the roadside service station at about 1:00 A.M., he saw "a car full of niggers going too fast up the highway."

On the first toe hill of the Appalachians, he pulled the car over and called for help.

James Earl Motley was in the backseat with a black woman.

All four people in the car, the deputy said, had been drinking.

When Connor asked the driver to step outside, Motley "wised off," Connor said. Motley got out of the car and walked toward the deputy, who pulled his billy club from his belt. It was a six-inch piece of leather into which a bar of lead had been stitched.

When Motley talked back, Connor said, "I told him, 'Nigger, keep your mouth shut!' and when he reached out to grab a hold of me, I hit him across the head."

Motley fell to his knees, he said, then reached up. When hit again, Connor said, Motley began bleeding.

With the help of the state trooper, he put Motley into his car, where he bled more. At the jail, the two law enforcement officers carried Motley inside and put him in a cell.

During the night, he said, Motley rolled off the bunk and hit the top of his head on the concrete floor.

Asked if he sought any medical help for Motley, the deputy said he didn't think Motley was badly hurt.

After an hour of deliberations, the jury found the deputy innocent.

That evening I told friends, including *New York Times* reporter Gene Roberts and *Los Angeles Times* reporter Jack Nelson and my editor, Ray Jenkins, that I felt I had done all the work for nothing. Roberts said, "No, you made the price of killing a black man mighty high in Alabama. I bet it'll be a while before another deputy sheriff does what that one did. He got off, but it cost him a lot of money."

I came away from those stories with a great friend. Norman Lumpkin and I covered several other civil rights stories together. He went up North for a while, reporting for a big city radio station. A few years later he telephoned on a Sunday morning. I met him downtown at the Greyhound bus station. He had just arrived. We had coffee while he said, "Guess what I'm going to be doing?" I shrugged and sipped. "I'm going to be WSFA's token."

WSFA-TV was the NBC affiliate and Montgomery's largest and most powerful television station. Norman was its first black reporter. But he was nobody's token. Doing investigative stories from Capitol Hill to the halls of industry, he distinguished himself as one of the finest journalists in Alabama. He never gave up working diligently, seeking the facts and the ultimate truth.

★

Not long after the Motley stories and trial ended, I was unlocking the door to my tiny apartment on College Street late one night when an attacker smashed me across the head with a blunt object. After a night in the hospital, where I was treated for a concussion, my editor at the *Journal* said it might be best if I moved.

I moved into a roomy apartment in an antebellum mansion called Winter Place on the edge of a mostly black section of Montgomery. It was an interesting place with crimson velvetlike wallpaper and huge rooms with high ceilings, and it was rumored to be haunted. Its owner said F. Scott Fitzgerald had actually met his future wife, Zelda Sayre, in the living room. Zelda had lived with her family about three blocks away on Pleasant Avenue.

About four blocks from Winter Place was the Laicos (*social* spelled backward) Club, a nightclub that looked like an old movie theater. I had met the owner-manager soon after starting to work for the *Journal*. Roscoe Williams was a charming, handsome, hardworking man who was also Dr. Martin Luther King Jr.'s best friend. His wife, Mary Lucy, was Coretta Scott King's best friend and had been visiting with Mrs. King and her less-than-two-month-old baby in January 1956 when the Ku Klux Klan bombed the front porch of the parsonage on South Jackson Street. Roscoe operated one of the town's most successful electric companies, wiring most of the houses in Old Cloverdale owned by well-to-do whites. On Friday, Saturday, and Sunday nights he managed the Laicos, to which he invited me and my friends. There we heard some of the best performers in the country: rhythm-and-blues artists from everywhere from Detroit to New Orleans. Otis Redding sang "(Sittin' On) the Dock of the Bay." B. B. King played blues guitar and growled out the numbers he had written through the years. Tina Turner took the stage one night and sang "Proud Mary." Blind soul singer Clarence Carter's "Patches" was like an anthem in the place. Late one Saturday night Wilson Pickett, who was born in nearby Prattville, showed up and sat at the table with me and Roscoe and Mrs. Williams. He talked about how life on the road was changing for black entertainers. "At least in some places up North, like Detroit, you can find a good place to eat and sleep and go to the bathroom." At the stroke of twelve, with a microphone in hand, he stepped under the light of a single spot and sang "In the Midnight Hour."

✩

In 1969, Morris Dees filed a suit he styled *Cook v. Advertiser Company*. Neither my managing editor, Jenkins, nor I were very secret in our delight. For years, Jenkins had been urging the publisher to shut down the Negro News page. When a black couple brought their wedding photo and announcement to the society office of the *Advertiser* and filled out all the proper forms, instead of running it in the Sunday society section, the editor would turn it over to E. P. Wallace, who wrote the Negro News, before putting it into my box for final editing and layout.

Even after Dees filed the suit our editor-in-chief, Harold E. Martin, a stubborn and hard-nosed journalist who had cut his teeth as a troubleshooter for I. E. Newhouse Newspapers after graduate studies at Syracuse University in upstate New York, refused to do away with the separate and unequal black section. He said he was damned if Dees was going to tell him how to run the newspaper, even if it did embarrass some reporters and editors.

In the meantime, Martin hired two former investigators who had retired from the Alabama Department of Public Safety to work out of his office. With the help of other reporters, they uncovered a commercial scheme that used state prisoners in drug experimentation. We also showed that the private laboratory, located in north Montgomery, collected blood plasma from prisoners and sold it through pharmaceutical firms. As a result, the Advertiser Company won its second Pulitzer Prize in 1970. This one was for investigative reporting. The first, awarded to Grover Cleveland Hall in 1928, was for editorial writing that protested gangsterism, flogging, and the racial and religious intolerance of the Ku Klux Klan.

Before a ruling was handed down in *Cook v. Advertiser Company*, Harold Martin's young son was killed in an automobile accident near Washington, D.C. That night Martin telephoned Jenkins and told him to print Negro obituaries in the column that included his son's obit. That ended the Negro News page. Although the federal court found that the 1964 Civil Rights Act did not prohibit such discrimination, we never again published separate news.

✯

As a reporter for the *Alabama Journal* I was privileged to know some of the best and some of the worst. I spent hours listening to George C. Wallace as he recounted the days when he ruled Alabama government. I sat on a pier overlooking the Choctawhatchee Bay with my friend Charles Morgan Jr., who left Birmingham to become the finest civil rights lawyer in the South. I watched Morris Dees and Joseph Levin try cases in Montgomery Circuit Court before they founded the Southern Poverty Law Center. I met Bill Baxley in the spring of 1963, and we became good friends long before he was elected attorney general and prosecuted the bomber of the Sixteenth Street Baptist Church. And I rode with Orzell Billingsley Jr. through the Black Belt and listened to his stories about his and J. L. Chestnut's exploits as young attorneys in the late 1950s.

My first years of reporting for the *Journal* put me directly into the trenches of the civil rights movement. It also put me into position to get up close and personal with Dr. Martin Luther King Jr., Edgar Daniel Nixon, Clifford and Virginia Durr, and many others. During those years I got to know personally and professionally a group of young people who came south to show us how civil rights journalism should be accomplished. Many of these editors, reporters, and photographers of the *Southern Courier* became my friends. We played together at the Laicos and worked together across central Alabama. I watched and I read, and my respect and admiration for them grew almost daily.

In this story of how civil rights prevailed over white-on-black violence in Alabama, the people I knew during my days and years at the *Journal* play a prominent part.

—Wayne Greenhaw
Rosemary, Montgomery, Alabama
Casa Naranja, San Miguel de Allende, Mexico

FIGHTING
THE DEVIL IN DIXIE

1

WILLIE'S FIRST DAY

On the morning of January 23, 1957, Willie Edwards Jr. and his family had many reasons to be happy. He had worked hard and gotten a raise. Today he would make his first trip as a truck driver for Hudson-Thompson, delivering supplies to Winn-Dixie, the largest supermarket chain in the Southeast. Edwards would drive from the warehouse in north Montgomery to Talladega in east-central Alabama, stopping along the way at every little town on his route.

Willie Edwards Jr., known affectionately to his family as Mookie, had witnessed many changes taking place in his world over the past year.

More than a year earlier, on Thursday night, December 1, 1955, a small-built black seamstress named Rosa Parks refused to give up her seat on a Montgomery city bus to a white man. Parks was arrested and charged with violating the city's ordinance requiring segregated seating on buses. Bailing Parks out of jail that night was Edgar Daniel Nixon, a Pullman car porter who had been leading voter registration drives in Alabama's capital city for decades and who had served as state president of the National Association for the Advancement of Colored People. It had been Nixon's dream that a courageous and steadfast black person would refuse to sit in the back of the bus, be arrested, and challenge the segregation law.

On Sunday morning following Parks's arrest, black preachers told their congregations that there would be a boycott of the buses. On

Monday morning, the buses were empty. Later that morning Parks was found guilty in city court. Representing her was attorney Fred D. Gray. Standing by her side was Nixon. She appealed the ruling.

On Monday afternoon a meeting of local black leaders formed the Montgomery Improvement Association and elected the Reverend Martin Luther King Jr., the twenty-six-year-old minister at the Dexter Avenue Baptist Church, its president.

That night a mass meeting was held at the Holt Street Baptist Church, where Reverend King spoke for the first time as the leader of the new movement, telling more than a thousand people that it was time to use "the tools of justice" to bring about a "day of freedom, justice, and equality." His voice rose to the rafters as he challenged: "We must stick together and work together if we are to win—and we will win by standing up for our rights as Americans."

That was the first of many mass meetings throughout a year when a legal battle in U.S. District Court filed by Gray, *Browder v. Gayle*, ended in the U.S. Supreme Court ruling that the local ordinance requiring segregation was unconstitutional.

In December 1956, little more than a month later, the town's black leaders—Reverend King, Parks, Nixon, Reverend Ralph David Abernathy, and a few out-of-town white ministers—stepped onto a legally integrated Montgomery City Lines bus for the first time.

During the yearlong boycott there had been a distinct change in the manner in which black people carried themselves in Montgomery. They no longer walked on city sidewalks with their heads hanging, gazing downward, afraid to look into a white person's face, dragging their feet as though they were plowing a field behind a tired mule. They held their heads high, squared their shoulders, picked up their feet and put them down in a cadence, like they knew exactly where they were going and what they were going to do when they got there.

★

Although he was far from a leader of his people, Willie Edwards Jr. felt like he was moving up in his world. For the past few months, Edwards had worked in the yard of Hudson-Thompson's wholesale warehouse on Jackson Ferry Road in north Montgomery. If he worked hard and tended to the customers on his route, soon he would be making enough to move his family out of the dirt-poor section of west Montgomery where they lived in a four-room, unpainted clapboard with no under-pinning. They would find a place far from Rice Street, where the shacks were built forty years ago by the Gulf, Mobile & Ohio Railroad for its workers. He told it all to his daddy, Willie Edwards Sr., who expressed pride in his son.

As he prepared to leave, Willie Jr. told Sarah Jean, pregnant with their third child, that he would be late coming home that day. The dispatcher had warned that his first day would be a long one.

As Edwards stepped into the cold outdoors, pulling his heavy green jacket around his body and his old gray felt hat down to his ears, he took his new cigarette lighter from his work pants. He was proud of the lighter that Sarah Jean had given him on Christmas morning. As the door closed behind him, he lighted an unfiltered cigarette.

In a pocket of low-lying land between downtown and the Alabama River known as Ward Five, the Little Kitchen on Jefferson Street was the regular meeting place for a group of white men.

Raymond C. Britt Jr. was a twenty-seven-year-old salesman for a flooring store. Britt sat at the large round table in the Little Kitchen every morning, talking with his fellow members of the secret society of the Ku Klux Klan about what they would be doing and where they would be going that night. Here, they felt their importance, believing the white community of Montgomery depended on the Klan to keep the black revolutionists, the Communist intruders, the Jewish hordes, and any other ethnic outsiders from taking over the world as they knew it. Their duty, they believed, was to protect the "Southern way of life."

James D. "Jimmy" York was a veteran of World War II. He worked for Montgomery's street department, drove a city truck and heavy road-building equipment, and took time off for a coffee break every morning. In Europe, he had fought under the command of general George S. "Ol' Blood and Guts" Patton, and he bragged that he had killed more Italians than Germans in the war.

As they sat together, they waited for another Klansman, Henry Alexander, who had called ahead that he had "some important news."

Above the table, an image of Jesus hung on the yellowed wall next to a framed notice: WE RESERVE THE RIGHT TO REFUSE SERVICE TO ANYONE— THE MANAGEMENT.

Ray Harrelson had operated the Little Kitchen since the end of the war. He lived next door on the corner of Jefferson and Hull, where he ran an on-again, off-again, all-night poker game upstairs.

The Little Kitchen was a half-dozen blocks from the center of town near the Court Square fountain at the western end of six-lane Dexter Avenue. Six blocks to the east, sitting high on Goat Hill, was the state capitol, with its snow-white dome and its bronze star, where nearly one hundred years earlier Jefferson Davis took the oath of office as president of the Confederate States of America.

The Little Kitchen sat in the middle of Ward Five, within shouting distance of the two-story frame house where singer-songwriter Hank Williams lived as a teenager before he became a world-famous troubadour. Two blocks to the north was the notorious Pollard Street, where, until the end of World War II, African American prostitutes catered to white clientele in houses of ill repute.

Montgomery was a proud old historic town. It was called the River City, located on a wide bend of the Alabama River that carried cotton grown on the area's plantations to the Gulf of Mexico. From the city's beginning, adventurous roughneck frontiersmen worked hard by day. At night, they drank and fought in the taverns that outnumbered churches ten-to-one in Montgomery's first decade.

In the early 1880s, African American slaves were brought into the region to work the vast plantations that surrounded the town up and down the river. Soon the black population outnumbered the whites two-to-one. But by the mid-twentieth century, blacks were in a slight minority. A significant number who had been born and raised in south Alabama had migrated north after World War II. Very few who remained could vote, and none held public office. The men who gathered at the Little Kitchen wanted to keep them powerless.

Since its incorporation in 1819, the same year Alabama became a state, this section of Montgomery had flooded seasonally after heavy rains in the spring and the fall. Oftentimes the river flooded its banks, and when the water receded it left knee-deep puddles of mud. When cotton wagons lined up along Commerce Street, waiting their turn to be loaded onto the steamboats after the fall harvest, boles and hulls blew off and settled in the puddles. The waste rotted and stank, and by the late 1820s the town lost half its population to what an early inhabitant, M. P. Blue, described as "a most malignant type of bilious remittent and intermittent fever." As a result, white residents moved up the hill to the south.

African American slaves stayed in the area north of Ward Five known as Newtown, where they lived next to stables in which they tended livestock for their white owners. As late as the 1860s, Thomas Calhearne, a journalist with the *Charleston Mercury* who had been sent to Montgomery to cover the beginnings of the Confederate government, described the town as "a pig sty, if there ever was one. Very few self-respecting swine in this day and time live under the conditions of our Confederate capital after a downpour. When the streets of the downtown outside the hotel where I am lodged become soaked with rain, it is a shame the conditions of travel. Large puddles stand like lakes and backwaters of the Carolina Low Country. But Charleston and its environs have never seen the size of mosquitoes like the ones that swarm around the poor livestock that try to traverse these streets. Commerce Street on which I stay—only a short walk to the Executive Offices of the Confederacy, or a short wade through mud and debris, for the menace of the filth is beyond compare—is like a dump outside Poor Town or the stench outside privies of most towns' slave sections."

By the mid-1950s, the area in and around Ward Five had been filled with gravel and covered with dirt. It still flooded when the river's banks overflowed, but it drained relatively quickly and did not smell as it had in the nineteenth century.

On the block west of the Little Kitchen was Tom Suitt's barber shop and the place where W. E. Robinson once sold groceries before he sold out to Tine Davis, a short, fat man with a high-pitched, squeaky voice who founded the Winn-Dixie supermarket chain that later covered the South and made Davis a multimillionaire. Halfway down the block, Ralph "Coots" McGehee, who claimed to be a full-blooded Creek Indian, kept a shaggy hound in the front yard. Few black people ever walked through Ward Five. If they did, McGehee's dog growled and howled and strained against its chains.

In mid-twentieth-century Montgomery, it was no secret that these so-called good old boys were members of the local klavern of the Ku Klux Klan. In the Little Kitchen, people talked openly about being card-carrying members. In 1957, numerous white Montgomerians even bragged about being members of the White Citizens Council, the States Rights Party, and the Knights of the Ku Klux Klan. Each member of the KKK was required to fill out a membership application stating "I believe in the ideals of Western, Christian Civilization and Culture and in the great people that created them, and in the Constitution of the United States. I am a White person of gentile descent. I believe in the aims and objectives of the Knights of the Ku Klux Klan. I swear that I will keep secret and confidential any information I receive in quest of membership." The application was always signed and dated and included the applicant's address, phone number, birth date, and occupation, along with his photograph.

The men at the round table wondered if anyone had heard from Birmingham. During the first three weeks of January, Birmingham Klansman Robert Chambliss, known as Dynamite Bob, made periodic deliveries of explosives to the capital city. Chambliss knew explosives. He had explained that the twelve-inch brown sticks of wood pulp soaked in nitroglycerine packed a powerful blast when detonated. Included with each bundle of four sticks held together by tape was a detonator designed by Chambliss and made in his backyard shop. Britt, York, and their fellow Klansmen used the explosives to blow up several black churches and the front porch of at least one black parsonage.

After the U.S. Supreme Court declared unconstitutional the city law requiring separate seating of the races on public transportation, the imperial wizard of the United Klans of America, Robert M. "Bobby" Shelton, ordered Klansmen throughout the United States—and particularly in the South and Alabama—to "turn up the heat against the lily-livered nigger-loving whites who aid and abet them and the black-hearted nigger leaders who are controlling them."

★

On Christmas Eve night in 1956, a young black woman boarded a city bus and took one of the front seats. When the bus stopped downtown at the corner of Dexter Avenue and Perry Street, a block east of the Court Square fountain, the woman stepped down onto the pavement. As she walked down the sidewalk, two cars pulled to a stop. Raymond Britt, Jimmy York, and three of their friends surrounded her and began beating her with their belts and homemade clubs. The woman fell to her knees, raised her arms, and screamed. A fifteen-year-old African American, Ollie Mae Collins, reported seeing the incident to police officers D. W. Mixon and F. B. Day. An unidentified white rider on the bus said that he witnessed the attack but could not identify the attackers. When police questioned the victim at the emergency room, she became hysterical and said she could not identify her assailants. Subsequently, no arrests were made.

One week after the first integrated bus ride, three nights after the beating incident, an unidentified white man fired a gun through the window of a bus being driven by W. H. Fullilove. The bullet pierced the window, ricocheted, and then struck twenty-two-year-old Rosa Jordan, going through her left leg and lodging in her right calf. After the shot, Fullilove did not realize anyone had been injured until other passengers shouted, "Stop the bus! A woman's been shot!" He then drove the bus to Oak Street General Hospital, where Jordan was treated. The bus, continuing on its route, was hit by another bullet. Passengers huddled on the floor while Fullilove drove to police headquarters downtown.

The following night, a bullet was fired into a side window of another city bus, frightening the riders. Later the white bus driver told a reporter from the *Montgomery Advertiser* that he saw a black man hiding in shrubs and suspected that he was the shooter. After all, he said, the incident occurred in a black neighborhood. A subsequent ballistic test showed that that bullet, as well as the second bullet fired into Fullilove's bus, was fired from the same .22-caliber gun that police investigator Jack Shows found in Jimmy York's car.

Henry Alexander, operator of a plumbing business on the Lower Wetumpka Road in north Montgomery, entered the Little Kitchen. Sitting down at the round table, he told the group about an African American "who thinks he's hot shit." Alexander said that a black man named Eddie or Edward Wells "made a pass at a white woman up in Sylacauga, where he delivers goods to Winn-Dixie from the Hudson-Thompson warehouse."

Shortly after nightfall, the men—Britt, Alexander, and York—met at Alexander's house at 1940 Yarbrough Street in Boylston, a section of north Montgomery carved from the land of Camp Sheridan at the end of World War I. Driving Alexander's two-year-old Chevrolet, they moved through a familiar maze of streets to the Hudson-Thompson terminal on Jackson Ferry Road, where trucks were loaded in the mornings to deliver groceries to Winn-Dixie supermarkets throughout central Alabama. Seeing no empty trucks parked in the lot, Alexander drove to the Lower Wetumpka Road and turned north into the rural countryside.

Alexander slowed. About a half mile from the turnoff, they approached the small frame house where the Klan periodically met to plan something big. Out front, a big round metal sign showed a hooded rider on horseback. Around the circle were the words: "Ku Klux Klan of Alabama." Britt suggested they pull in and wait in the dark. When the truck passed, they could run it down.

Alexander said he would rather keep moving. Traveling very slowly through the darkness, he glanced into the rearview mirror. They were surrounded by darkness. With thick brush growing on both sides of the narrow pavement and tree limbs hanging over the road, it was impossible to see the full moon. About a mile farther, they passed Hitson's A&H Grocery in the Flatwood community. Several naked exterior bulbs burned in the empty gravel parking area. They kept moving south. Finally, Alexander turned again, creeping along at a snail's pace.

As they passed the quiet rural store again, a truck sat under an outside light.

Alexander slowed. The men saw WINN-DIXIE was painted on the side of the truck. The front door was open. Inside, the driver was studying something beneath the dome light. Alexander turned into the lot.

As soon as the Chevy moved in front of the truck's headlights, Britt got out with a gun in his hand and walked to the passenger side and opened the door.

Willie Edwards Jr. looked up, startled.

York reached into the cab, grabbed his arm, and jerked Edwards out. The Winn-Dixie logbook fell to the floorboard.

"Edward?" Alexander asked.

"My name's Willie Edwards Jr."

Edwards shifted his body, trying to pull away from York's grip.

Britt swung, slamming the short barrel of his pistol into the man's face. Then he hit Edwards again.

Blood squirted from the man's nose. Losing balance, he leaned against the trunk of a large oak. He grasped the bark to hold himself upright, his nose still bleeding.

York grabbed Edwards's arm.

Edwards tried to free himself, but York held tight and pulled hard.

"If you don't come, I'll shoot you right here," York said.

Edwards straightened and coughed, wiping his nose with the brim of his hat and the sleeve of his coat.

York jerked him toward the car and shoved him into the backseat.

Alexander pulled out of the lighted parking lot. Edwards was wedged between Britt and York on the backseat.

"You been fooling with a white woman?" Britt asked.

"No, sir," Edwards said.

"Don't give me no sass!" Britt snapped.

"You see this?" York asked, holding his revolver in front of Edwards's eyes. Before Edwards answered, York slammed the butt of the gun against his jaw.

Something cracked.

"Son of a bitch!" Britt reached out and slapped Edwards twice. "We'll teach your black ass to fuck with a white woman!"

Edwards pleaded. He swore that he had never touched a white woman. He told them he had a wife and two little children. He said he would never touch a white woman.

His hands shook. Tears washed down his cheeks.

"We oughta cut your nuts out," York said. "That's what we do with niggers who mess with white women."

York lowered the revolver and pushed the barrel between the man's legs.

Edwards jerked back. He cried out that he had never done anything to hurt anyone.

Alexander turned onto the dark, empty, narrow highway heading north toward Millbrook, a community in Elmore County. The Tyler-Goodwin Bridge was an old, ill-conceived, poorly engineered passage over the Alabama River. Nobody used it but a few locals: drunks returning from the out-of-the-way riverbank honky-tonks and lovers trying to hide from jilted spouses. Even in broad daylight the bridge was not easily navigated. Built with iron girders and a wooden ramp, it sat crooked to the highway; going north, a driver approached straight on, then turned left onto the bridge, and on the northern end, a driver maneuvered to the right to pull back onto the curving pavement of the highway. An old-timer once said that when the bridge was brand new, back in the 1920s, a heavy barge hit one of its concrete pilings, knocking it cockeyed, and nobody ever bothered to fix it.

Alexander pulled the Chevy onto a dirt road used by fishermen to drive down to the water's edge. As he turned the lights out, Britt pulled Edwards from the car and pushed him toward the highway and the bridge.

Edwards stumbled and almost fell. Alexander kicked him in the back of the right leg. He stumbled again. He put out his hand and gripped an iron railing to keep from falling. "Please don't hurt me," he pleaded, his lips quivering, his entire body shivering.

York pushed him toward the middle of the bridge.

"I'm telling the truth. I swear I am. I've never touched a white woman. My wife's my woman."

"Lying son of a bitch!" Alexander spat, then kicked him twice in the shins.

Shivering, Edwards swore that he was innocent, didn't know a white woman, and had never touched a white woman. He told them that he had just finished his first trip outside of Montgomery in the Winn-Dixie truck. When they found him, he said, he was studying his logbook. He wanted to make sure he had finished all of his deliveries before returning the truck to the terminal.

The three men formed a wall around the truck driver, whose red-rimmed eyes shifted nervously from one to another. He could not escape. York pointed his pistol at Edwards's head. One of the white men said, "Hit the water!" Willie Edwards Jr. climbed up onto the iron railing. The rumble of the river was heard far down below. Willie Edwards Jr. jumped, screaming all the way down through the darkness to the water.

The white men made their way back to the dark car. In the backseat, Britt touched something on the floorboard. He reached down and picked up an old felt hat. Then he tossed the hat out the window into the scrub brush.

In the little house on Rice Street, Sarah Jean Edwards was awakened by the baby's cooing. Willie was not in the bed.

After feeding the children, she bundled up, instructed her daughter Malinda to watch after the baby, and walked down the street to a pay telephone. Sarah called her father-in-law, Willie Edwards Sr., who lived on Fourth Street in Greater Washington Park. She told Daddy Edwards that Willie had not come home. Would he go to the warehouse terminal and see what had happened? The elder Edwards told her not to worry; something probably happened to the truck.

At about the same time Sarah Jean was talking with her father-in-law, Lee Ernest Williams, a driver for Winn-Dixie, was on his way north out of Montgomery in his truck on the Lower Wetumpka Road. At Hitson's A&H Grocery in the Flatwood community he saw another Winn-Dixie truck parked near a big oak tree with the driver's door open.

Williams pulled into the gravel parking area, stopped, and looked around. Seeing no one, he went inside and asked a man behind the counter if he knew anything about the truck.

"It was parked out there when I got here about a half hour ago," Wilbur Adams said.

Williams telephoned the Winn-Dixie office and reported finding the empty truck. Back in his own vehicle, Williams continued northward on his route.

When Willie Edwards Sr. arrived at the warehouse, he was told that the truck his son was driving the previous day had been located. But nobody had seen or heard from Willie Jr.

At the store on the Lower Wetumpka Road, Edwards walked around the truck, his eyes scanning every inch. At the open door, he looked inside and saw an open book on the floor. He leaned down and read Willie's name written across the top of a white sheet.

Edwards walked slowly around the truck again. At the oak tree he saw what appeared to be a good-sized splotch of liquid. He moved close and reached down and touched it. To him, it smelled like blood.

In the store, a clerk said that he had found the truck exactly the way it was then. He had seen no sign of the driver or anyone else.

Back in town, Edwards parked on Madison Avenue. At police headquarters he found a captain and reported his missing son. The man wrote Willie Jr.'s name on a pad but asked no further questions. Edwards told him the truck his son was driving was sitting in the parking lot of Hitson's A&H Grocery in the Flatwood community. The captain simply nodded. Edwards told him he thought there was blood at the base of a large oak tree near the truck. Again, the captain nodded. He made no further notes.

When Edwards repeated the story to Sarah Jean, telling her how he was treated at police headquarters, she was furious. She shook her head. "We're just poor damn niggers, that's what they all think," she told him.

When a friend took her into town, Sarah Jean walked into police headquarters and confronted a lieutenant, who told her that her husband "has probably run off somewhere."

"Where?" she asked angrily.

The man shrugged and walked away.

For the Edwards family, these scenes were repeated over and over again.

During the next week Edwards went back to the police headquarters with his brother. He was told nobody knew anything about his missing son. The two men drove back out on the Lower Wetumpka Road to the store. By now, the Winn-Dixie truck had been moved. Inside the store, Edwards again asked the clerk if he had seen anything on the night of

January 23. The man answered that he never saw anyone. He found the truck sitting near the tree the morning of January 24. The driver's door was open, but nobody was inside.

Down the road, the two men rode toward the Tyler-Goodwin. Near the bridge, Edwards said, "Stop." Outside, he ambled toward a briar patch. He leaned down and reached into a bush. He pulled out an old hat, gray and weather torn. He looked it over, brought it up to his face, and then slapped it against his side. At the car, he said, "I think this is Mookie's." Holding the hat, his hands began to shake. He dropped the hat onto the floorboard.

He and his brother walked over every inch of the sorry land between the bush and the bridge. It was sandy and rocky—nothing but scrub brush grew there. They found no other sign of Willie Jr. To Edwards, the bridge looked spooky and unsafe, the way it sagged in the middle and was uneven with the road on the southern end. He didn't venture out onto the wooden plank runway. He looked at it from a distance and shook his head.

Later, Edwards visited the downtown office of a private investigator. He paid the man one hundred dollars to find his son. Two weeks later, the PI told him he came up empty-handed and asked for another fifty dollars to continue the search. Disgusted and distraught, Edwards refused.

On the afternoon of April 23, 1957, while tending to her three-week-old baby boy, Willie Edwards III, Sarah Jean heard a knock at the front door. She listened intently. Hearing it again, she gingerly placed the tiny child into the crib. She hesitated, straightening her dress where it had wrinkled from handling her two babies and from Malinda's pulling on her skirt.

When she opened the front door, she looked into the faces of two uniformed policemen.

"Sarah Jean Edwards?"

She said nothing as she stared into the brown pasteboard box the officer held in his hands. In it were Willie's tattered clothes. She recognized what was left of his jacket, now water soaked and in shreds. On top of the jacket sat the cigarette lighter she had given him last Christmas, now bent and aged with rust.

Her lips quivered as the man said words she didn't hear. She could not think. Her vision faded as her eyes filmed over with moisture.

Suddenly, her sister-in-law, Mildred Harris, appeared next to the men. She stepped to Edwards's side and held her arm and said, "Sarah Jean, they found Mookie."

As time passed, she learned that two fishermen found the body floating in the Alabama River near a fishing camp in Lowndes County southwest of Montgomery. Harris accompanied the policemen to the morgue, where she identified Willie's remains. When the police questioned Willie's father, he verified that his son had an amputated finger on his left hand.

When Edwards told the police that he had found a hat that Sarah Jean identified as Willie Jr.'s, they told him to keep it; it wouldn't be of any use to them.

The next day, after the Howard and Howard Funeral Home took the body, the *Montgomery Advertiser* ran a two-paragraph story in the Negro News section of the paper about a man identified as Willie Edwards Jr. found drowned in the river. A week later, Sarah Jean, her babies, and the rest of the family put her husband to rest in the New Pleasant Valley Cemetery in Hope Hull in south Montgomery County.

Years later, speaking separately to different people, Britt and York recalled the happenings of the night in rural north Montgomery County. Their recollections differed only slightly. Robert Lewis Mulder, who was married to Henry Alexander's first wife, Edna, for two and a half months, told investigators Jack Shows and Tom Ward that Henry Alexander and Sonny Kyle Livingston "threw the Winn-Dixie Negro in the river."

On February 20, 1976, Shows was working as chief investigator for the Alabama attorney general Bill Baxley. After Shows told Baxley about the unsolved killing he and his partner Tom Ward had worked years earlier, Baxley told him to solve it. When Shows confronted Britt, Britt signed a sworn affidavit telling how he and three other Klansmen, including nineteen-year-old Livingston, had abducted Edwards, carried him to the bridge, and made him jump. A week later the other three were arrested and charged with murder.

As they were putting together the case to be prosecuted, Baxley knew he would need more than one witness. He told Livingston that if he would take two lie-detector tests administered by the nation's leading experts, he would consider the results as evidence. If Livingston passed, Baxley said, charges against him would be dropped. If he did not, he would be tried. After hours of questioning, Livingston passed. Traveling back to Alabama from San Diego, California, Livingston told Shows, "Jack, you got me with the wrong nigger." Then he laughed. It was obvious to Shows that Livingston had been involved in similar incidents of racial violence but not the death of Willie Edwards. As in most polygraph examinations, the investigators were not allowed to probe into other crimes.

Back in Montgomery, circuit judge Frank Embry threw the case out of court, declaring the evidence did not prove that Edwards was a victim of homicide.

Years later, Baxley said that he read carefully the results of both polygraph tests and considered them from every angle. The interrogations had been extensive, going into every aspect of Willie Edwards's death, questioning Livingston about times and dates and others who may or may not have been involved, and he had an answer for every question. "I came to the conclusion that Livingston had not been in the car with Alexander, Britt, and York. They had probably been with him on other similar missions but not the one in which Willie Edwards Jr. was killed," Baxley said.

In the 1990s, Raymond Britt's widow called Shows, who had retired from his state position. On his deathbed, after suffering months with cancer, Britt had confessed to his wife that he and the other two had killed Edwards forty years earlier.

On July 28, 1997, Willie Edwards Jr.'s daughter Malinda wrote to Montgomery district attorney Ellen Brooks and pled with her to reopen the case. Brooks talked to Britt's wife. Edwards's body was exhumed for another autopsy. After examining the remains, Dr. James Lauridson, the state medical examiner, concluded that Edwards was a victim of a homicide. Lauridson told the court that he found that Edwards had been assaulted before he was found floating in the river. After Brooks filed a motion, circuit judge Charles Price ordered the State Department of Vital Statistics to change the cause of death to homicide.

Finally, after exploring the evidence presented by the district attorney, the grand jury refused to bring indictments. Brooks told the *Montgomery Advertiser* that the reason given was that the key witnesses were dead.

In late November 2009, Jack Shows met with FBI agents who came to his house in Montgomery to question him and explore his notes from more than fifty years earlier. "They wanted to know everything I knew about the Willie Edwards Jr. case," Shows told me. "I showed them what I had and told them everything I knew." The agents spent several hours perusing his information and questioning him. Among his files were copies of both polygraph tests taken and passed by Sonny Kyle Livingston, the only possible suspect still alive.

When asked about the FBI's interest, an agent assigned to the Montgomery office would not comment.

2

THE LEGACY OF WILLIE EDWARDS

Only a small circle of family and friends grieved for Willie Edwards Jr.

He never demonstrated for civil rights. He was too busy working, trying to feed and clothe his growing family. He worked at various jobs in and around Montgomery. He had not been an outstanding student. In fact, he never finished high school, choosing instead to get a job and help his father and stepmother, who were having a hard time making ends meet trying to feed and care for five children.

"Willie was a good boy," his mother, Ella Edwards, remembered. "He never got into trouble. From the time he was old enough to hold a rake he was working, cleaning white folks' yards, clipping hedges, hauling stuff for stores around here. He worked for the old Jewish man, Louis Kushner, who had a meat market on Holt Street near the Mobile Highway. Mr. Kushner was a caring person who showed that he truly cared for Willie. Willie couldn't keep his mind on studies in school, he had to be out in the world doing something.

"As soon as he was old enough to drive he got a job driving trucks for different folks. He drove for Schloss & Kahn wholesalers. He had been working for Hudson-Thompson, the warehouse suppliers for Winn-Dixie, for just a few months and had just started driving a truck for the company when he disappeared. We didn't know what happened to him. He just vanished. But then, after, we began hearing rumors that the Ku Klux Klan had done it. His daddy knew something bad happened. That man worried his heart out for his missing son. It wasn't like him to pay a hundred dollars out of his pocket to some jackleg private detective, but he did. He didn't know what else to do when the police just wouldn't do anything, just looked at him like he wasn't even a man. I tell you, I never saw no man grieve so hard or so deep.

"As soon as he found Mookie's hat—knowing it was his hat from the second he picked it up out of the bush that day—he said he could feel something in that hat that told him something terrible bad had happened to his boy."

Day after day, Willie Edwards Sr. sat in the old rocking chair on the porch of his home at 2819 Fourth Street in the Greater Washington Park section of southwest Montgomery. He sat and rocked, holding the flop-brimmed hat he had found on the side of the road near Tyler-Goodwin Bridge. He gazed out into the distance and wondered when, if ever, he was going to learn what happened to his boy, whose presence he could feel in the worn felt hat as he slid it between his gnarled fingers. Even after the fishermen found the decomposed body that was identified as Willie Jr., the old man's deep-down feeling in his bones told him that someday he would learn what truly happened. He knew Willie Jr. would not have simply fallen off the bridge and he would not have jumped unless he was forced. The young man had too much to live for, was proud of his family, and had felt a joy in his new job.

One day during his search for answers, Willie Edwards Sr. came upon a woman who seemed to be talking crazy. He had seen and heard women who talked gibberish, talking in what some of the church people called "tongues," but this woman appeared as sane as anyone else on the street, other than her fast-moving tongue spitting out words. When he calmed her down, he asked what she was trying to tell him. Her eyes rolled, then focused on his face. "My boy been cut," she said. Willie Sr. touched her shoulder softly, steadily, with purpose. "He ain't all there," she said, pointing toward her head. Willie Sr. waited. He knew a retarded boy in the neighborhood who wore a cowboy hat and carried a cap pistol he aimed at people and called out, "Bang! Bang!"

Willie Sr. considered him simply a poor unfortunate who couldn't help himself and who would never harm anyone. He had not seen the boy in several weeks.

"Some of them Klan men took Sonny Boy out on the Old Selma Road and pulled his britches down. He tried to break and run, but they held him down on the ground while one of 'em took a knife and cut out his manhood. He bled like a stuck pig, hollering and screaming, hurting and scared they were gonna kill him. Then they poured turpentine all over his middle. Poor thing! He jumped and hollered, screaming at the top of his lungs. He was found hours later, still writhing in pain. Poor thing! He was taken to the hospital, where they tended to him.

"A white man come to the hospital and told the folks, 'This here boy spoke sweetly to a white woman. Now, this is what happens to nigger boys that do things like that. Y'all tell ever'body, this is what happens. Tell 'em, so they'll know.'"

As he listened, Willie Sr. grimaced and felt the torture in his mind and wondered if his own son had undergone such pain. "Where is he now?" he asked.

"He won't come outta the house. He's scared. He still hurts. I don't know what'll become of him. The thought of it all bears down hard on me. It's about to run me crazy."

Willie Sr. felt her anguish and touched her hand and told her he understood.

Across town, rumor had it that a white teenage girl had gotten pregnant by a black man. Klansmen searched the community for the girl and the man. When they found him or her, it was said, he or she would pay a deadly price. A sixteen-year-old girl in Boylston ran away from home. Kinfolks said she had gone to Atlanta, where she planned to live with relatives. Whether the rumor was true, no one knew. Decades later, survivors of that time of terror on the streets of Montgomery would say, "Do you know that the Klan killed a young white girl who got pregnant by a black man?" "Who?" you would ask. But the teller of the tale would not say or did not know. A half century later, it was still a rumor.

In the mid-to-late 1950s, the feeling of mystery lay on the atmosphere of the community like a fog. It was a town of little more than a hundred thousand, more than a third African American. Rumors spread quickly and lingered, especially among the black activists and white liberals who had grown accustomed to the nighttime violence. Membership rolls of the Ku Klux Klan grew rapidly. But in Montgomery and across the South, a white upstart didn't have to be a card-carrying member to be an active terrorist. All he needed was hate in his heart, a weapon in his hand, and a mode of transportation. Most of the time the latter was a car or pickup, but in the case of some, it was a motorcycle.

"Motorcycle gangs cropped up all over the South," according to Alabama Bureau of Investigation expert Sam Rainey. "In Phenix City, called the Sin City of the South, prior to our closing down most of the organized criminal activities in the early 1950s, a gang known as the Dixie Mafia was organized and spread rapidly to Atlanta, Greenville, Nashville, Memphis, Little Rock, and down into Louisiana and Mississippi. In the early 1960s its activities became as widespread and as dangerous as the Klan. And it had the extra benefit of mobility. We called them 'hit-and-run terror groups.' They were always on the lookout for white and black activists. They'd move in, strike, and move on toward another target before law enforcement could organize and capture them. That was worse than the KKK, who tended to be locals you could infiltrate and watch. These guys were always on the move."

In the early days of 1957, after Willie Edwards Jr.'s body was found floating in the Alabama River, Rosa Parks and her husband, Raymond, a quiet barber, received a barrage of death threats. In the aftermath of her December 1, 1955, refusal to give up her seat on a city bus and her subsequent arrest, Rosa Parks was branded a troublemaker by the white power of Montgomery. The white men who frequented the hangouts in Ward Five took racial matters a step or two further. As troublemakers, she and her husband became their target. Young white men drove by their home at 634 Cleveland Court, honking their horns and shouting racial epithets. In the middle of the night an unidentified woman telephoned and screamed, "My husband's gonna kill your sorry nigger ass."

One night in mid-April, a group of white-hooded men erected a cross in the small front yard and torched the wood that burned until it crumbled after midnight. Raymond tried to comfort his wife, but the threats continued. Finally, Raymond told her there was only one thing left to do: leave their home in Montgomery. He telephoned Rosa's brother, Sylvester, who insisted they move north to Detroit, Michigan, where he had lived since the end of World War II. After friends in Montgomery organized an event that collected eight hundred dollars for them, Rosa, Raymond, and her mother moved north to be near relatives and to escape the cruel behavior of some whites in their Southern neighborhood.

The Klan and its leaders lived in every type of neighborhood across the South. Jesse Benjamin "J. B." Stoner Jr., an attorney, ran his National States Rights Party out of a two-story brick building in Marietta, Georgia, north of Atlanta, where he proudly flew the Confederate flag. James Venable of the National Knights of the Ku Klux Klan was elected mayor of Stone Mountain, Georgia, for three terms and bragged about his KKK affiliation. Robert M. "Bobby" Shelton, self-identified at various times as the imperial wizard or grand cyclops of the United Klans of America, operated a service station on University Avenue in Tuscaloosa, Alabama, when he wasn't donning the scarlet robes of the U.S. Klans and later the Knights of Alabama and the United Klans of America. Shelton formed the latter when he broke with the national group, openly defying law and order as it was written in the Klan code.

Around Marietta, Stoner wore a jeweled Confederate flag on the lapel of his suit coat and a revolver strapped around his waist. Venable campaigned relentlessly and angrily in his KKK cloaks. And Shelton spoke to rallies throughout the South, proudly wearing his red satin gown with a dragon emblazoned across the chest.

Shelton joined the U.S. Klans in the late 1940s. At the time the state klaverns were headed up by grand dragon Alvin Horn, a Holy Roller preacher who traveled with the branch heads of the state and recruited thousands of members, telling them about "the unholy alliance of the devil and the nigger leaders in Montgomery" when James E. "Big Jim" Folsom was governor from 1947 to 1951, and later, during the boycott in 1956. White people gathered to hear Horn and his words of hate, even though he had been arrested and charged with murder in Pell City, Alabama, in 1950. He ranted on and on about Folsom, saying the governor was walking "in lock-step with Martin Luther Coon." After Horn was acquitted of the murder charge, his first wife committed suicide. In the late 1950s, after Horn married a fourteen-year-old girl, he was arrested for contributing to the delinquency of a minor. When it was discovered the couple was legally married, the charges were dropped. After both instances became public knowledge, Horn was ousted from the Klan, and Shelton took his place as grand dragon. Shelton left the U.S. Klans and formed the Knights of Alabama, an organization whose workers assisted the state attorney general, John Patterson, in his successful bid for the governor's chair in 1958. Still later, Shelton's organization became the United Klans of America.

In the 1970s, Shelton told journalist Patsy Sims, author of *The Klan*, "Of course, I do think of myself as a racist. That's nothing to be ashamed of. I'm proud I'm white. Being a racist is an individual that is proud of his heritage, his integrity, and his own culture and ethical background. But they have smeared the word 'racist' to associate it with something like the Gestapo or Hitlerism or Nazism." As I read Shelton's words, I thought of my own personal run-ins with racism and racists.

When I was a teenager, growing up in Tuscaloosa in the 1950s, I saw Klansmen in their robes parading through the streets of Holt, a suburb near the Gulf States Paper Mill on the Black Warrior River. My great-uncle John Hewitt, a storeowner in a mostly black neighborhood, pointed and said, "That's Bobby Shelton. His daddy owns a grocery store on Fifteenth Street." On another occasion I recognized two of my mother's male cousins who worked at the Goodrich Rubber Plant on the western edge of town. They were dressed in their Klan getup and were obviously very proud of their positions as they marched through the streets of Northport on the other side of the river from Tuscaloosa. I asked my father about the fact that we had Klansmen in the family, and he said it "was something you ought to just forget." I asked my mother, who replied, "Those boys never had a lick of sense. When they were growing up, I could always tell they were different: they hated. You could see it in their eyes. They were never very good with the farm animals. You're not like that. Don't let something they do that's mean and bad sink into you. Just turn the other way and do good for people."

I never forgot either my mother's or my father's words. Each time I saw my cousins, which wasn't often—at my grandparents' funerals or large family gatherings—I would relive that day when I saw them stepping along Main Street behind Shelton.

Later, after I became a reporter for the *Alabama Journal* in Montgomery, I was talking with my editor, Ray Jenkins, and I told him what I remembered about Shelton, my cousins, and the Klan. As I told him, Ray grimaced and said, "Why don't you write about it?"

I didn't feel like bringing it out in the open at that time. "Maybe later," I said. And later I did write a piece about the Klan that was published on the op-ed page of the *New York Times*, but I never mentioned the cousins. Somehow, I felt that I should bury that part of my family history. Through the years, however, as I learned more and more about my own father's friendship with numerous racist leaders, I began to feel I should reveal these family stories, because they are as much the story of Alabama and the South during this period as they are a part of my family history.

During those years as a journalist, after I began writing books and exploring my background, I revisited that land of northern Tuscaloosa County, where my mother's cousins grew up. It was hardscrabble land of sandy loam, good for little but growing corn from which they could feed hogs or make moonshine liquor. For generation after generation, after their forefathers made their way across the Atlantic from Ireland and pushed southward through the wilderness from South Carolina to Alabama, my ancestors settled on this land that no one else would have. They brought with them knowledge of how to raise their own fruits and vegetables they preserved and kept for eating in the winter, make sauerkraut from cabbage, and store and cure the meat of animals they raised or killed in the wild. Few black people lived here, miles north of Alabama's cotton-rich Black Belt.

My family raised hogs that fattened on leftover corn and scraps from the dinner table. Hog-killing day was a seasonal ritual, when my grandfather and grandmother would join her brother and sister-in-law and other family members who would take part in the activities. At first frost every fall one of those cousins would take his rifle to the barnyard, shoot the hog in the head, and raise the plump body onto a scaffold. The morning's ritual included a washpot full of boiling water to pour onto the animal's skin, which would be scrubbed clean of hair. My great-uncle would cut the pig's belly open, and the hounds would go mad with delight as the entrails spilled onto the ground. My grandfather would carve the meat, and my aunt and my grandmother would prepare it for storage in the kitchen or smokehouse.

Killing, such as the bloody sport of coon-hunting, was a part of their world. On long winter nights the men would lope across the ridges of western Alabama, listening to the baying of their hounds on the scent of a raccoon. Sipping from their bottles of homemade corn liquor, they would follow the hounds to a tree where the frightened coon had taken refuge from the barking dogs. Finding the black-masked little animal in the light of their lantern, they would shoot until it dropped. Before its body hit the ground, the hounds would grab and tear, ripping it to bits, lapping up its remains. And under the moon, my uncle and cousins would laugh and wander farther into the woods, calling the sated dogs to find another prey.

For the most part, my kinfolks killed for food. They shot and harvested deer, rabbits, and squirrels. However, when I saw them parading down Main Street in Northport in their KKK regalia, it was obvious that they enjoyed their roles as racists. It occurred to me that they might kill for other reasons, too.

I remember my beloved grandfather, H. D. "Bub" Able, my mother's father, telling about a time in the 1930s in Sheffield in northwest Alabama, after he got a job with the Tennessee Valley Authority building coffer dams, when he was invited to a KKK meeting. "I went, thinking it would be good for my new job and help me get acquainted with the new community. I listened to the leader standing in front of about two dozen men. All he did was talk hate, hate, hate. It made me feel dirty. And when I looked around at those men who were sitting and listening, I saw they were the lowest form of human being. As soon as I could, I got out of there and never went back. I told your Nanny I hoped nobody knew who I was, I didn't want anybody knowing I was there. I'm telling you now in hopes that you'll never stoop so low."

Later, when I asked him about my cousins, he said, "They don't know any better. I hate to say it, but our deep-seated Scotch-Irish ancestry is filled with a lot of violence. Our folks tilled the soil and worked with our hands. My own daddy learned the turpentine trade in South Carolina from his father who'd come to this country as a farmer. Daddy moved to south Alabama when I was a boy and set up a turpentine still in the Piney Woods near Florala on the Florida state line. Our folks worked hard, made do for themselves, learned whatever they could, and clawed their way up from the dirt-poor beginnings. While we worked, other ignorant poor whites lay on their backsides and didn't break a sweat, living in shacks, not knowing or caring if there was a future. For them, the lowest on the totem pole of humanity, the only folks they had to look down on was the Negro. So they pointed to the black and said, 'He ain't even human.' Well, you and I know better. Unfortunately, some of our own family don't know that that's not true. Colored folks are human beings, just like you and me, and you ought to treat them in a Christian way, just like you'd want people to treat you."

That speech was made in 1956, when I was sixteen, after I told my mother I could not go back to the Covenant Presbyterian Church, where we had worshipped for the past four years.

As a youth, I had spent nearly a year in a body cast, undergoing two major surgeries to correct scoliosis, a weakening of the spinal column that resulted from infant polio, and had become deeply and devoutly religious. In the children's clinic, I prayed daily, usually three or four times a day. I read the Holy Bible and believed in the Scripture.

On numerous occasions, our minister, Will Ormond, visited my bedside, held my hand, and prayed. When I had a question, he counseled, speaking honestly and forthrightly.

My best friends were from Sunday school. On the eve of going under for the first seven-hour operation, I wrote my friends that I was not afraid because the Lord would be watching over me. Together, we recited the Lord's Prayer and believed in those well-known words, "The Lord is my shepherd, I shall not want . . ."

Aware of the civil rights happenings in Montgomery, Will Ormond invited a group of black professors from nearby Stillman College to worship at our church. I heard disturbed rumblings among the white adults of the congregation, but I had no idea their feelings were so strong that they would put up an argument, much less react adversely.

When the professors arrived on a spring Sunday morning I was in the vestibule of the sanctuary behind Brother Ormond, who stepped up to greet them.

It was not until I turned to walk inside that I noticed the congregation had shrunk and that those remaining were squeezed together on the first rows. No space remained in those rows for anyone else.

When the African American couples filed onto a row behind the whites, I sat next to them.

My aunt and uncle, both teachers whom I admired greatly, pivoted and glared at me. My mother and father glanced my way, then quickly shifted back to the pulpit, where Brother Ormond was standing in his black pastor's robe. He spread his arms and looked out over the people and, after the obligatory hymns, read a passage in the Bible about "brotherly love."

I don't remember all the words, but the message was "Love thy neighbor."

Afterward, I watched the visitors shake the preacher's hand. Then he went back inside. A few minutes later he reappeared. He put his hand on my shoulder and said, "Always be forgiving. Love your fellow man."

When I found my parents I discovered that the church's ruling board had fired Will Ormond immediately after his sermon. "They warned him not to invite *those people* to our church," Daddy said.

"What do you mean?" I asked.

Of course, I knew what he meant. I grew up around bigotry and had seen it manifest itself in many forms in my everyday world. Throughout my life I attended segregated schools. But I had always been taught to treat everyone the same. If I said a hateful word about someone because of the color of his or her skin, my mother would take me to task immediately and thoroughly. I truly believed there wasn't room for racism in our lives.

That afternoon I decided I would not return to the church. I told my parents I simply could not enter that place without feeling the absence of the minister whom I respected and admired. I could not go inside a church filled with hypocrisy. In my estimation the board's decision to fire our minister was unchristian.

My mother begged me to wash such feelings from my brain. My father said I had no choice but to return. If I didn't, he said, I would be shunned by all of my friends. He added that my actions would disappoint him greatly. But I didn't go back. I made my stand.

3

KLAN ON TRIAL

On the afternoon of January 10, 1957, Robert "Dynamite Bob" Chambliss and one of his Birmingham buddies delivered a trunkload of dynamite to a north Montgomery hiding place.

Detectives from the Montgomery Police Department, Jack D. Shows and T. J. Ward, had already begun snooping around, getting closer and closer.

The good old boys from Ward Five realized that Shows was a well-trained investigator. Born and raised about fifty miles south of Montgomery, he served in the navy during World War II; when he came back home he knew immediately that he did not want to stay in Luverne, his small hometown in Crenshaw County. In Montgomery, the largest city in central Alabama, Shows applied for a job with the police department and was hired immediately. He rose through the ranks, proving not only that he could do the work of a policeman but also that he had an extraordinary ability to play departmental politics. He discovered who was related to whom, who had friends in high places, and where the money and the old favors were stashed. He recognized the pecking order of politics from the dispatcher's office to the chief's secretary, from city hall to the governor's office, from the janitor in the basement of the capitol to the man who hoisted the flag every morning on top of the silver dome. He knew that politicians came and went but the bureaucrats stayed in place, and he made friends with all of them.

It was not long before he made himself familiar with the underbelly of the city, easing his way through the boudoirs of the cathouses on Pollard and Columbus streets and spending time in the bar and the backroom of Willie's Pool Parlor, where many bookies operated and second-rate hoodlums came and went. He knew the gambler Johnny Connor and the showgirls who danced at the Steamboat Lounge.

Shows and Ward enjoyed the fresh shrimp, oysters, and red snapper in the Seven Seas Restaurant on the northwest corner of Montgomery and Lee streets, where another contingent of Klansmen met nightly, behind the lighted aquarium. Shows knew every taxi driver on a first-name basis. He let it be known with a grin and a wink that he appreciated a well-chosen tip about who was stepping on whose toes, whether a new dude was moving onto old turf, coming into Gunn's Club on the Atlanta Highway and running new girls into the local rackets—gambling, stealing, fencing, or whoring.

He even kept up with the criminals he sent to prison. It was not unusual for him to visit Kilby, the state penitentiary in the northeastern quadrant of town with its high concrete walls and corner guard towers on U.S. 231, toward the former Creek Indian town of Wetumpka. He took cigarettes and sandwiches when he visited the prison, and he knew that convict gossip was some of the best in the criminal world. The inmates knew which crimes were committed by what outfit and how many were involved and how they fit into the scheme of things. It was all information that helped him in his profession. And Shows strived to be the best.

The boys of Ward Five considered Shows one of their own. He talked like they talked, with a Southern drawl. But they weren't so sure about Ward. He spoke the way people talked in New York or Boston. Raised in the blue-collar area of South Boston, Ward had served as a military police officer. He was stationed at Montgomery's Maxwell Air Force Base when he was discharged from the service.

The boys of Ward Five didn't trust Yankees. What they didn't know was that Ward was a dedicated, hardworking investigator who never quit until he solved the crime and nabbed his man and sent him away. He was like an old bloodhound that got a whiff of something and wouldn't stop until he was on top of the scent. He didn't know politics and cared less. He did know police work and enjoyed it immensely. Like Shows, he had no respect for the bullying bigots who terrorized the black community—he wanted to catch them and put them behind bars, where he was sure they belonged. First, however, he had to prove what he believed and what he felt in his bones: that the men who were hanging around the Little Kitchen were the ones causing the trouble.

Late on the night of January 10, 1957, Leila Ann Ramsey, sleeping in a cramped little apartment in Montgomery's west end, awakened to a sudden blast. Instinctively, she moved to the nearby crib where her six-month-old baby lay sleeping. As she put her hands down to feel the child, Leila Ann shivered, feeling fright more than the chill of the winter air as she heard another crash in the distance.

In the morning she learned that dynamite had exploded and blown away a corner of the Bell Street Baptist Church. The choir loft behind the pulpit collapsed in the blast.

On the same night, another explosion damaged a wall at the Hutchinson Street Baptist Church.

Another hit the Mount Olive Church and tore a four-foot hole in the northern wall.

While the minister of First Baptist, Colored, Ralph David Abernathy, was in Atlanta, staying with Martin Luther King Jr. at King's parents' home, he received a call from his wife, Juanita, that their home had been bombed. Juanita and the couple's baby daughter, Juandalynn, were asleep in the bedroom when dynamite had blown out the front windows and destroyed the walls of the living and dining rooms. For the moment, they were physically unharmed.

When Abernathy called back that he had gotten reservations on the next airplane headed for Montgomery, Juanita told him that someone had planted the bomb beneath the porch of their house near the bedroom wall. If the bomb had been placed three inches to the right, the fire marshal told Mrs. Abernathy, it would have ignited the main gas line, and the entire house would have exploded, killing everybody inside. She also told her husband that policemen were combing through the debris and were looking for any other explosive that might have been placed by the terrorists.

While they were talking, Juanita heard another crash in the distance.

Holding the phone away from her face, she asked a policeman, "What's that?"

A uniformed cop glanced down at his watch, then said, "That would be your First Baptist Church."

In his autobiography, *And the Walls Came Tumbling Down*, Abernathy wrote, "She had stared into the coldest eyes she had ever seen, and suddenly the full horror of the situation dawned on her. The police had known all along. They were in on the plans. There would be no real investigation and no one would be arrested or indicted. And the same would have been true had she and the baby died."

Later that night, the home of the Reverend Robert Graetz, a white pastor of the all-black congregation at the Trinity Lutheran Church on Cleveland Avenue, was wrecked by exploding dynamite. Graetz, who sympathized and worked with the leaders of the bus boycott, had been the target of another bombing the previous summer. It had not slowed him in his efforts to assist the black community, showing them his devotion and love for their cause.

After the church bombing, governor James E. "Big Jim" Folsom issued a press release criticizing the violence and offering a two-thousand-dollar reward for the capture and conviction of the bombers.

✶

By now, Shows and Ward had their informants in place. From time to time, these men contacted the detectives, met them at a rural location, and related the stories that the KKK planned a big blow soon. According to the informants, the Klan was talking about a bigger target. At the right time, they planned to blow up the entire house of the number one black leader, King, who lived on South Jackson Street.

With such a plan in mind, the Kluxers stored enough dynamite to destroy the entire family and any friends who might be visiting. If they accomplished their goal, they rationalized, they would be rid of their most persistent and profound enemy. In doing away with him and his family, leaving behind nothing but a bombed-out crater, they would silence the entire black community. Then they would go back to life the way it was before King and his demonstrators created the civil rights movement.

★

Although some members of the Montgomery Police Department were part of the plan to disrupt the black community, as Mrs. Abernathy had seen and heard, Shows and Ward were steadfast in their investigation. While some of the police officers belonged to the Klan, Shows and Ward worked to curtail the violence and uncover evidence that would bring the culprits to justice.

The detectives sifted through the wreckage at every bomb site. They smelled out every trace of evidence. They found shoeprints and portions of dynamite sticks that had not exploded. From these fragments they lifted portions of fingerprints that could be studied and compared with fingerprint records on file at headquarters.

Ward, a meticulous note-taker, made a notation of every smidgeon of evidence they gathered. He kept his records in a small notebook stored in his back pocket for quick consultation. Late at night, he copied them onto three-by-five cards on his desk at home. He would separate the cards and study them and then put them together like a puzzle. Each of several dozen small filing boxes was crammed with detailed information he collected during his many investigations.

Years later, Ward recalled the investigations. "At night, after I copied my notes, making certain they were correct and thorough, I took them apart and put them back together again. Sometimes one card would find its way to another that had been hidden earlier. Sometimes one set of prints fit another, showing that one person had worked with another in certain bombings. I lay awake until after midnight, thinking about what we'd found. Sometimes I'd dream about the scenes and the people the evidence implicated. I'd wake up, roll over, and make notations in my notebook. Early the next morning I would go over each detail again, keeping it fresh in my mind." Like Shows, he believed in hunches.

The pair interviewed witnesses, delved into memories, discovered repetitious happenings—automobiles seen near multiple scenes where the bombings had taken place, snatches of evidence they put together like a lopsided jigsaw puzzle. Their information led them to two hiding places. One was a gravel pit near Maxwell Air Force Base to the northwest. Another location was six miles north of town off the Lower Wetumpka Road near the site of Camp Sheridan, where World War I soldiers trained. In both of these locations, the stockpile of explosives grew weekly. Shows and Ward watched both, not wanting to disturb them and waiting patiently for the right moment to move in.

As Reverend Abernathy drove up to the site of his church late on the morning after the bombings, he "saw a sign that made me physically ill. It read CONDEMNED. This fine church, the jewel of the black religious community, was a shattered husk of what it had been the last time I saw it. Several of the great windows had been blown out, and the whole building listed to one side, like a great ship about to sink into the sea." In the next four years the church underwent major restoration that cost a total of $250,000, all collected from the meager congregation.

A few days later, when King arrived back in the city, he "found the Negro community in low spirits. After the bombings the city commission had ordered all buses off the streets; and it now appeared that the city fathers would use this reign of violence as an excuse to cancel the bus company's franchise. As a result, many were coming to feel that all our gains had been lost; I myself started to fear that we were in for another long struggle to get bus service renewed," he wrote in *Stride Toward Freedom*. "Discouraged, and still revolted by the bombings, for some strange reason I began to feel a personal sense of guilt for everything that was happening."

At a mass meeting on Monday night, King broke down in public for the first time. He invited the congregation to join him in prayer. As he was asking for God's guidance, his voice rose and fell as he said, "Lord, I hope no one will have to die as a result of our struggle for freedom in Montgomery. Certainly I don't want to die. But if anyone has to die, let it be me." In the audience, people shouted, "No! No! No!" As he struggled to find more words, his throat clamped shut. His hands fluttered. His tongue thickened. Several ministers stepped up to the pulpit, put their arms around his shoulders, and whispered for him to take a seat.

"Unexpectedly," he wrote later, "this episode brought me great relief. Many people came up to me after the meeting and many called the following day to assure me that we were all together until the end. For the next few days, the city was fairly quiet. Bus service was soon resumed, though still on a daytime schedule only."

Early on the morning of January 27, the People's Service Station and Cab Stand, a major transportation outlet during the bus boycott, was bombed. Within minutes, explosives ripped the porch from the home of a sixty-year-old black hospital worker. Several hours later, a neighbor found a bomb made of twelve sticks of dynamite taped together and smoldering on the porch of the parsonage where Reverend King and his wife and his baby daughter lived. King was staying with friends in another part of town. Coretta and their daughter were in Atlanta with relatives.

Late in the afternoon of January 28, only five days after Willie Edwards Jr. disappeared, Shows and Ward arrested eighteen-year-old Sonny Kyle Livingston on charges of bombing the First Baptist Church, Colored, and the Hutchinson Street Baptist Church on January 10 and the People's Cab Company on January 28. Sandy-haired, rawboned, and cocky, Livingston was well known by the men at the Little Kitchen, where he often hung out with Alexander, Britt, and York, although the older men joked that he was not old enough to be a Klan member.

After Livingston was taken into custody, Shows and Ward transported him to the city jail on the Lower Wetumpka Road. This was the same rock-and-brick jailhouse where Rosa Parks had been booked after she was arrested more than a year earlier, charged with violating the city's law requiring segregation of races on city buses. Shows told Livingston, "If you want out of here soon, you need to tell us what you know about the bombings." Then Shows left him alone in the small cell.

"Ward and I were not back at our offices downtown [at police headquarters on the corner of Perry Street and Madison Avenue] more than a few minutes when the phone rang. It was Sonny Kyle. He said, 'I want to get out of here. There's a Klan meeting tonight. I need to be there.' I said, 'Are you going to tell us exactly what happened?' He said, 'Just come and get me now. I'll tell you and I'll show you where we stashed the stuff.'"

After calling the circuit solicitor and telling him what was happening, Shows and Ward returned to the jail and checked Livingston out. Outside the jail State Toxicologist Vann V. Pruitt, who had been examining the forensic evidence found in the bombing cases, met them in the parking lot. They followed Livingston's directions down Jefferson Street, past the Little Kitchen café, through the downtown warehouse district, over a number of railroad tracks, beyond Sabel Steel, where huge piles of scrap metal waited to be melted down and formed into railroad cars, past the Whitfield Pickle Company's canning plant, and out North Court Street toward the Alabama River. In a deserted field, Livingston led the two detectives into a gravel pit, where he pointed toward a cache of explosives in an abandoned well. While the slender young man pointed, the toxicologist took photographs that would later be presented at trial.

Ward climbed down into the shallow well and lifted out four pieces of dynamite wrapped in a detonation chord. He found loose dynamite and two half-pound cans of TNT. Although Livingston said there should be seventeen boxes of dynamite, they found only four and portions of another.

Back in town, Shows and Ward took Livingston to a room in the Jefferson Davis Hotel, where they interrogated him. After less than an hour, circuit solicitor William F. Thetford and associate solicitor Maury Smith showed up.

Shows told them that Livingston was ready to make a statement. Thetford said that was "a good thing for the prosecution," and then he and Smith left.

Following directions by Shows, a stenographer wrote:

I, Kyle Livingston Jr., 3447 Texas Avenue, Montgomery, Alabama, wish to make the following free and voluntary statement to Detectives J. D. Shows and T. J. Ward, who have identified themselves to me as such officers. I was not threatened in any way to get me to make this statement and any statement made by me may be used in a court of law.

I came back from Prattville, Alabama, on the night of January 8, 1957, in a car with Raymond Britt and, I think, Mr. Jimmy York. I was invited to Mr. Britt's house on the night of the 8th.

On that night it was discussed that we drop those bombs and I asked if the bombs were at his house and he said he had to pick the bombs up. We all agreed to meet between 1 A.M. and 1:30 A.M. at Glenn's Grill, Madison Avenue, January 10th. After we got there, Mr. Britt and Mr. York arrived in Mr. York's pickup truck.

The bombs were passed out from that truck to the cars that were waiting for them. They were taken out in a green canvas bag. Mr. Britt and Mr. York passed out the bombs. From there Mr. Britt and I drove to the Hutchinson Street Baptist Church, where I tossed a bomb on the door steps. I had a two-minute fuse on my bomb and heard it go off when I was approximately at the corner of Decatur and Grove streets. I rode to Glenn's Grill and got my car and went on home.

Shows: "What kind of car did you ride to the Hutchinson Street Baptist in?"

Livingston: "A yellow Oldsmobile convertible."

Shows: "What did the bomb look like?"

Livingston: "I imagine it was from six to ten sticks of dynamite wrapped around a rod approximately eighteen inches which had two fuses and two caps."

Shows: "Did you light both of those fuses?"

Livingston: "Yes."

Shows: "Did you get out of the car to light them?"

Livingston: "No."

Shows: "Did you get out of the car to throw them?"

Livingston: "Yes."

Shows: "How was the dynamite held to the rack?"

Livingston: "It was taped together. It looked like masking tape."

After receiving the statement, Shows and Ward drove Livingston to the homes of his friends W. T. Gilley, H. T. Little, and C. E. Jenkins, who agreed to sign his bond.

While Livingston was interrogated, Britt was booked at city jail at 6:30 P.M. Later that night the detectives talked with Britt, but he said he would not talk to them about the bombings.

Shows and Ward left the jail. They did not see Britt for two days, but on the afternoon of January 30, Britt sent word that he wanted to meet with them. They picked him up at the jail and took him to the same hotel room where they had interrogated Livingston. After two hours of questioning, during which Shows showed Britt several handwritten references to the Hutchinson Street Baptist Church they had found during a search of his house two days earlier, Britt admitted that he participated in the bombings.

Britt directed Shows and Ward to a trash dump near Dannelly Field Airport southwest of Montgomery, where he pointed to a cardboard box containing several sticks of dynamite. Again, the toxicologist took photographs. Britt told them the box had been discarded by him, Alexander, York, and Livingston. "We had the box filled with dynamite in the backseat of my car while we were following that nigger preacher, Martin Luther King," Britt told them. "We were gonna blow him and his whole family to smithereens, but we decided to wait until another time," he said. Asked why the group had abandoned the box, he said, "Because Officer Ward was following us, and we thought it best to ditch the stuff for now, until he gave up the hunt. We could always go back and find the nigger preacher at some later date." Subsequently, Britt led the two detectives to the other two locations they had already discovered near Maxwell AFB and near Camp Sheridan. Later that night Britt was released on a $7,500 bond furnished by the Dean-Pettus Bonding Company.

A day later, James D. York and Henry Alexander were indicted and charged with dynamiting the occupied residence of the Reverend Ralph David Abernathy and bombing an unoccupied building. The first offense was punishable by death and the second by a maximum of ten years imprisonment. Alexander was also charged with assault to murder.

Three others, Eugene Hall, Charlie Bodiford, and Donald Dunlap, were arrested and charged with conspiracy in the throwing of bombs that failed to explode. Since the maximum penalty for the misdemeanors was a one-thousand-dollar fine plus six months imprisonment, they came under the jurisdiction of D. Eugene Loe, the city recorder and ex officio justice of the peace.

Police Chief G. J. Ruppenthal told reporters covering the case that twenty-four-year-old Dunlap was an ex-convict, having been convicted of grand larceny in 1950 and sentenced to thirteen months in Kilby State Prison north of Montgomery. Previously, Dunlap had been arrested on a grand larceny charge that was turned over to juvenile court. He had also been convicted twice of disorderly conduct.

Reverend King signed the warrant against Dunlap, charging him with attempting to bomb the house where King, his wife, and his infant daughter, Yolanda, lived at 309 South Jackson Street.

Bodiford, a twenty-nine-year-old foreman with a local furniture company, was charged in the bombing of the home of the Reverend Robert Graetz, who signed the warrant against him.

Forty-five-year-old Hall, who worked as a printer, was charged in the bombing of the home of the Reverend Robert Johnson, who signed the arrest warrant against him.

Finally, the team of investigators presented the evidence they had found, including the statements of the defendants, to Circuit Solicitor Thetford.

On February 12, circuit judge Eugene W. Carter charged the grand jury that it was their duty to look into every detail of the recent bombings. "If the evidence justifies it, it is your duty to return an indictment or indictments."

The eighteen white men, led by foreman Herbert R. Nation, a printing company executive who had once been chairman of the Montgomery County Democratic Executive Committee, began their deliberations behind closed doors. Thetford laid out the state's evidence, primarily the testimony of the two city investigators and the state toxicologist, as well as the physical evidence.

A week later the grand jury issued four indictments of the principal defendants.

Britt and Livingston were scheduled to go on trial on February 28 in Montgomery County Circuit Court, but on February 21 Judge Carter granted a request from defense lawyers John Blue Hill and Joe Pilcher, the town's two most accomplished and well-known criminal lawyers, that the trial be delayed until May. Hill told the judge that he needed the assistance of his partner, John Harris, who had recently undergone major surgery. Harris was another of Montgomery's premier legal minds.

In May the trial was called to order. Hill, a short, stout, dark-haired man with an expressive face with a square jawline and thick, dark brows, immediately asked that the signed confessions of both defendants be declared inadmissible.

Solicitor Thetford put Officers Shows and Ward on the stand. Each testified that he had not coerced either of the defendants. Shows, a big man with broad shoulders, nodded as Thetford asked him to tell how Livingston began his statement. Later, Ward, short and stocky with a dark, bristly flat-top, military-style haircut, answered Thetford's questions in his brusque Yankee brogue.

When Hill said, "You manhandled Raymond Britt roughly, didn't you, Officer Ward?" Ward snapped his head sideways and stated, "No, I did not."

"You like to get rough with prisoners, don't you?" Hill asked.

"No, I do not," Ward said.

"You were a military policeman, weren't you?"

"Yes."

"Did you not browbeat Mr. Britt?"

"I did not."

"You and Detective Shows, y'all get a great deal of joy in questioning prisoners, don't you?" Hill asked.

"No," Ward said.

"Y'all like to keep prisoners up late, keep 'em from eating so they'll get hungry and tell you what you want to know?"

"No, sir, we do not."

"If they get tired, go hungry, they'll say just about anything y'all want 'em to say, won't they?"

"That's not the way we do it. If they're tired, they can sleep. If they're hungry, we give 'em food."

Under redirect from Thetford, Ward said there was always food available at the jail or in the hotel room.

Later, Hill called Georgia Britt, Raymond's wife, to the stand. She said that when her husband returned home from the city jail at 1:30 A.M. he was "filthy dirty, hadn't eaten since early the day before, and was so nervous he couldn't go to sleep."

Defense attorney Pilcher, tall, slender, and sandy-haired, introduced a copy of the search warrant obtained by the detectives on the same day both defendants were arrested.

Both Shows and Ward testified that when they searched Britt's home on Gilmer Avenue they found several handwritten references to the Hutchinson Street Baptist Church.

"Did the warrant authorize you to search the house for such notes?" Pilcher asked in his Dallas County, Alabama, drawl. When he asked it, his eyes swept over the twelve white male faces of the jury, all residents of Montgomery County.

When Shows did not immediately answer, Pilcher shook the paper that he placed in front of him. "Read the wording, Mr. Shows," he said.

Shows read that it authorized a search for firearms and explosives.

"It doesn't say anything about pieces of paper, does it, Mr. Shows?"

"No, sir," Shows said.

When the defense once again asked that the confessions be thrown out, Judge Carter ruled that the search warrant did not include handwritten notes; therefore parts of Britt's confession were inadmissible. Still, he said, it was a confession. Asked if they wished to proceed with the prosecution, prosecutors Thetford and Smith said they felt that the state had enough evidence to convict.

Then the defense asked the judge for a ruling on Livingston's confession. Judge Carter said that only the parts dealing with the crime with which Livingston was charged would be admissible. When he spoke to other charges, those sections would be stricken.

On the second day, the prosecution called a lanky railroad switchman, Walter L. King, to the stand. King spoke in a low voice and clasped his bony hands in his lap. As he talked he twisted his fingers together nervously.

He told about attending a meeting at the home of Raymond Britt the night before the bombing of the Hutchinson Street Baptist Church. Inside the home, he said, he saw dynamite caps and other bombing material.

Speaking in a low voice, almost a whisper, Walter King said, "I told them, 'You know, you can go to jail for bombing places.' One man there said he'd kill me if I said anything about it." He identified the other people attending the meeting as Britt, Livingston, and Alexander.

"As we stood way up on the bank of the Alabama River, Britt looked down at the dark water and said, 'That river down there is mighty swift and deep, and you throw something in there, it might not ever come up.'"

On cross-examination, Hill asked, "Why didn't you report these incidents to the police, Mr. King?"

"I was scared to," he answered.

"You're such a good citizen, I'm sure the police would have listened to you," Hill said.

"What would you do?" King asked.

Hill stood with his feet apart and glared at the witness before dismissing him.

When several spectators in the courtroom laughed aloud, Judge Carter stopped proceedings and warned, "I know who just laughed, and if you do that again you're going to jail. Is that understood?"

The audience was silent.

After the state rested, the defense called witnesses who had worked with Walter King. Charles Smitherman, a seventy-one-year-old retired railroad worker and currently an elevator operator in the courthouse building on Dexter Avenue, testified that he had known Walter King for many years and knew him to be "a consummate liar. I would not believe him under oath," he said. Then L. C. Childre, a clerk for the Atlantic Coast Line Railroad, testified that he would not believe Walter King under oath.

The defense called Reverend King to the stand. The short, square-built man's face and voice had become familiar to the nation and to the world during the previous year as the Montgomery bus boycott became daily headlines in newspapers and on the six o'clock television news. For more than an hour, defense attorney John Harris hammered questions at King about the Montgomery Improvement Association, the organization of the MIA, the finances of the group, its relationship with the National Association for the Advancement of Colored People, and statements allegedly made by King concerning integration efforts throughout the South. As each question was asked, deputy solicitor Robert Stewart rose to object. After each, Judge Carter sustained the state's objection.

Finally the judge allowed King to answer that the MIA had spent $225,000 from the beginning of the boycott until it ended in December 1956.

Standing ramrod straight in front of the jury box, facing the witness, defense attorney Harris asked, "After your house was bombed, how many contributions poured into the coffers of the MIA?"

Again, Stewart rose. Again, he objected.

The judge instructed the jury to disregard the question.

"Every time a church is bombed, the MIA benefits, doesn't it?"

Again, Stewart stood. Again, he told the witness not to answer. Again, he appealed to the judge, who told the jury to forget Harris's words.

"Does the MIA have a bombing committee?" Harris asked.

Once again, Stewart appealed to the judge for help.

After several snarling questions, Judge Carter said, "Mr. Harris, this is your witness. You called him to the stand to testify for your case."

When Harris asked another argumentative question, Stewart stood again. He asked the judge to stop this line of questioning designed "solely to influence the jury." He added that the defense knew that none of the questions were relevant. Judge Carter agreed.

The defense paraded forty-three witnesses testifying that they knew Britt and Livingston and that the defendants had a good reputation in the community.

In closing arguments, defense attorney Hill strode back and forth in front of the men whose eyes were riveted on his every move. He spoke of "the sanctity of the Southern way of life" being "in jeopardy. These good men," he said, gesturing toward Livingston and Britt, "have been fighting for you and your families."

Thetford spoke softly. He outlined the facts of the case: the confessions, the testimony of law enforcement officers and a forensic expert, and the details of the bombings.

After deliberating less than two hours, the jury reported that it had reached a verdict. While Britt and Livingston stood next to their attorneys, the foreman of the jury stated, "Not guilty" in both cases.

The crowd of white observers packed into the courtroom exploded with applause and whoops of joy. Although Judge Carter rapped his gavel, the spectators leaped to their feet and surrounded Britt and Livingston, congratulating and hugging them. Outside on Dexter Avenue a photographer from the *Advertiser* took their photos, and a cameraman from WSFA-TV followed them down the sidewalk.

Jo Ann Flirt, who covered the arrests and the trial for the *Advertiser*, remembered, "I really felt sorry for the prosecution and for the investigators. They tried so hard and believed they had a solid case against both of the defendants. I don't think there was ever any question about their guilt. It was a matter of emotions."

"It was the first major victory for the white people of the South in more than a year," Joe Azbell, city editor of the *Advertiser*, wrote in his column, "City Limits." "Raymond C. Britt Jr. and Sonny Kyle Livingston became the symbol of what the white community felt near and dear. They were the embodiment of the white soul of Montgomery."

Looking back, Shows said, "It didn't matter if Britt and Livingston had taken the witness stand and admitted to every bombing of the past year, that jury would not have found them guilty. White people back then just didn't care about law and order. To them, blacks didn't count. In their minds, blacks weren't people. When I look back on it, I think our people in the South had to go through some of the most horrible violence to make them see and make them feel and make them know that blacks were human too. It's an awful thing to comprehend, but I think it's true."

4

HOUND-DOG DETERMINED

In the days following the Confederacy's defeat in the Civil War, a small group of Confederate veterans met in a law office in Pulaski, Tennessee, to organize a good ol' boys club. By their second meeting shortly after Christmas 1865, they decided on a name: the Greek word *kuklos*, for circle. When they added Klan because of their common Scotch-Irish ancestry, it became the Ku Klux Klan. It was not long before famed Confederate cavalry general Nathan Bedford Forrest became their symbolic leader. His self-promotion as the quickest and most effective guerilla tactician against the Union Army had reached legendary proportions. His image, with a rakish, silver-gray, wide-brimmed hat cocked on his handsome head as he sat astride a jet-black stallion, was well known to his admiring public. And he attempted to brand the KKK with the same romantic vision.

Small clubs, or klaverns, cropped up across the South. These white men took it upon themselves to provide vigilante justice, usually against freed slaves who they thought were showing disrespect, getting out of hand with their newfound freedom, or being plain "uppity." The Klansmen often spoke out as representatives of an unnamed fundamentalist religion. They were also known as nightriders because they would storm through black shanty enclaves under cover of darkness, often yelling at the top of their lungs and frightening African Americans, who bowed their heads and shied away from open defiance of white rule.

One Confederate veteran, Ryland Randolph, a native of Mesopotamia, Alabama, owned a plantation with fifty slaves near Montgomery. Before the Civil War he sold his property and joined the Montgomery Rifles. He rode with the company throughout the war, rising to the rank of colonel. After the war, he moved to Tuscaloosa and became editor and publisher of the *Tuskaloosa Independent Monitor*. He wrote scathing editorials against the Reconstruction government, carpetbaggers, and scalawags, and soon he was elected grand cyclops in the local klavern. On special occasions he wrote poetry, displayed on the front page of his newspaper. By reading certain words, members of the klavern would discover the time, date, and location of the next Klan meeting. It was said that Randolph wore twin revolvers he named Alpha and Omega, the beginning and the end. It was also said that the firearms had caused the death of many men, both black and white.

During Reconstruction, when the people of Tuscaloosa elected a freed slave, Shandy Wesley Jones, to the Alabama Legislature, Randolph watched his every political move. He even followed Jones to Montgomery, where, Randolph claimed, he signaled Jones how to vote. In his editorials Randolph often referred to Jones as "the black monkey."

The original Klan began to dissipate in the 1880s and '90s, when the Southern states began enacting Jim Crow laws "to put the Negroes in their place and keep them there," according to James K. Vardaman while serving as Speaker of the Mississippi State House of Representatives in 1894. After he became governor and U.S. senator, Vardaman applauded Alabama's rewriting of its constitution in 1901, arguably one of the most racist documents ever passed by a constitutional convention.

In the years following Reconstruction, Bourbon Democrats, well-to-do white landowners who developed out of the plantation society of the Black Belt that ruled when cotton was king, dominated Alabama politics. These men were the opposite of the federal government's black Reconstruction government and the Republican Party that fostered black voting. When rewriting the state constitution, the authors managed to disenfranchise most of the black population that had been given the vote after the Civil War. In the fourteen Black Belt counties there were 79,000 registered black voters in 1900. Three years later, this number had dropped to 1,081. On January 1, 1903, although Dallas and Lowndes counties had a 75 percent black population, only 103 African Americans were registered voters. At the same time, throughout the state, only 2,980 black citizens were listed as "qualified to vote," although 74,000 were listed as "literate."

William Joseph Simmons, born in 1870 in Harpersville in northeast Alabama, was working in a field on his father's farm when he was suddenly stricken with a fever. Bedridden for weeks, young Simmons dreamed of men dressed in white, defending a wall. In 1898, when president William McKinley called for volunteers to fight against the Spanish Army in Cuba, Simmons enlisted. He believed military service was the answer to his vision, but ultimately the Spanish-American War did not fulfill the prophecy.

In his journey to find an answer, Simmons attended seminary and became a Methodist minister. From the pulpit, he spoke often about his youthful vision, believing that God had put him on earth for a definite purpose. In 1914, the Methodist church removed him for "inadequacies." Back in the sick bed at his parents' farm a year later, a friend brought him a poster of an upcoming movie, D. W. Griffith's *Birth of a Nation*. Gazing into the poster with its image of a white-gowned Ku Klux Klansman wielding a lighted torch on the back of a raring horse, Simmons became convinced that this was the answer to his vision, that his calling was to defend the white "Southern way of life." He rose from the bed and traveled to Atlanta for the premiere of the movie that romanticized the Klan, showing the organization as a glorious tool to fight for national patriotism and Christianity. On the eve of the film's opening, Simmons convinced twenty local white men to join him in a display of unity. With Simmons leading the way, they climbed nearby Stone Mountain, a huge granite dome that jutted high over the earth's floor, more than sixteen hundred feet above sea level. Atop Stone Mountain they burned a huge cross to symbolize the rebirth of the KKK. Calling himself Colonel, although he never reached the rank while a soldier,

Simmons also claimed to have studied medicine at Johns Hopkins and was called Doc by some of his followers.

In the years after the first cross burning, Simmons employed public relations professionals from New York to California to market the Knights of the Ku Klux Klan as protectors of American values, stating the organization was "100 percent Americanism." From Georgia to New York, across the Midwest to California, Simmons preached that his organization "will deliver us from evil" as he spoke to and signed up tens of thousands, organizing outings, children's divisions, and Klan auxiliaries for female members. He and his followers preached against Negroes, women's rights, divorce, drinking and carousing, Jews, Catholics, immigration, and "any sin against the Holy Bible." Groups and individuals cropped up in communities across America to take the law into their own hands, riding at night to frighten black men who had simply looked at white women, to beat white men who drank too much, or to lynch black men who failed to meet the Klan's rigid social standards. They wore white gowns and hoods, carried burning torches, and erected huge crosses they burned with flames licking into the dark nights. In the 1920s, membership in the KKK grew to monumental proportions. Across the South, its political power was enormous. In Alabama, Bibb Graves, the exalted cyclops of the Montgomery klavern, was elected governor in 1926 with Klan support. The same year, Klan member Hugo Black was elected U.S. senator from Alabama. Later that year, when violent Klan activity became more and more widespread throughout the state, both men renounced the organization.

A member of the U.S. House of Representatives during this time, James Thomas "Cotton Tom" Heflin of Alabama was an outspoken racist on the floor of Congress. In 1908, when a black man confronted him on a streetcar in the nation's capital, Heflin shot and severely wounded him. Although indicted, Heflin never faced trial. For many years, he bragged that the shooting was one of his greatest accomplishments. One of the only bills he actually passed as a congressman recognized Mother's Day as a national holiday.

In 1927, after Heflin became a U.S. senator, he cursed the state of New York for passing a law allowing marriages between people of different races. Grover Cleveland Hall, whose eloquent editorials exposing the Klan won a Pulitzer Prize, wrote in the *Montgomery Advertiser* that Heflin was "a bully by nature, a mountebank by instinct, a Senator by choice. . . . Thus this preposterous blob excites our pity if not our respect, and we leave him to his conscience in order that he may be entirely alone and meditate over the life of a charlatan whose personal interest and personal vanity are always of paramount concern to him." After Heflin refused to support the Democratic candidate for president, Al Smith, because he was Catholic, the party would not allow Heflin to run under its banner when he came up for reelection, and he lost.

By the 1930s, after an extensive investigation by the U.S. House of Representatives that uncovered numerous illegal and immoral activities, the Klan was so splintered across the United States that it was rendered virtually powerless. However, during World War II, although the U.S. military was fighting one of the most dreadful and hateful empires of evil the world had ever seen in the Nazi regime of Adolf Hitler, white supremacist groups began to form in the armed services. Jack Shows had seen it while serving in the navy. "When some of those white soldiers saw black troops mingling with blond women, you could see that it made their blood boil," Shows remembered. "They'd go into the saloons and drink a snootful of good German beer. When a black serviceman would enter, a pretty little blond hanging all over him, those white guys would seethe. They didn't have to be from the South. They were from all over. I'd see the hate in their eyes, their expressions, and later their words."

Jack Shows and Tom Ward did not let the Montgomery bombers' not-guilty verdict stop them. "We were hound-dog determined to keep the violence to a minimum, if we couldn't catch them in the act of actually setting up and detonating a bomb in a church or at a house," Shows said. "In some incidences we found their cache of explosives and destroyed it. Some we just threw into the river and watched it sink."

The two had already begun to build a network of informants. Through their questioning of the suspects in the church bombing they had determined which members of the local Klan would talk when separated from their fellow members. Often Shows would pick up a known Klansman in north Montgomery and take him for a ride out on the road toward Tyler-Goodwin Bridge, where the Klansmen had taken Willie Edwards Jr. on his last ride. "We'd talk," Shows recalled. "Just talk. About anything. The weather. Sooner or later, I'd lead him around to what was happening with the Klan. Who was doing what to whom and where. Where Dynamite Bob was last seen in Montgomery. Where the latest cache of explosives was hidden. Who was saying what at the Little Kitchen."

Sometimes Shows would go out to the Kilby Prison compound. The inmates he had arrested, testified against, and put away for hard time behind the high concrete walls were usually glad to see him. He would bring a candy bar, a Coke, or a pack of cigarettes. They were always glad to get smokes. He would talk in his easy, slow, country way. His voice was a familiar baritone to them. Although he was "the law," they trusted him.

After the not-guilty verdict in Montgomery Circuit Court, the KKK was so eager, anxious, and arrogant, a rally was called. In long white gowns and high, pointed hoods, more than a thousand gathered at twilight in a field off the Old Selma Road west of Montgomery.

Bobby Shelton came down from Tuscaloosa donning his crimson satin gown. From Georgia appeared J. B. Stoner in his customary business suit and Confederate flag lapel pin. With him was James Venable, grand wizard of the Georgia Klan and mayor of Stone Mountain. It had been his uncle who had opened his property to William Joseph Simmons and his band of cross burners back in 1915 to stage the rebirth of the KKK.

On this night, the gathered group planned to burn the biggest cross ever. Workers had built a huge cross from eight-by-eights, standing more than forty feet high.

"We are here to send a message," Shelton told the multitude who cheered his every statement.

"We want the scalawagging white law enforcement to know that we will not be pushed around," Shelton said.

The crowd applauded.

"We are the law," Shelton said into the microphone that broadcast his words to the people whom Shows and Ward learned had come from South Carolina, Georgia, Mississippi, Tennessee, and Arkansas.

"We are the law of the white people. We will keep the Negro from running amok, as the federal court wants him to run. We will show those people who are trying to control us that we will not stand for such turmoil as they wish. We will take control of our lives, thank you.

"Where sinners trod this good earth, promoting communism and ungodly acts, like race-mixing, fornication, and out-and-out adultery, we must stand tall on a higher moral ground. We must provide the law in a land of the lawless.

"Now, in the name of the Lord of the Universe, the white man's God who shall prevail over the South, the North, the East, and the West . . ." He pointed toward the huge cross. Three men in gowns, each holding a lighted torch, marched through the crowd that parted for them. As the spotlight was switched off, the men lowered their torches to the base of the cross, which suddenly exploded in a fire that climbed up and out, lighting the dark sky.

As soon as he heard the not-guilty verdict at the end of the trial, Jack Shows knew it would give the KKK a boost. Talking with investigators in Birmingham, Mobile, Selma, and Tuscaloosa, he learned that underworld activity started a new and energetic buzz as soon as the verdict was learned. Now, in the dark of night, just beyond the reach of the spotlight that circled the group of Klansmen, city investigators Shows and Ward sat with two officers who had been recruited to help in their KKK investigations. The four watched and listened and recorded from their car parked on an unpaved road next to a dairy. "There was nothing we could do," Shows remembered. "We were basically helpless, unless the KKKers got out of hand and started a riot and committed crimes right there in front of us. We knew we couldn't arrest them for saying words that they chose to say."

Police watched the gathering until near midnight and saw a carload of Kluxers in their robes ride onto the Old Selma Road and turn east toward Montgomery. Shows decided to follow at a distance. If they got out of hand, the four policemen would arrest them. Even if they couldn't be convicted, perhaps a few hours in city jail might slow them down and make them think about their actions.

They followed the car through north Montgomery. When it entered Newtown, where black residents had lived for more than a hundred years, Shows, Ward, and their fellow officers turned off their headlights but continued to watch.

Newtown was a section of Montgomery off the Lower Wetumpka Road that had been stables and carriage houses in the nineteenth century. Blacks enslaved by townspeople had lived here and tended to livestock. They had kept buggies and horses next to the small houses where they lived. In the mornings, the slaves would saddle the horses or hook up harnesses to buggies. They would ride to town and wait near the houses on Perry or Hull or McDonough streets for their white "masters."

On this night, the KKKers slowed and came to a stop, as did Shows. Hooded Klansmen got out of their car in their robes. At a house on French Street, two Klansmen approached the front door. The men did not bother to knock. They slammed their shoulders against the door and entered, shouting. Within moments, they dragged a black man out of his house, across his front porch, and down the steps.

While the black man wept, Shows, Ward, and their fellow officers surrounded the group. Within moments, the policemen had the two Kluxers in handcuffs. Their friends in the car sped away, the wheels of their car squealing against the pavement.

While his men were placing the Klansmen into the rear of their police car, Shows tried to comfort the victim. As the man trembled, Shows assured him he would not have to testify against the KKKers.

The officers took the culprits to the city jail, where they were booked and charged with breaking and entering an occupied dwelling at night. Within several hours, three of their friends signed their bonds, and they were released.

The Klansmen were never brought to trial. The district attorney refused to prosecute white-on-black crime after the all-white jury's not-guilty verdict in the bombing trial; he considered it a waste of time and money under the circumstances. Shows spread the word that while the prosecution might not be able to convict Klan members in court, he and his officers would continue to arrest them if and when they broke the law. They would spend many nights in the Montgomery city jail and would leave behind bond money every time they were released. Every time they were arrested, he said, it would cost them.

5

"FIGHT EVERYTHING SEGREGATED"

The African American leaders in Montgomery were angry. Their constituents and congregations were confused, hurt, and mad. For more than a year they had refused to ride city buses. They had suffered. They were criticized and cursed by many whites. When the preachers told them to stay the course, they listened and followed. Few had cars of their own. They walked from one end of town to the other. They caught rides with strangers. They organized an efficient system of carpools to transport people who could not walk longer distances. And finally, they won a huge battle with the U.S. Supreme Court declaring the city's segregation law unconstitutional. To most, it was a significant victory.

Now, however, an all-white jury spoke for a cheering white community, saying basically that violence against the black community was OK. For many local blacks, the Montgomery Improvement Association that had been quickly organized on the Monday after Rosa Parks was arrested on Thursday, December 1, 1955, had outlived its usefulness with the integration of the city buses. But in the mind of its first president, Reverend King, it was still useful.

King knew that he would be able to raise a great deal of money in the aftermath of the not-guilty verdict. That verdict echoed in headlines and on six o'clock television reports across the nation and the world.

Within hours King flew out of Montgomery and made speeches in Atlanta, New York, Chicago, and Los Angeles. In each, he reiterated the facts and the drama and the bitter disappointment of the trial. In each, he appeared on television and spoke out, telling the people of the world about the daily atrocities in Alabama. In each, he raised funds to keep the civil rights movement alive.

"Before the end of the boycott, our struggle had mushroomed into an international happening. Now, the people of the world were concerned—not only about our situation but about the situation of all black people everywhere. They poured out their hearts and opened their pocketbooks," King said. "We were no longer local. Our headlines became news in Great Britain, France, Germany, and throughout the world. When I spoke to audiences in the big cities of our nation, I was speaking to the world. Every television network carried our message in prime time. Although the trial of the two men in Montgomery was a tragedy, I had to accelerate to reiterate our message of hope. I continued to believe that ours was a success story, even though violence continued to simmer and burn all around us. We had to overcome the obstacles that were born out of the violence of racism. I had to believe that in their heart of hearts, the white people would push aside their hatred and find love. It was my true belief. I had to keep preaching it."

On February 18, 1957, *Time* ran a cover story about King and the victorious boycott. Lee Griggs from the Atlanta bureau wrote, "Personally humble, articulate, and of high educational attainment, Martin Luther King Jr. is, in fact, what many a Negro—and, were it not for his color, many a white—would like to be." Griggs followed the preacher through a long, tiring day, ending with a mass meeting where he spoke to hundreds. After a hymn, King said, "If we as a people had as much religion in our hearts as we have in our legs and feet, we could change this world." At the meeting, he told the crowd, "Our use of passive resistance in Montgomery is not based on resistance to get rights for ourselves but to achieve friendship with the men who are denying us our rights and change them through friendship and a bond of Christian understanding before God." Griggs's article expanded King's audience greatly, selling out the issue in which it appeared.

From the pulpit of Dexter Avenue Baptist, King described "the birth of a new nation," how the people of Ghana on the Gold Coast of Africa were able to sing out at last, "Free-dom! Free-dom! Great God Almighty, I'm free at last!" He told his congregation that "freedom only comes through persistent revolt, through persistent agitation, through persistently rising up against the system of evil. The bus protest is just the beginning. Buses are integrated in Montgomery, but that is just the beginning."

He urged, "Let us fight passionately and unrelentingly for the goals of justice and peace, but let's be sure that our hands are clean in this struggle. Let us never fight with falsehood and violence and hate and malice but always fight with love," adding that soon "we will be able to live with people as their brothers and sisters." He said he wanted to come back home to Montgomery but first he needed to travel to New York and Los Angeles, London and Paris, and to the Gold Coast of Africa to spread the word. It was the gospel that had begun on the early Monday morning streets of Montgomery, Alabama, on December 5, 1955, when black people refused to ride the city buses.

However, for Edgar Daniel Nixon, the problems were local. The former statewide president of the NAACP, Nixon had been instrumental in organizing the bus boycott and putting King into the leadership position. "I understood what King and Abernathy and all of them were trying to do on a national and worldwide level. At least, I tried to understand. Still, I had to watch out for the folks right here at home. It was here that the violence was happening, where the white men who wanted to do it felt that they could do it, no matter what, and they would get away with it. Who was gonna stop 'em? Surely not the law, 'cause it was a white man's law. I had to shake my finger in Jim Crow's face." As he spoke in his ancient, gravel-gruff voice, he leaned forward and gazed into my eyes.

"That's what I got out of the verdict from the twelve white men." Nixon's voice rose in a bitter refrain. "For me, the years after the bus boycott were years of hell. I wasn't too well [physically]. I felt like my old body was just pure wore out. But it wasn't long before I got up out of the sick bed and went back to work," he said. For many years Nixon had enjoyed his life's work as a Pullman car porter on various passenger trains that ran into and out of Montgomery. He especially enjoyed his trips up East, when he met with his mentor, A. Philip Randolph, the leader and organizer of the Pullman Car Porters Union, whom Nixon had listened to in a speech in the 1920s and had become inspired to become an activist back home in Alabama.

In the early 1940s, Nixon enjoyed a friendship with First Lady Eleanor Roosevelt, who helped him through social changes back then. He walked with Rosa Parks from the Montgomery Municipal Court on the Monday morning after her arrest. He sat on the front porch of the Dexter Avenue Baptist Church parsonage with twenty-five-year-old King and talked him into taking the reins of the bus boycott that evolved into the civil rights movement. Then he saw and heard the testimony in the Montgomery Circuit Court.

"When I listened to the two white detectives tell what they'd learned, I felt like this thing was surely turning around," Nixon said. "I thought: Now's the time. But it wasn't to be. When I heard the jury's verdict, I knew it was gonna be hell."

Within three nights of the not-guilty verdict, and after Bobby Shelton spoke to the large gathering of the KKK, three more houses were bombed in the black community. Little property damage was done, and no one was injured. Still, the sounds of explosions resonated through the community and told the African American citizens that things were no better than a year earlier.

"While we were definitely frustrated, we were not complacent," said Johnnie Rebecca Carr, who stood steadfast by the side of her childhood friend Rosa Parks. Like Parks, Carr had been a volunteer in Nixon's office when he was the local president of the NAACP and had helped in organizing efforts for what became the civil rights movement. Slowly but positively, she became one of the stalwart leaders in the community.

As she spoke to me years later in the living room of her home on Hall Street, she remembered the days of the 1950s. "We knew that sooner or later we would lose Reverend King. He was becoming too important to the entire world of the people of color. His stature was greater than Montgomery, Alabama, and we knew it. We also knew we wanted to keep him here as long as we could. For the time being, he could fly out on Monday and fly back in later in the week. For the time being, we'd settle for that. Mr. Nixon and others tried to cheer us on, all during the time when explosions were waking us nearly every night. We didn't drop our heads. We didn't cry out. We clinched our fists and swore to be more determined than ever before."

★

In June 1957 the white government of Montgomery was feeling the strength of its superiority. In the wake of the all-white jury's verdict, the city commission passed an ordinance that it titled simply "Segregation." It declared that any black person using a white park or a white swimming pool would be guilty of a misdemeanor and could be fined and imprisoned for a year.

Early in 1957, King wrote a friend, "After living in the South all my life, I have come to see through grim experience that the southern reactionaries will never fall in line voluntarily; it will only come through proper, moral, and legitimate pressure." In August he called together more than a hundred African American leaders to convene in Montgomery to organize against similar segregation measures throughout the South. Those gathered became the founding members of the Southern Christian Leadership Conference. Its first initiative would be the Crusade for Citizenship, a voter registration drive across the South that would show, King said, "a new Negro, determined to be free, emerging in America." In the meantime, the founders raised $250,000 for the first year's operating budget, opened an office in Atlanta, and named King its chairman. As one said, "King *was* the Southern Christian Leadership Conference."

Among the first delegates of the SCLC was a man who would soon become known as the Wild Man from Birmingham, the Reverend Fred Lee Shuttlesworth, who not only listened to but had already become enthralled with King's preachings. A graduate of Selma University and Alabama State College, he was minister at the Bethel Baptist Church in Birmingham, where he announced to his congregation late in 1956 that he planned to test Birmingham's city ordinances requiring segregation. Soon thereafter, he announced that his organization would be called the Alabama Christian Movement for Human Rights.

Sue Ellen Clifford remembered, "Reverend Shuttlesworth was not as poetic or as thoughtful as King, but his words were just as strong. He had a fire that burned hot inside his soul. That fire spilled out when he stepped into the pulpit. Later he showed that his actions were just as strong as his words." Clifford, who was a child in his congregation in the late 1950s, said that her father and other men would sit around on Sunday afternoons and talk about what Shuttlesworth had told them that morning in church. "They knew that Reverend Shuttlesworth was laying the groundwork for a battlefront of a revolution. It was only a matter of time. I lived it, saw it, felt it, and later became a part of it."

Back in Montgomery, in September 1957, sixteen-year-old African American Mark D. Gilmore was cutting through Oak Park, a forty-acre wooded playground, petting zoo, swimming pool, and picnic area, when a policeman spotted him. The path through the park was young Gilmore's shortcut to Jackson Hospital, where he worked after school. Not wanting to be late to work, he took the shortcut.

When the white policeman nabbed him, young Gilmore was beaten, arrested, and charged with violating the city's ordinance against segregation of city parks. He was held in jail without bond. Two weeks later, he was found guilty in city court.

In the Montgomery County Courthouse in late November, Georgia Gilmore, the boy's mother, approached Solomon Seay Jr., a young lawyer with a new license to practice. He had graduated from Howard Law School in Washington, D.C., that spring, returned to Montgomery in the summer, studied for the bar, and passed the exam. In October 1957 he became the seventh African American lawyer in the state of Alabama. He went to see his friend Fred D. Gray, who practiced with Charles D. Langford. They were the only other black lawyers in the capital city. Others in the state were Arthur Shores, Peter Hall, and Orzell Billingsley in Birmingham and Vernon Crawford in Mobile.

Seay immediately recognized Georgia Gilmore, who was famous as a cook. During the long days of the bus boycott, she cooked for and fed tired and hungry protesters. Her kitchen was always open to her people. She knew Seay as the son of a local minister and had seen his photograph in the Negro News section of the *Montgomery Advertiser* as the town's new black lawyer.

Early in 1958, Seay wrote a petition signed by Mrs. Gilmore and many other black leaders. In the spring the attorney filed the petition with the city commission, asking the three white men to integrate all fourteen parks, including swimming pools, tennis courts, and other recreational facilities. In August the commissioners recognized the petition and agreed to rule on it.

At a hearing, Seay ran into the kind of hostility he had known through life and would face for years. In the second-floor room in city hall, he was asked by the petitioners where they should sit. Seay said wryly, "At the back, if you are black." Moments later, police commissioner Clyde Sellers stepped to Seay's side, pointed to the opposite side of the aisle, and said, "Niggers sit over there." Seay and his group moved across the aisle.

A few minutes later, after the petition was read, mayor W. A. "Tacky" Gayle stated curtly, "The commission will not operate integrated parks."

On the following morning, Seay met with his partner Fred Gray, who lived and practiced law in both Montgomery and Tuskegee. By now Gray was experienced with handling hardheaded decisions by the stubborn white government. He had represented Rosa Parks in city court, had filed *Browder v. Gayle* questioning the constitutionality of Montgomery's law requiring segregation of riders on city buses and carried it from federal court in Montgomery all the way to the U.S. Supreme Court in Washington, and had represented Reverend King in numerous court proceedings. Early in his career, Gray swore to himself that he would "fight everything segregated that I could find."

On December 22, 1958, Gray and Seay filed *Gilmore v. City of Montgomery* in U.S. District Court in Montgomery. Soon after the suit was filed, the city commission closed all of Montgomery's parks to all of its citizens.

Gray and Seay felt that if the white politicians operated in such an obstinate way, they would be just as stubborn. The attorneys would push the case forward in the federal court.

Nine months later, U.S. district judge Frank M. Johnson ruled that operating segregated public parks was illegal and unconstitutional. He enjoined the city from operating them in such a manner, if they were ever opened again.

The commission ordered the parks permanently closed. Bulldozers filled the pools. Some parks were sold to private developers. In several cases, the land was simply deeded to individuals free of charge.

In the same year, when public libraries were ordered to open their doors to people of all colors, the city took away all the chairs in the public rooms. One could not sit and read in the libraries. It was impossible for black and white children to sit together at the same table.

Across Alabama, the few African American attorneys had their hands and minds full, trying to put out the Jim Crow fires the white governments were setting.

In Selma, Fred Gray, Orzell Billingsley, and Peter Hall defended Lewis Lloyd Anderson, pastor of the Tabernacle Baptist Church, where he used his pulpit to preach the righteousness of the civil rights movement. As he was driving a very short distance home one day, the Reverend Anderson accidentally hit and killed a black man named Tom Reese. Although it was an accident, the local white establishment determined to silence Anderson by charging him criminally and sending him to prison. As attorney Gray wrote later, "Under normal circumstances, the law enforcement officials of Selma and other cities in Alabama were not very concerned about the death of an African American person and certainly not one that was the result of an automobile accident." In 1959, Anderson was convicted of manslaughter and sentenced to prison. His attorneys appealed the ruling. At one stage, city powers said they would drop the case if he would leave town. He refused.

Gray, Billingsley, and Hall appealed all the way to the U.S. Supreme Court, which reversed the case. In the end, Anderson was exonerated. He continued preaching civil rights and became a leader in the early 1960s when demonstrations became a part of daily life on the streets of Selma and the country towns of the Black Belt. As the Selma-to-Montgomery March was being planned, he proved himself an effective leader.

When the white power bosses of Macon County continued an age-old tradition of keeping political strength out of the hands of African

Americans, although blacks outnumbered whites nearly two-to-one, Fred Gray took up the case of Dr. Charles G. Gomillion, dean of students at Tuskegee Institute. As president of the Tuskegee Civic Association (TCA), Dr. Gomillion led the black citizens to boycott white-owned shops in Tuskegee to retaliate for the actions of white politicians. As a result, Alabama attorney general John Patterson filed suit against TCA, asking that it be enjoined from illegal boycotting. When Gray called Patterson to the stand, he tried to show through the politician's testimony that he was using the suit to promote himself as a candidate in the governor's race the following year. Patterson would not admit it, but it came true just as Gray had foreseen it.

In 1957, state senator Sam Engelhardt, executive secretary of the White Citizens Council of Alabama, who also represented Macon County in the Alabama Legislature, introduced a bill that changed the boundaries of the City of Tuskegee from a square to what Gray called "a twenty-eight-sided sea dragon." Passing unanimously, the bill removed about four hundred blacks from the city. Residents of these black neighborhoods could not vote in subsequent municipal elections. One of the disenfranchised was Dr. Gomillion.

When Gray filed *Gomillion v. Lightfoot* he was joined by Birmingham attorney Arthur Shores, a small but fiery veteran fighter for civil rights. They argued the case before judge Frank Johnson, who dismissed the complaint.

When they appealed to the Fifth Circuit Court of Appeals, two of the three judges on the panel affirmed Judge Johnson's ruling.

Gray and Shores appealed to the U.S. Supreme Court. By now, *Gomillion* had attracted nationwide attention. In the more than three years it took to work the case up to the U.S. Supreme Court, other, more seasoned attorneys became attracted to the case. Robert Carter, general counsel for the NAACP, with whom Gray had worked on other legal matters, became cocounsel.

As he prepared for the high court, Gray could feel the excitement growing within him. He wrote later in his autobiography, *Bus Ride to Justice*, "I argued first. As I began, the Chief Justice wanted to know the meaning of the map. I explained that behind me was a map of the City of Tuskegee showing the old city limits with the new city limits superimposed thereon. Justice Felix Frankfurter immediately asked,

'Where is Tuskegee Institute? I know it is still in the City of Tuskegee.' I pointed out to Mr. Justice Frankfurter where Tuskegee Institute was on the map. I told him that Tuskegee Institute was gerrymandered outside the city limits.

"He said, 'You mean to tell me that Tuskegee Institute is outside the city limits of the City of Tuskegee?' I said, 'Yes, sir, Mr. Justice Frankfurter.' I believe that was the determining factor in getting Frankfurter's vote."

In the meantime, Gray and Carter argued that the Fourteenth and Fifteenth Amendments, due process and equal protection, as well as the right to vote, were being denied their client. The unanimous opinion of the U.S. Supreme Court, written by Justice Frankfurter and handed down on November 14, 1960, stated, "When a legislature thus singles out a readily isolated segment of a racial minority for special discrimination treatment, it violates the Fifteenth Amendment."

With its weighty decision, the case was sent back to Judge Johnson, who granted Gray's motion and found that the act passed by the Alabama Legislature was indeed unconstitutional. The previous boundaries of the City of Tuskegee were reinstated.

Gray wrote, *"Gomillion v. Lightfoot* is perhaps the most important civil rights case that I have had the privilege of handling. In fact, this case was my brainchild and the one I thought from the beginning we would win in spite of overwhelming odds."

He added, "Finally, this case was a personal victory. Not only did I have the opportunity to appear and argue the case before the U.S. Supreme Court, but we won. I felt that I had come a long way from riding the buses in Montgomery, Alabama, and seeing injustice being done to African Americans, to standing before the highest court in America. I had, to a great degree, accomplished my goal of destroying everything segregated I could find. In this case, the court announced a rule of law which would live on and be a mighty weapon for destroying racial discrimination."

In his own inimitable way, rising above the segregationist atmosphere in which he was born and raised, Gray continued a distinguished career that had begun in the throes of the Montgomery bus boycott. He had stood with Rosa Parks and Edgar Daniel Nixon before the city court on the Monday after she was arrested on December 1, 1955. He had filed *Browder v. Gayle*, in which an African American woman had sued the mayor of Montgomery, and the court had declared that the segregationist statute on city transportation was illegal. Now he had laid the groundwork for legal work to end jury discrimination in the future of the South.

★

In March 1953, Selma was awakened abruptly when the young white wife of an airman stationed at Craig Field cried out that she had been raped by a black man. She reported to police that a black man wearing a mask had broken into her home, pushed her onto the floor, held a knife to her throat, and repeatedly raped her. As the word spread through the white community, white men threatened to take the law into their own hands.

Several months after the first rape was reported, the mayor's daughter, a young married woman, told police that she awakened to find a black man with a knife straddling her body. When the news spread, the white community panicked. Although she fought and took the knife and her assailant fled, white men began patrolling the streets.

Every night police reported receiving five or six calls saying, "There's a nigger in my house!"

Police rounded up dozens of black men, took them to jail, questioned them, and sometimes kept them overnight.

One night several white men found a black man walking alone down an alley near a white neighborhood. They took him to the police. William Earl Fikes was a resident of nearby Marion, a small Black Belt town in the middle of plantation country. Married and the father of four, he was known in his community as borderline retarded. He was taken from the Selma jail to the state prison fifty miles southeast in Montgomery "for his protection," according to authorities. Locked in a cell, he was questioned for fourteen hours a day for several days, after which he confessed to the crimes.

Charged with rape and attempting to rape, both capital crimes, he was tried first for rape. Although the wife of the airman said she could not identify him because her assailant had been wearing a mask, twelve white men found him guilty and sentenced him to ninety-nine years in prison. Because he was not given death, the white community screamed that justice had not been done.

Standing up for Fikes was Sam Boynton, a graduate of Tuskegee Institute who had come to Selma as a U.S. agricultural extension agent. He and his wife, Amelia, a home economics extension agent, had worked with black farmers and their families. They had talked with numerous black and white people who knew Fikes and did not believe he was capable of such a crime. Also, the Boyntons believed the white community was acting irrationally.

As a result, Boynton sought the help of the NAACP Defense Fund to represent Fikes in his second trial. Traveling to Dallas County from Birmingham were attorneys Peter Hall and Orzell Billingsley, who would be the first African American lawyers to try a case in a Dallas County courtroom.

When he heard about the case, Selma native J. L. Chestnut Jr., who was studying at Howard Law School, came down to watch the action. Chestnut met Peter Hall at the Elks Club, where "he was sitting at the long mirror-tiled bar, drinking whiskey and looking for respectable, educated blacks to testify that they had never been called to serve on a jury," Chestnut remembered. He never forgot Hall's words: "I don't know if Fikes is guilty, but it's damn sure the system is. I intend to try the system while the circuit solicitor is trying Fikes."

The next day in the courtroom, Chestnut was impressed with what he saw. Hall's "appearance was striking. Whites and blacks in Selma rarely saw a black man in a suit other than the standard black ones preachers and undertakers wore. Peter—tall with light skin and a mustache—was movie-star handsome and sophisticated. He carried himself in a way that suggested Duke Ellington or Billy Eckstine. Though he was raised in Birmingham, he had gone to law school at DePaul University in Chicago, and he didn't speak with a Southern accent. He spoke very formal English, referring to Fikes as 'the defendant.'"

Chestnut watched as Hall came in "a little late, probably for effect. He walked with a slight limp—he had a cork leg—at a determined but unhurried pace up to the bench, where he planted that cork leg and started arguing a flurry of pretrial motions.

"From that moment, it was obvious that Peter Hall was the smoothest, most competent lawyer in the room—and that Peter Hall knew it. He dominated the white judge, the white lawyers. Orzell was impressive, too, as a researcher in that trial. While Peter would be making a legal point, Orzell would be flipping the pages of a law book and would have it open to just the right citation when Peter turned around and reached for it."

After asking the judge to quash the indictment and dismiss the jurors on the ground that blacks had been systematically excluded, Hall examined county officials on the witness stand. Each testified that no blacks had served on juries in Dallas County for as long as they could remember. Sam Boynton was one of a number of educated blacks who testified that they had never been called to jury duty. Although he was refused at every turn, Hall managed to lay the groundwork for suits that would be filed in the future.

Although the mayor's daughter testified that her assailant had had a towel wrapped around his head and she could not positively identify him, the confession was allowed, and the jury took forty minutes to find Fikes guilty and sentence him to death.

Ultimately, the motions that Hall made during the trial gave the U.S. Supreme Court enough evidence to overturn the conviction. The defendant displayed limited mental and verbal capacity, and his isolation for nearly a week and the repeated questions by police gave the court reason to dismiss the confession. However, the first conviction by the all-white jury stood. Although the prosecution decided not to retry him on the second case, Fikes remained in prison on the first conviction.

In July 1957 a mentally challenged fifty-five-year-old black handyman, James H. "Jimmy" Wilson, was convicted in Marion in the heart of Alabama's Black Belt of robbing an elderly white widow of $1.95. He was then sentenced to death by the all-white, all-male jury.

On September 3, 1958, Martin Luther King Jr. and his wife, Coretta, went to the city recorder's court in Montgomery. They were standing outside the courtroom when a policeman stepped up and told them to move on. "I am waiting to see my lawyer, Fred Gray," King said. "If you don't get the hell out of here, you're going to *need* a lawyer," the police-man said. When King didn't move, the white officer said, "Boy, you done it now." Calling another policeman to assist him, the two grabbed King, twisted his arms behind his back, and pushed him down a flight of stairs to city hall on the first floor. When the first policeman turned to Mrs. King, he said, "You want to go to jail too, gal? Just nod your head if you want to." King said, "Don't say anything, darling." After the police shoved him around and kicked him, the first officer wrote a ticket charging him with failure to obey an officer of the law. Then he released King on his own recognizance.

In city court two days later, King stood with Gray in front of judge D. Eugene Loe, who found him guilty and fined him ten dollars or four-teen days in jail. King then asked if he could make a statement. Loe said, "Go ahead."

King took a piece of paper from his coat pocket, unfolded it, and read. In spite of having his arms twisted and being choked and kicked, "I hold no animosity or bitterness in my heart for the arresting officers," he said. He would not pay the fine. He would go to jail instead. "I make this deci-sion because of my deep concern for the injustices and indignities that my people continue to experience. Today, in many parts of the South, the brutality inflicted upon Negroes has become America's shame."

King pointed out that "at this very moment in this state James Wil-son sits in the death house condemned to die for stealing less than two dollars. Can anyone at this court believe that a white man could be con-demned to death in Alabama for stealing this small amount?

"The Negro can no longer silently endure conditions of police bru-tality and mob violence. We cannot do so because we are commanded to resist evil by God that created us all. Let me hasten to say, your honor, that I am confident that Negroes will adhere to the same quality of Christian love and nonviolence to overcome these conditions that were used in our long protest. I am sure that there are thousands of white persons of good will throughout the South who in their hearts con-demn mob violence and inhuman treatment of Negroes. I call upon these persons to gird their courage and speak out for law and order."

When he stood in line to be taken to jail, the policemen would not take him. When he stepped onto the vehicle carrying other convicted defendants to jail, the policemen led him off. Ultimately, he was told someone had paid his fine. Later, he discovered police commissioner Clyde Sellers had paid the fine and then issued a statement saying he wanted "to save the taxpayers the expense of feeding King for fourteen days."

In the meantime, the Associated Press, United Press International, and other national media reported the story and quoted King's statement, which he had sent to numerous journalists.

Less than three weeks later, on September 29, governor James E. Folsom held a press conference and announced that he had commuted the death sentence imposed on James Wilson to life in prison.

Although another important battle was won in the fight for civil rights, throughout the South the Ku Klux Klan was gaining strength by the day. Klaverns from southern Illinois and Indiana to the suburbs surrounding New Orleans were adding more and more members to their rolls.

In north Montgomery on the Lower Wetumpka Road, the same road on which Willie Edwards Jr. rode with the Klansmen to the Tyler-Goodwin Bridge, a six-foot-wide round sign hung on the side of a small framed building. On it was painted a hooded and gowned figure riding a horse rearing up on its hind legs. Around the rim the legend read, KU KLUX KLAN OF ALABAMA. Inside the building, the North Montgomery klavern met frequently to plan their activities.

Less than a mile down the same road, a larger concrete-block, whitewashed building housed the off-duty meeting room of the Montgomery Fraternal Order of Police. It was here where off-duty police officers met to drink beer and barbecue, where their families gathered, and where they enjoyed time away from the staid headquarters five miles to the south. In 1960 it was an all-white police force that watched over black and white Montgomery.

On the eastern edge of Tuscaloosa was a sign that read, WELCOME TO TUSCALOOSA, THE UNITED KLANS OF AMERICA.

On a rural road in north Alabama another small sign read, NIGGER, DON'T LET THE SUN SET ON YOU IN CULLMAN COUNTY.

And on a highway north of Birmingham was a full-sized billboard: JOIN & SUPPORT THE UNITED KLANS OF AMERICA.

6

THE MAKING OF A SEGREGATIONIST

George Corley Wallace was a member of the Alabama Legislature from Barbour County, where he had been elected in 1946 by an overwhelming majority after returning home from World War II. As a floor leader for progressive governor Big Jim Folsom in his first term, Wallace too was known as a progressive. In 1948 he refused to walk out of the Democratic National Convention with the Dixiecrats and stuck with the loyalist Democrats who supported the reelection of president Harry Truman.

On Christmas morning in 1949, Governor Folsom told his statewide radio audience, "As long as the Negroes are held down by deprivation and lack of opportunity, the other poor people will be held down alongside them. Let's start talking fellowship and brotherly love and doing unto others. Let's do more than talk about it. Let's start living it." Wallace applauded that speech as one of the most courageous he had ever heard from an Alabama politician.

⋆

During the summer of 1954, when I was fourteen, I first met Wallace. He was south Alabama campaign chairman for Folsom, who was running for his second term as governor. I was traveling with my father, Harold, a beauty and barber supply salesman who never met a stranger. I saw immediately that Wallace—short, bouncy, and energetic—was endowed with the same personality trait as Daddy. When he shook my hand, he looked directly into my eyes. I sat nearby and listened while he and my father talked. Wallace talked mostly about himself, but he did manage to say a few words about Folsom. He went on and on about how the good people of Alabama were sick and tired of having the federal government shoving ideas down their throats, though he wasn't specific in his ideas. Back in Daddy's car, which always smelled of aftershave lotion and permanent-wave mixture, Daddy said, "That man's not going to stop until he's governor of Alabama."

About two years later, when Wallace, by then a judge, revved up his old Chevrolet and hit the rural highways of the state to begin his own campaign for governor, my father and I met him again, in a barbershop in south Alabama. As I wrote in the prologue of my 1976 biography, *Watch Out for George Wallace*, "When Wallace came through the door, he bounced straight over to me, his arm outstretched, and he said, 'How are you, Wayne?' And again, he and my father spent time bantering about what was on their minds. I liked George Wallace. If I could have voted, I would have voted for him. I knew no other adult who remembered my name after meeting me only one time and not seeing me for two years. He was an impressive man. When he stood in front of my father he looked like an erect dwarf. My father was tall and heavyset. Wallace was a half foot shorter, his chin was thrust upward, his lips full but taut, and his dark hair slickly combed with a wave beginning at the top of his forehead and sweeping back."

Later, Wallace recalled in one of many interviews with me, "I was a hungry politician. I could and would drive all day and all night, if necessary, to talk to three or four people. And when I got to where I was going, I wouldn't be in a hurry. I'd sit there or stand there and talk to those folks. They were worried. They saw their way of life being taken away from them. At that time, I thought they were just scared for no reason. In 1957 and during the campaign of 1958, I didn't recognize the pure fear that the white folks felt deep down in their bones. I thought it was just a surface thing. I'd talk to them about the need for more roads, just like Jim Folsom did back in the mid-1940s. I talked to 'em about the need for better schools. I talked to 'em about a whole long list of things I thought they were interested in.

"When Alabama attorney general John Patterson swept the field, he had the support of the Ku Klux Klan and the White Citizens Council and every other right-wing group. In the runoff, I realized too late that he was talking the talk that the folks of Alabama wanted to hear. Ku Klux Klan members handed out his literature in every country store in the state. At the same time, they took my material and destroyed it. He could not have had better support."

Analyzing the election, Wallace determined that Patterson's support by the Ku Klux Klan, the White Citizens Council, and other segregationist groups had put him over the top. In reality, Patterson was a favorite son. He had the sympathy vote just as he had it four years earlier. His father, Albert, a lawyer in Phenix City in east Alabama, had become the Democratic nominee for state attorney general. He campaigned on the promise to clean up his corrupt hometown, known as the Sin City of the South, filled with saloons, gambling houses, and dens of prostitution. Soon after his election, the elder Patterson was gunned down, apparently by mob hit men, and his son was named to take his place. John became the youngest state attorney general in the nation.

As attorney general, Patterson had completed his father's promise to clean up Phenix City, and the voters adored his fresh face and his squeaky-clean persona. There was no way the majority of the voters in 1958 were not going to vote for him. After all, when a movie called *The Phenix City Story* was released with Richard Kiley playing the young Patterson, showing his romanticized heroic exploits as he cleaned up the mob-riddled town, Alabama audiences poured into the theaters. Within a year, the movie became a hit at the drive-in theaters. Every teenager in the state had sipped Coca-Cola and watched the handsome young hero. They were enthralled with John Patterson.

But Wallace saw his opponent as a tool of the segregationists. "The people really didn't give a damn about all of my highfalutin campaign talk. All they really wanted to know about was black folks, and that's what I started givin' 'em after the 1958 race," he told me during one of many bedside interviews in his last years. "I looked back at that huge gathering of the White Citizens Council in Montgomery. I remembered the people who wanted to preserve their Southern way of life. Deep down in my heart, I felt like them.

"In the runoff in 1958, I [had] followed the advice of my friend Grover Hall Jr. [editor of the *Montgomery Advertiser*], who suggested I use the bed on the back of a truck." Wallace had traveled from town to town. In each, he climbed onto the truck and made his speech next to an elevated bed. He talked about good things he wanted to do for Alabama: improve education and construct more schools, build more highways, and develop community colleges for young people in Alabama's small towns. At the end of each speech, he lifted the covers halfway, peered into the darkness, and said, "Who are you in bed with, John Patterson? The Ku Klux Klan? The Big Mules? Where are you, John Patterson?" He looked at me with a profound nod of his head and allowed, "It was a good gimmick, but it didn't work. What I didn't realize at the time was: Grover Hall was an intellectual. And intellectuals don't win elections."

The man who drove Wallace from town to town during that campaign was no intellectual. He was another Barbour County native named Oscar Harper. A lanky, blue-eyed countryman with an easy way of talking and a wry sense of humor, Harper was the small town Alabama neighbor who just plain knew people. "George Wallace was born thinking about politics," Harper told me. "That's the first thing that enters his mind in the morning. It's what he's thinking about at night. And I believe he dreams about politics. He couldn't have been knee-high to a june bug when he knew he was going to spend his life as a politician.

"I've known George Wallace all his life. I really got in with him during the 1958 governor's campaign. He wanted somebody to drive him around the state, take care of him, and get some money somehow or another. He wanted my brother, Henry, to do it. Henry was in law school at the University of Alabama. He knew George better than I did, but I didn't want Henry to drop out of school to run the campaign. I had had to drop out early. I was working and making some money and sending him to school.

"I took George Wallace to Scottsboro on first-Monday trade day when all the people came to town with all their goods to sell and trade. The streets were just crowded with folks. We went up there and did real good, and we worked our way down the state. He talked to people at every crossroads.

"I've never seen anybody push like he pushed. He'd be up early and go until after midnight. It really wore him down to a frazzle. I know it about got the best of me. I think it really about got him. He lost the race, but he never stopped running for the office. He kept on going."

By then, Harper had become Wallace's closest friend. In the years ahead he would become his chief crony and closest adviser. He even introduced the politician to one of his later wives. No wonder his remembrance of the hours, days, and weeks after the defeat contradicted the remembrances of others. According to close observers, Wallace became physically ill after he read the final returns. At first, he actually took to the sickbed with his wife, Lurleen, his mother, Mozelle, and his sister, Marianne, tending to him.

But Wallace did not remain bedridden long. He had too much nervous energy. He drove himself to Montgomery and checked into the Greystone Hotel, where his younger brother, Gerald, met him. Gerald suggested that, after George left the judge's bench, his name be added to the door of Gerald's law office on Washington Avenue in the capital city. George, who had never been able to consume more than one alcoholic drink without becoming visibly tipsy, if not knee-walking drunk, joined friends at the Casino Lounge at the Elite (pronounced E-light), a popular restaurant with the local political and business insiders. "Every night for several weeks, he got drunk and ranted and raved, cursing the electorate, saying that he would never again be outmaneuvered on the race issue," recalled Frank Long Sr., who had known Wallace since college days.

Finally, Gerald went to his brother and told him Lurleen had had divorce papers drawn up. "She plans to file 'em with a court down in the Black Belt," Gerald told him and added, "unless you straighten up." The threat hit him hard. He sobered up, called Lurleen, and began planning the next governor's race. Montgomery attorney John Peter Kohn, who soon became a staunch supporter, was with a group whom Wallace called together at the Greystone. "While we sat and watched and listened," Kohn said, "he marched up and down the room. You could see him thinking as he talked about running. Among other things, he said, 'I'll tell you one thing right now: I'll never be outniggered again. They did it once, but it won't happen again. I know exactly what to do this time around.'"

Early in January 1959, just days before he would step down from the bench as circuit judge, Wallace recognized a chance to make statewide headlines and catapult himself into the governor's office. The newly created United States Civil Rights Commission had begun examining the voting patterns in select counties around the South. It would ask: are the Negro citizens of these counties being allowed to register to vote? Among the thirty-six counties it would investigate were Barbour and Bullock, which made up Wallace's judicial circuit. As the news media reported the quest of the Civil Rights Commission, editorialists like Grover Cleveland Hall Jr. at the *Montgomery Advertiser* lashed out at the federal government for once again meddling in local affairs. When they read Hall's editorials, the white citizens of south-central Alabama grew weary and then angry. Wallace picked up on the thrust of public opinion expressed by the white people on talk radio and in letters to the editor. Immediately, he decided to speak out on behalf of what he called "the little man."

The circuit solicitor, or prosecuting attorney, was Seymore Trammell, a longtime Wallace friend who was raised in the rural Barbour County hamlet of Midway and who had remained uncharacteristically silent during the election. Wallace knew Trammell had been quietly helping Patterson back home, and he was anxious to solidify Trammell's support for the future. "Ol' George called me and said, 'Seymore, you've got to help me.' Then he outlined a scenario in which he and I would be principal players. It would be pure drama, but it would work if we both played our parts. He said he had every move planned. When the Civil Rights Commission subpoenaed the voting records of Barbour and Bullock counties, he would refuse. As circuit judge, he would impound the records and hold them as confidential. He would get big headlines, then I'd slip around and turn over the records behind his back to keep him from going to jail," Trammell remembered. "It was soap opera being performed by two of the best actors ever on the Alabama political stage." Trammell always enjoyed the dramatic. Years later, when I was a reporter, he would telephone and set up secret meetings and pass information about Wallace's political campaign of the moment.

On January 8, 1959, Wallace held a press conference packed with reporters from state newspapers and television stations. Rex Thomas of the Associated Press was an old acquaintance from Wallace's days in the legislature and knew Wallace was sharpening his skills for the 1962 race for governor. As soon as the cameras were ready, the judge strode before them. He stood with his chin raised defiantly, his eyes squinted, his lips clamped shut. He lifted the U.S. Commission's subpoena, shook it until it rattled, and called it "a Roman holiday investigation, held in a federal courtroom, surrounded by a circus atmosphere with television platforms and ladders, newsreel cameras and hired publicity agents." Shaking the papers again, he snarled, "I will stand up and defend the rights of the people of Alabama, regardless of the personal sacrifices. That is the motto on which this great state was built: We dare defend our rights."

On January 9, a representative of the U.S. Justice Department went into U.S. District Court in Montgomery and requested U.S. judge Frank Johnson to order Wallace to make the voting records available for scrutiny by investigators of the Commission. Subsequently, Johnson issued the order, giving Wallace four days to comply or answer why he should not be jailed for contempt.

Wallace and Johnson were not strangers. They had been acquaintances at the University of Alabama and friends in law school. Wallace had frequently stopped by the apartment where Johnson's wife, Ruth, made good country-style suppers for them. "He always had a good appetite," Ruth Johnson remembered with a smile years later. Johnson, a native of Winston County in northwest Alabama, where his family had been hard-rock Republicans for ages, had been appointed to the federal bench by president Dwight Eisenhower. He was already known as a jurist who sat on the three-judge panel that ruled Montgomery's segregation law unconstitutional three years earlier.

On Sunday night before Wallace was to appear in court, a mutual friend from law school days, Glen Curlee, called Johnson and asked if Wallace could visit with him in his home in Montgomery. Johnson agreed.

Shortly after eleven, Wallace rang the doorbell of the judge's ranch-style brick home in the fashionable Haardt Estates. As Wallace walked into the foyer, he said, "You've got my ass in a crack, Johnson."

The judge led him into the paneled den, where a pot of fresh coffee awaited. As the two men sipped, Wallace said, "If you'll give me a light sentence, you can find me in contempt. I know I wouldn't be able to spend more than a week in jail."

Johnson told him, "If you don't hand over those records, George, I'm going to send your ass to jail."

Wallace rose and paced. Years later, Johnson told writer Jack Bass, "He asked me to send him to jail 'just a little while'; it would help him politically. He said, 'If you send me for any length of time, it'll kill my mother; my wife won't care.' I said, 'George, I'm going to send you for as long as I can. You've made it too big an issue. I've got to protect the integrity of the court.'"

Wallace replied, "What if I turned them over to the grand juries and let them give them to the Commission?"

"If you can do that by morning," Johnson said. "I don't care how you manipulate it. That's your business."

Back home in Clayton, Wallace phoned Trammell. Wallace told him that Johnson had threatened him with jail. "Get to work on your end of the deal right now," Wallace said. Trammell remembered that Wallace was "very frightened, very shook, his voice trembling." The time was 2:00 A.M.

Four hours later, Trammell met with Wallace at the courthouse. According to Trammell, they handpicked eighteen "rednecks, nigger-haters, footlog walkers, and possum-hunters. They were the kinda folks who'd do anything we told 'em to do without thinking twice. That's what he needed; that's what we got. It would work just as he'd planned from the beginning."

Later in the day, after Judge Wallace met with the special grand jury and gave them the voting records, he said he would defy the court's order. In his office, he met with reporters and told them that he had instructed the jury to keep the records secret.

While he was talking to reporters, Trammell was meeting downstairs with the grand jury. "I was giving them the lowdown on what they would do. The foreman asked, 'You want us to go against Judge Wallace?' and I said, 'No, not exactly.' Then I told 'em that tomorrow morning investigators from the Civil Rights Commission would come to see them, and they'd tell them, 'Go ahead and look at the records.' It would be OK, I told 'em; they would not be going against Judge Wallace."

Upstairs, as soon as Wallace dismissed the reporters, he sat down at a typewriter and typed out a report for the jury. This report would be read in open court. Copies would be given to reporters. It praised the circuit judge and the circuit solicitor. "We commend the courageous action of the Honorable George C. Wallace, who risked his very freedom in the federal courts in carrying out his duties and oath of office as a Circuit Judge." The report ended, "The great need of the South today is for more men of the foresight and determination of Judge George C. Wallace."

That night, Wallace telephoned the director of the Civil Rights Commission's Office of Complaints, A. H. Rosenfeld, who was staying at Maxwell Air Force Base in Montgomery. "If you send your men down here at nine-thirty in the morning, I believe they'll be able to see the records." When they arrived at nine-thirty, they began perusing the records.

As the agents read the records, however, Wallace continued his ruse of defiance, telling reporters that he had ordered the records "sealed in secret."

That afternoon, after the foreman of the jury, Wynn Martin, read aloud the report praising Judge Wallace and Solicitor Trammell, Wallace thanked him and the others for their service. "He might as well have looked over at me and winked," Trammell recalled years later.

On Thursday, four days before Wallace would officially leave office to be succeeded by his brother Jack, Judge Johnson heard an attorney from the Justice Department say Wallace was continuing "questionable and childish conduct" while "all records were produced, if in a jumbled-up form."

If Wallace failed to prove to Johnson that he was not in contempt, the Associated Press reported, Wallace would face up to six months in jail and a thousand-dollar fine.

On the morning of January 26, Wallace and his attorney, John Kohn, stepped before the bench in U.S. District Court.

Asked how the defendant pled to the charge of contempt of court, Kohn threw up his long arms and pronounced, "We plead guilty, your honor."

Johnson remembered staring down in disbelief. "I had already been told by the U.S. Civil Rights Commission that the voting records of Barbour and Bullock counties had finally been turned over to them by the grand jury." Now Wallace was telling the judge he was guilty of contempt.

Johnson stared down into Kohn's regal face, then toward Wallace's downturned eyes.

Looking down over his half-moon reading glasses with deep brown, piercing eyes, Johnson began reading in his flat, nasal, hill country drawl. "This court finds that, even though it was accomplished through a means of subterfuge, George C. Wallace did comply with the order of this court concerning the production of the records in question. As to why the devious means were used, this court will not judicially determine. In this connection, the court feels sufficient to observe that if these devious means were in good faith considered by Wallace to be essential to the proper exercise of his state judicial functions, then this court will not and should not comment upon these methods. However, if these devious means were for political purposes, then this court refuses to allow its authority and dignity to be bent or swayed by such politically generated whirlwinds."

With his wife on one side and Kohn on the other, Wallace stood in the late morning sunlight on the steps of the courthouse. He raised his fist in defiance.

"Since there was a grave constitutional question involved, I had hoped to take it to a higher authority," he stated, while the flashbulbs sparkled and the television cameras rolled.

"But now I have been acquitted. I believe this justifies my militant stand against the efforts of the Civil Rights Commission to take over the courts of Alabama.

"I was willing to risk my freedom in order to test the question at this time. I felt an opinion should be rendered on this important question. The whole matter arose as a result of my doing my duty and pleading guilty to the failure to bow to the wishes of the court, and if the judge says this is not contempt, then I have no control over such conclusion."

Later, with Kohn and others at the Greystone, Wallace told them Johnson was "a no-good goddamn lying son-of-a-bitching race-mixing bastard."

Within days, meticulously planning his campaign for governor, Wallace believed that he had now laid the perfect foundation on which to run. He told the press that the federal judge in Montgomery was "an integrating, carpetbagging, scalawagging, race-mixing, bald-faced liar."

Oscar Harper remembered, "I pitched in some money with some more folks to get him over the hump of the three years or so after his judgeship ran out and the 1962 race started."

Gerald added George's name to the front door of his law office and gave him a desk, but George seldom worked there. When he was there, arriving between stops in every little town in the state, he exchanged pleasantries with his brother. He used Gerald's telephone to call supporters around the state. On other occasions, he and others sat around and talked about what was happening on the campaign trail.

To Harper, "It was never any doubt in his mind that he was going to win the 1962 election. He took off into it headlong, never looking back. When he started running this time he had more money than back in 1958, when he was always broke except for the money me and a few others took out of our pockets and gave him. I mean, he didn't have money to pay for little sidewinding bands from Birmingham to play at rallies. But in 1962 he had more going for him. And he was in better shape physically. He had gotten himself ready to run. Like I said, he had been running all the time. He didn't really stop. He proved himself a natural-born campaigner, but he had been doing that all his life. Hell, he even had Minnie Pearl coming down from Nashville and campaigning for him."

However, early in 1962, only two weeks into the rigors of the climax of the campaign, Wallace had to be hospitalized. He had become convinced that the campaign was so low on funds that it couldn't continue. Campaign workers, including Harper, checked him into St. Margaret's Hospital in Montgomery in the middle of the night. "The collar of his coat was turned up. The brim of his hat was pulled down so that nobody would recognize him. He looked like a Dead End Kid," Harper said.

But the depression did not last long. Within days, Harper wrote a check for five thousand dollars. Wallace's old friend, whom he called

"Uncle Billy" Watson, a shrewd, well-to-do Barbour County landowner who had been a staunch supporter since his first campaign, showed up at his bedside with twenty thousand dollars in cash that he had raised from well-wishers. Uncle Billy's actions proved more powerful than any other medicine. According to Harper, "George got rejuvenated about as quick as I ever saw."

7

THE PAIR FROM HOWARD

In the summer of 1958, while the Ku Klux Klan and the White Citizens Councils were gaining strength almost daily and while George Wallace was fanning racist flames on the gubernatorial campaign trail, J. L. Chestnut Jr. drove from Washington, D.C., where he had recently graduated from Howard Law School, to his hometown of Selma.

In the late 1950s, Selma was the same sleepy old town on the banks of the Alabama River that Chestnut remembered from his days as a boy there. Throughout his life he had heard its history, and he knew its attitudes and the personalities of both whites and blacks.

In antebellum days Selma was a bustling port where African American slaves loaded cotton onto steamships from dawn to dusk. In 1860 alone, more than sixty thousand bales of cotton were sent to market on steamers that took the product downstream to Mobile, where it was transported onto ships that took it around Florida and up to New England to textile mills. In 1879 former mayor John Hardy wrote in *Selma: Her Institutions and Her Men* that from 1830 to 1850, slaves were brought to the town in "large droves, some hundreds daily." Hardy wrote that "several large buildings were erected in the town especially for the accommodation of Negro traders and their property." The largest of these, he wrote, sat on the corner of Water Avenue and Green Street. "This was a large three-story wooden building, sufficiently large to accommodate four or five hundred Negroes. On the ground floor, a large sitting room was provided for the exhibition of Negroes on the market, and from among them could be selected blacksmiths, carpenters, bright mulatto girls and women for seamstresses, field hands, women and children of all ages, sizes, and qualities. To have seen the large droves of Negroes arriving in the town every week, from about the first of September to the first of April, no one could be surprised that the black population increased in Dallas County, from 1830 to 1840, between twelve and thirteen thousand." In the city's first history, Hardy wrote that the building was used for twenty years until 1854. During this time the average slaveholder in Dallas County owned seventeen slaves. In Montgomery County, the average slaveholder owned ten.

A hundred years later, the slave mentality had passed down from generation to generation. J. L. Chestnut had heard it from his neighbors as they talked the talk, and he had seen them bow their heads when addressing a white person, not looking them directly in the eye. He had seen it, and he had wondered about it and thought that such attitudes should change and would change. But when? Many young blacks had fled to the North in search of jobs and a better way of life. However, many remained behind, stayed on plantations, continued to pick cotton, doing whatever work they could find. Many women worked in white people's houses as domestic servants. Few were educated. Fewer had registered to vote.

As in Tuskegee, twice as many blacks as whites lived in Selma. In rural Dallas County, it was estimated that there were over three times more African Americans than whites. As in pre–Civil War days, the Black Belt whites clung to the old myth of extreme individualism perpetuated historically by the so-called Southern aristocrats. In his excellent economic study, *Plantation Politics*, professor J. Earl Williams pointed out that the white Southerner "increasingly maintained [that] his less fortunate neighbors were fully responsible for themselves; their plight was neither his responsibility nor the product of the social system." This mode of thought remained strong in Alabama's Black Belt in the mid-1950s. In the entire state in 1958, statistics showed that only 14.2 percent of voting-age blacks were registered to vote. The total was less than seventy thousand. In the Black Belt, the percentage was estimated at less than 5 percent.

As a boy growing up here, Chestnut had dreamed about being king of the Drag, a short strip of shot houses and gambling dens that decorated his neighborhood. He idolized his uncle, Preston, a fancy-dressed dude who prided himself on being the finest gambler in the town, the state, and probably the entire South.

As a teenager attending Knox Academy, a school built by Presbyterians, Chestnut had come under the influence of a bright and hard-nosed educator named John Shields, who questioned the "Southern way of life." He preached that segregation was neither natural nor ordained by God. "Why is it," he would ask, "because they're white they ought to have that, and just because we're Negro we ought to have less?" Shields forced young Chestnut to think and to question.

After graduating from Knox, Chestnut attended Talladega College but found it lacking in intellectual stimulation. He looked elsewhere and found Dillard University in New Orleans, where he discovered not only a backdrop for thought but a world where his beloved jazz filled the night air. An aficionado of Count Basie, Duke Ellington, and Lionel Hampton, Chestnut was asked to join a jazz group and played saxophone on weekends at local joints.

When she heard Chestnut's name mentioned in conversation, a young woman who had also been raised in Selma, Vivian Davis, looked him up. They began dating, fell in love, and were married before they graduated.

In 1953, with two baby daughters, he and Vivian moved to Washington, D.C., where he attended Howard Law School and discovered a place where his intellectual imagination was tested at every turn. Thurgood Marshall and other NAACP attorneys who had argued *Brown v. Board* before the U.S. Supreme Court spoke to the students. They outlined in detail their arguments against *Plessy v. Ferguson*. They listened seriously to students' questions. They sparred with them about the law, which became a living, breathing thing for Chestnut. These men explored verbally the idea that the Fourteenth Amendment, granting equal protection for all people under the law, could be used in many circumstances, particularly incidents arising from laws requiring segregation.

In January 1953, after one semester of law school, Chestnut received notice that he would be drafted into the army. He was devastated. Just when he was getting into the depths of law, he would be jerked out of school.

Asking how he could obtain a student deferment, he was told it would be difficult, even though he and Vivian now had three children after the birth of their son. Knowing that his white Alabama congressman would be no help, he got an appointment to see U.S. representative Adam Clayton Powell Jr., who represented Harlem in New York. Powell listened and made a call on his behalf. Still, Chestnut was refused. However, he had made an acquaintance of Powell and would later rekindle the friendship.

For two years Chestnut was assigned to Aberdeen Proving Ground in Maryland. He worked nights and weekends as a disc jockey at a local jazz radio station. Two months ahead of schedule, he received word of his discharge. It had been obtained by Congressman Powell's office.

Chestnut returned to Howard and graduated in the spring of 1958. When he and Vivian and their three small children crossed the Edmund Pettus Bridge into Selma, Chestnut was looking forward to becoming the first and only black lawyer in the town and the county. He knew that there were thousands of black Dallas County citizens who had a world of legal problems. Also, there were two black doctors, three dentists, many teachers, preachers, and other black professionals. He wanted all of them as clients.

That summer, Chestnut found Selma similar to the town he had left. Downtown on Water Avenue, running parallel to the Alabama River, the ancient brick stores sold the same dry goods and hardware to farmers who came in on lazy Saturday mornings. In this slow-moving country town where everybody was known to his or her neighbors, it was not unusual to see an occasional farmer in tattered overalls driving his wagon pulled by a pair of mules to market. Now and then a hardshell Baptist preacher from Marion Junction parked his pickup truck and stood in its bed and quoted the Holy Bible in his raspy tones as people gathered in the shade of the wide awning over the sidewalk outside Lathem's General Store, watching the man in his long-sleeved coat as he talked and sweated in the late morning sun.

Chestnut watched and listened and wondered why white preachers refused to take off their long-sleeved coats, even in the June heat. "It showed me something about the nature of man," Chestnut told me one day as we sat in his office near downtown. "White preachers are different from black ones. A black preacher will shed his coat when the humidity gets so great that sweat will run off his forehead and drench his shirt. A white one won't. It does make a difference, you know." Then he laughed deep down in his throat, and he nodded. He wanted it to be known, even to a young white newspaper reporter, that he was a close observer of the nature of man.

Shortly after his return, word spread through white Selma that Chestnut had been educated and sent back home to cause trouble in the name of the NAACP. Probate judge Bernard Reynolds called him to his office and accused him of verbally abusing the white women in his office. Angry, Chestnut told him, "I have never been disrespectful of a lady in my life. Unlike you, I also respect black women."

Although he learned later that the all-white Dallas County Bar Association sent a representative to the local banks asking them to refuse Chestnut a loan for money to open an office, he received a loan from a black Elks credit union. He was also given office space in the Elks building in the black business district.

As the town's only black lawyer, he found that many of the whites in positions of authority used their rank to oppose his presence, to say nothing of his power. When he asked the court for a petition that would be a normal occurrence for a white attorney, the judge told him outright, "I'm going to overrule you. No lawyer would come in here and even propose that." Another judge knew Chestnut's family and treated him as he would any other lawyer in his courtroom, but many judges simply referred to him as "J. L." while calling white lawyers "Mr." However, not everyone in the courts discriminated against Chestnut. One white defense attorney, T. G. Gayle, offered valued advice and often talked law with him. One night, while drinking liquor together, Gayle told Chestnut, "Well, in time they'll get used to you, if you let them. But you've got to know how to act, and don't push too damn much."

Peter Hall, the black attorney from Birmingham who had defended William Earl Fikes in the attempted rape case that Chestnut had traveled back home to watch several years earlier, came to Selma to try a case. Chestnut stayed by his side. Just as Orzell Billingsley had assisted Hall previously, Chestnut worked with him in the Dallas County courtroom. Chestnut watched every move Hall made and remembered every word. "Peter showed me the crucial importance of dominating the courtroom," Chestnut wrote. "He was master at that. No way was he going to sit quietly in the audience. He'd be inside the rail, damn near in the witness box, and would be insulted if anyone suggested he sit anyplace else. He wasn't about to wait his turn either. He'd walk up and ask the judge, 'Where's my case on the docket?' If this was the city or Dallas County court, there might be fifty cases and Peter's might be number thirty-five.

"'Well, Judge, I have to be back in Birmingham,' he'd say. 'You need to move it up.' And they'd do it. Watching him taught me a whole lot about being aggressive, that if you take the step and take it with authority, more often than not those who want to oppose it are uncertain. If not given time to think, they'll likely back away."

To Chestnut, Hall had risen above the position assigned to black lawyers by his brilliance and his arrogance. "I watched him talking with the judges, and it wasn't the condescending conversation—white judge to black lawyer—they had with me. It was two esteemed members of the bar speaking."

Chestnut saw that Hall worked with a basic superiority over all people, black or white. He would not abide laziness or tardiness. "He was the meanest man and the best trial lawyer I've ever seen," Chestnut wrote.

Chestnut had been practicing law less than a year when a black woman from rural Lowndes County showed up in his office. Overweight and pregnant, Mary Aaron was so distraught that she stood in front of his desk and wrung her hands. She told him nervously that her husband, Drewey, had been arrested in Montgomery for raping a white woman. Over and over, she told him that her husband was innocent and would never do such a terrible thing.

On the spot, Chestnut told her he would take the case. As soon as she left, he telephoned his former classmate from Howard, Solomon Seay Jr., who by now was familiar with the courts in Montgomery. Like

Chestnut, Seay too had listened to the brilliant black lawyers who often visited the D.C. classrooms at Howard, outlining how the law could be used to turn Jim Crow around. He too had felt intellectually challenged by the older, more experienced men.

On the following morning, as Chestnut drove toward Montgomery on U.S. 80, he detoured onto a county road and found Mary Aaron's shack, which looked like so many others that dotted the rural Black Belt: unpainted, tiny, with no underpinning or plumbing. An outhouse stood in the grassless backyard, and three little boys played on the shotgun porch. He told Mrs. Aaron that Seay would be joining him in the case. And he discovered what he already knew: neither she nor her husband had a dime to pay for the defense.

In Montgomery, Chestnut and Seay found their client in a cell at Kilby State Prison, where he had been taken for his own protection, they were told. A police officer said there had been armed men parading around the city jail when they arrived with Drewey Aaron. The officers were afraid for his safety.

Aaron swore that he did not rape the white nurse, who had told the circuit solicitor and his assistant that she had been tending to her baby in the nursery when she opened a closet and a black man jumped out, grabbed her, flung her to the floor, and raped her.

Meeting with Martin Luther King Jr. and Ralph David Abernathy at the Montgomery Improvement Association headquarters, Chestnut and Seay were told by the ministers that they did not think it wise for the MIA to get involved in a criminal case. The lawyers got the same news from NAACP officials in New York.

Armed with their splendid educations and little else, the pair of young black lawyers stepped into the Montgomery courtroom to face a white judge, two white prosecutors, twelve white male jurors, with their frightened black client sitting between them and his pregnant wife and three young sons sitting behind them in the black section of the courtroom.

When Aaron was arrested, he had been driving a truck in which he hauled gravel for a local quarry. Police said he had splinters from the nurse's closet in his trousers. After being taken to the state prison, the accused was put in a lineup. When the victim looked at the black men standing side by side, she could not identify her assailant. Later, she was brought back and watched as Aaron was made to repeat the words her assailant had said when he raped her. This time she identified him.

In court, Chestnut and Seay held their own with the white prosecutor. When they sparred, Chestnut recalled later, "It delighted me to whip his white ass."

Throughout the trial, while Chestnut did most cross-examinations of witnesses, Seay was injecting bits and pieces of legalese into the trial; they had learned at Howard to insert these details in order to bring them up on appeal and argue for reversal at the appellate level.

As he watched, Chestnut learned. He discovered that white jurors were fascinated with black lawyers. Now and then, he would lapse into an actor's role, playing to the human side of the jurors, making them laugh and trying to pull their heartstrings.

At the conclusion, Chestnut said, "That trial confirmed to me that all-white, all-male juries simply were not compatible with justice where black people were concerned. Certain things they just would not listen to. A black person's word didn't carry the weight of a white person's. We put on several black alibi witnesses, people unrelated to Drewey who had no reason to lie and were mistaken at worst. One of the jurors literally turned his back on them, and others wore expressions of great disdain."

In the end, as both defense attorneys suspected, the jury convicted their client and sentenced him to death in the electric chair. But the lawyers knew the appellate court was where they were headed. Together, Chestnut and Seay raised many legal points that kept the case alive until years later the U.S. Supreme Court outlawed Alabama's existing death penalty law. At least they had saved the life of their client.

Although they did not try a case together again, for a brief while in Montgomery, Chestnut and Seay were known as the Pair from Howard. Although the two had lost the first round of their case, the white attorneys of the capital city had learned the two were formidable lawyers.

✳

As it turned out, the Aaron case was only a warm-up for both lawyers. Back in the Black Belt, Chestnut teamed up with Orzell Billingsley, trying cases under the auspices of the NAACP Defense Fund. When a poor black was charged with a crime against a white, Chestnut and Billingsley would show up to take the case. Back in Birmingham, Peter Hall, who had the connections through his years of work throughout Alabama and the South, would collect meager fees for their work.

In Chestnut's opinion, "While Peter gave the impression of a sophisticated jazzman, Orzell's persona was more like that of a blues singer, earthy and direct. He was shorter, darker-skinned, and Negroid all the way. He'd graduated five or six years ahead of me at Howard. There was something fierce about Orzell's manner around white people, an intensity that made them uncomfortable. His very presence would be saying, 'You racist son-of-a-bitch. You give me a chance and I'll fix you good.' He was one of the very few blacks then who would say to white people's faces exactly what he'd say about them in the company of only blacks.

"Orzell would not be talking with white lawyers and judges about the law as Peter did, and he wouldn't be trading jokes with them as I did. I don't think you could find a white person in the Black Belt who ever had an easy conversation with Orzell Billingsley. Yet the moment we'd cross the railroad tracks into the black community, a change would come over him. He'd relax. Around black people, he was easy to laugh, easy to smile, easy to know. Unlike Peter, he genuinely liked people."

As I talked with Billingsley, he said, "J. L. was a bright, hungry young lawyer with a razor-sharp mind who didn't mind using it for the welfare of his people. He was shortly out of school when I first worked with him. He quoted all the big dogs up in D.C. He didn't have the imagination I brought to law, and he took himself very seriously. I don't think he knew exactly what I was doing when I'd go on the attack like a mad bulldog. I'd go in gnarling, ready to snap at the first sign of opposition. That's just the way I was. J. L. was more laidback and easy-going. I could see him thinking, his mind working at a mile a minute."

In 1960 the plantation system still prevailed in Alabama's Black Belt as it had since slavery days. Over and over again, Chestnut and Billingsley witnessed the incredible faith that their black brothers and sisters had in the white landowners on whose properties they worked and lived. Usually the blacks would farm the land as sharecroppers. At the end of each growing season the worker would owe the landowner more than the share he collected, having borrowed on future crops. "It never ceases to amaze me, when I look back on those days," Chestnut confided. "It is a wonder any progress whatsoever was made. I mean, most of our people still lived like they had lived since they were brought over from Africa in the beginning. You have to live in this area to realize the pressure the Negro was under. They had lived in this oppressive society for generation after generation. It was an everyday thing, not something out-of-the-way and unusual. When you've grown up in an atmosphere where you could get whipped for not saying 'sir,' it's highly uncomfortable to be arguing your convictions with a white person."

For example, when a white man claiming to be a voodoo doctor took an eleven-year-old from her mother's house and kept her in his rural trailer for weeks, the girl's brother returned from Columbus, Ohio, went to find her, and beat up the voodoo quack, who had a reputation of favoring young black girls. The brother, whose name was Lucius Sims, was arrested and charged with assault and attempted murder.

Sims's mother went to the white man on whose land she lived and begged him to help her son, promising that if the sheriff allowed him to return to work in Ohio she would guarantee that Sims would return for trial.

When Sims was allowed to go free, the sheriff put him on a bus heading north. However, when the bus stopped, Sims stepped down, went to his mother, and said he wanted her and his sister to return to Columbus with him. The mother refused, saying she had promised the landowner that she would stay, guaranteeing his presence at trial.

When Chestnut and Billingsley heard her story, they told her they would represent her son. But they could not believe that she would put her trust in the white landowner. If she and her daughter had gone north with Sims, both lawyers knew, Alabama would never have gone after the young man. To Chestnut, "If he didn't come back, Alabama was not going to spend a quarter or a stamp to get him extradited. If he returned, his chance of getting a fair hearing before an all-white Perry County jury was as remote as Orzell's and my chance of winning a case there."

However, when his mother refused to leave, Sims did return. In the meantime, the attorneys subpoenaed the court clerk and court records.

In the past twenty-five years, it was shown, no white man had ever been prosecuted for trying to protect a white woman. Only three whites had been prosecuted for a crime against a black. None had been convicted. To the lawyers, this showed that their client was not only denied due process but equal protection provided under the Fourth and Fourteenth Amendments of the U.S. Constitution. If he were found guilty, as both suspected he would be, they would put into practice the lessons they had been taught in their Howard classrooms.

In the Perry County courtroom in Marion, Chestnut and Billingsley entered to find it packed with black spectators. Most were there, they learned, to see something none had ever witnessed: black lawyers in action.

As the white judge took the bench, the two black lawyers stood next to the black defendant, and two white prosecutors stood nearby. Soon, twelve white male jurors were chosen and seated in chairs behind a railing.

After a witness testified that the white voodoo doctor had a reputation for hanging around young black girls, the court was recessed. Following a short break, Billingsley found several white deputies standing in the aisle. "I just picked myself up," Billingsley recalled, "and walked up to 'em. They looked like your average Black Belt lawmen: potbellied, smart-assed, hooking their thumbs around the handles of their guns. I said, 'You know what ought to happen?' and one said, 'What?' I said, 'One of y'all ought to beat the shit outta that smart-ass white voodoo doctor sonofabitch, that's what.' And one of them acted like he hadn't heard me, but the other said, 'Maybe we ought to whip your black ass.' And I said, 'How you gonna do that?' And then he practically shouted, 'If you—you smart-ass goddamn nigger—don't watch, we'll whip your ass right here.'"

Stepping back onto the bench, the judge listened and watched. He was obviously astounded. He pounded his gavel and demanded order.

When the deputy shouted other slandering profanity, Chestnut stood and asked for a mistrial, gesturing toward the jury, all of whom were staring wide-eyed toward Billingsley and the deputies.

Within moments, the judge declared a mistrial and dismissed the jury.

Soon the lawyers learned that the prosecutors had dropped the case. They did not plan to reopen it. Billingsley and Chestnut would have to wait to bring up the legal issues on appeal. As they walked out of the courthouse, they heard murmurs of congratulations from the blacks who had watched and listened as Billingsley cursed a white deputy without being jailed or killed as a result.

In Wilcox County in the lower end of the Black Belt, they were confronted by legendary sheriff P. C. "Lummie" Jenkins, a crusty old unreconstructed rebel who had the reputation of never wearing a sidearm and never having to search for a wanted man—particularly not if the man was black. "If Lummie wanted you," recalled Carlton Simmons, a longtime resident of Camden, the seat of Wilcox County, "he just put the word out, and the person usually would show up at the courthouse before nightfall. He was known throughout the community as the most racist lawman in the Black Belt. If you know anything about the Black Belt in the 1950s and '60s, you know that's a helluva reputation."

While Billingsley and Chestnut were searching through county records in the courthouse, Jenkins entered the clerk's office and asked what they were doing. After they told him, he said, "Well, get your black asses out of here. We don't need no sorry-ass outside niggers messing around Wilcox County." When they continued, he stomped off. A half hour later he returned. He leaned against a filing cabinet and gazed at them. When they said nothing, he said, "I was just sizing y'all up. We got several coffins down at the morgue. They'd probably fit y'all just fine."

When they left that afternoon, Billingsley noticed that a sheriff's car followed them all the way to the county line.

Later, they heard that Jenkins had arrested two black federal marshals who came to Wilcox County on business. When asked by a federal judge if he harassed and arrested them because they were black, he said, "Naw, I did it 'cause they forgot they was black."

Throughout their early days of attempting to bring justice to the Black Belt, Chestnut and Billingsley continued to meet and to be harassed by white law enforcement officials. Now and then they would attempt to explain that they were not only citizens of Alabama but natives of the state. Most, Billingsley said, "didn't want to hear our talk.

But we'd talk anyway. Whenever we could, we'd tell 'em, 'We're the Pair from Howard,' and that'd confuse 'em more than you could imagine."

During this time, while Chestnut and Billingsley were roaming the Black Belt, Solomon Seay Jr. was working with his law partners, Fred Gray and Charles Langford, fighting segregation and filing lawsuits for justice in and around Montgomery.

As his friends and fellow Howard graduates faced problems at every crossroad, Seay had his own problems. He too found the plantation system operating in Butler County south of Montgomery. A young black man named Roosevelt "PeeWee" Howard, who was a lifelong cotton picker working for a plantation owned by Vandiver Lazenby, lived with his mother and father in a shack on the large farm and knew no other life. Lazenby demanded that all of his workers buy groceries and other goods from the plantation store he owned. Lazenby also kept the records of all purchases and payments.

Early in 1960, when PeeWee came to the store and asked for two dollars' worth of sugar, Lazenby told him the records showed PeeWee had already extended his credit beyond his limit. After an argument, PeeWee returned with a .22-caliber rifle, stood at the back window of the store, and shot Lazenby through the heart. Witnesses later said they saw PeeWee carrying the gun to the store.

In February 1960, an all-white jury convicted the defendant and sentenced him to die in the electric chair. When Seay was hired, he filed notice of appeal. As he was studying court records in Greenville, the seat of Butler County, the circuit clerk told him that judge T. Werth Thagard would like to see him. In the judge's chambers, Seay was greeted. The judge stood, shook his hand, and introduced him to the circuit solicitor who would prosecute the case. "As far as we can remember, you are the first Negro attorney to appear in a case in the Circuit Court of Butler County, Alabama," Thagard said. He added that he wanted to assure Seay that he would be treated fairly. "If you encounter any problems, you just let me know."

Like all courthouses in Alabama at the time, this one had WHITE ONLY and COLORED ONLY water fountains and restrooms. Soon, Seay made a motion to desegregate all facilities inside the courthouse. From the bench, Thagard ordered all signs removed. Without a further motion, the judge stated that spectators could sit anywhere in the room. Usually blacks sat on one side of the center aisle and whites on the opposite side.

At the end of the first day in court, Seay found the front tires on his car slashed. Inside, he told Judge Thagard about the problem. The judge called, Seay's car was towed, and new tires were put on at the court's expense.

Every afternoon, when Seay left the courthouse, a motorcycle policeman followed him. After several blocks the policeman stopped him, asked for his license, walked around the car, then handed the license back and sped away. On the fourth afternoon, Seay said, "It is the same license I have had all week," to which the policeman said, "Don't get smart with me, nigger."

Rather than continue on his way to Montgomery, Seay turned around, went back to the courthouse, and reported the incident to the judge. Thagard called the chief of police, ordered the motorcycle policeman to his office, and chewed him out in front of Seay and the chief. "Lawyer Seay has business with this court," Thagard said. "I am not going to tolerate any more harassment of him." If it happened again, he said, the policeman would be held in contempt. Then he said, "Seay, I'm really sorry this happened, but I am sure it will not happen again."

At the end of the trial, PeeWee Howard was found guilty and sentenced to life in prison.

Seay later wrote, "I had witnessed two formidable triumphs of courage over fear in Alabama's Black Belt. First, a fair-minded and honorable white judge whose actions spoke as loudly as his words; next, a principled, all-white jury refusing to back down on an unpopular decision."

8

"SEGREGATION FOREVER!"

As George Wallace's second campaign for governor was beginning, Oscar Harper introduced the candidate to a true-believing, hardcore racist who had proven the mantle of his hatred on the civil rights battle-front of the mid-1950s.

Asa Earl "Ace" Carter was a seasoned warrior who had marched with the Ku Klux Klan, had formed his own Original Ku Klux Klan of the Confederacy, had spoken on behalf of the White Citizens Council, and had been fired from a radio station for expressing his radical views as an anti-Semitic firebrand. He had even been arrested for egging and attacking black singer Nat King Cole on the stage of Birmingham's Municipal Auditorium. Once, he and a well-chosen gang of terrorist sidekicks beat Reverend Fred Shuttlesworth and stabbed his wife. Each time he attacked someone like Cole or Shuttlesworth, Carter was accompanied by a group of three or four. His accomplices always landed in jail while Carter was arrested, questioned, and set free.

A professional law enforcement officer with the Alabama Department of Public Safety wondered aloud in the 1990s if Carter had actually been an undercover spy for Public Safety. He pointed out that after the attacks on Cole and Shuttlesworth, Carter spent only an hour or two at police headquarters while his accomplices were charged and threatened with trial and possible jail time. More than once, Carter bragged that he had "sicced my mad dogs on a retarded nigger houseworker who'd acted like he was gonna cause trouble." His henchmen took the man into the woods north of Birmingham and castrated him with a butcher knife. To Harper, Ace Carter's credentials were impeccable for the Wallace campaign. Besides, the man could write like an angel and think like a devil.

Born and raised on the hardscrabble earth of the Appalachian toe hills north of Oxford in northeast Alabama, Ace Carter was a brilliant if narrow-minded student. He cut his literary teeth on the works of Sir Walter Scott, whom he considered "the great white Protestant patriot," but he failed to notice that the character of Rebecca in *Ivanhoe* was arguably the first sympathetic Jewish creation in English literature.

Carter shaded his past with complicated tales of his origin and his early career. He claimed to be one-quarter Cherokee Indian, which his brother later denied. After time served in the U.S. Navy, he attended the University of Colorado but never graduated. He claimed to have worked with Gerald L. K. Smith, for whom he wrote anti-Semitic treatises. To muddy his personal history appropriately, it was also rumored that Carter had been a member of the Communist Party; he said he "infiltrated the party to expose the real communists." He perpetuated his reputation of having been an announcer on an acknowledged right-wing radio station in the Rocky Mountains.

Carter showed up in Birmingham in 1954, heavyset, with thick dark hair and a stubble beard he had to shave frequently because he said he always wanted to give the impression of being "clean shaven." It was the one constant part of his persona, which he was otherwise always changing. He was soon hired to be the spokesman for the American States Rights Association by its guru, Sidney Smyer, a rawboned blond country boy from Cherokee County who had graduated from the University of Alabama Law School and had become a successful real estate attorney in Jefferson County. Smyer worked his way up the conservative political ladder in Birmingham, taking his place as a leader of the Dixiecrat movement in the late 1940s and hosting its national convention after the Deep South delegates walked out of the Democratic National Convention. In Birmingham, the Dixiecrats placed Strom Thurmond of South Carolina at the head of the ticket. However, by early 1955, Carter had spewed publicly his hate-the-Jews rhetoric one time too many. After a hate-filled, half drunk, rambling radio session, he was forced off the air by moderate members of the local chamber of commerce who were annoyed by his remarks, saying they were antibusiness.

Later the same year, Smyer and his friends rehired Carter as spokesman for the North Alabama White Citizens Council and put him on the road to talk against organized labor. In February 1956, Carter showed up as an instigator of riots in Tuscaloosa against Autherine Lucy, a young African American who was attempting to integrate the University of Alabama. Soon after, the recently merged American Federation of Labor and Congress of Industrial Organizations issued statements condemning White Citizens Councils, saying their current popularity grew out of the domestic Nazism of the 1930s.

By late spring of 1956, Ace Carter declared that he had organized a new KKK in north Alabama. He dubbed it the Original Ku Klux Klan of the Confederacy. Carter prevailed upon old friends who were talk show hosts on small radio stations in towns north of Birmingham. Appearing on these stations, Carter said his group of about thirty-five men "is the true Klan" and would "forever carry the torch for the white citizens of Alabama and the South." After the initial announcements, Carter disappeared from public for months. Acquaintances said that he went on a drinking binge in Oxford, where he was arrested and charged with driving while intoxicated. On another occasion, he was arrested in nearby Anniston and charged with public intoxication.

During the next five years, before Oscar Harper introduced Ace Carter to George Wallace, the Original Ku Klux Klan of the Confederacy was in and out of the news. Most of this time, Carter was a behind-the-scenes player. His old assistant, Jesse Mabry, was one of the key officers. By the time Wallace won the Democratic nomination for governor in the spring of 1962, Carter had been hired by Harper, who gave him an office in his building on Mount Meigs Road in Montgomery about a dozen blocks east of the state capitol. This was headquarters of Harper's National Services Inc., a printing, publishing, and office-supply company. In those days the Democratic primary race in Alabama essentially determined who would be governor. The Republicans seldom put up a nominee. If they did, it was usually only a token candidate who received a small percent of the vote.

In the hours after Wallace's victory in the Democratic primary, Harper's company was awarded the first concession for the new administration. It would prepare, sell advertising for, and print what became a 296-page official inaugural program. Three women were given the task of selling ads for the book. They went to every county commission, every city council, every lobbying group, and every agency that was a potential client of the future administration. In his cubbyhole, Ace Carter wrote copy, telling the Wallace story in detailed, colorful prose. It was estimated by an advertising executive that Harper profited over a half million dollars on the program, which was given to supporters at the inauguration the following January.

As the inauguration date neared, Harper gave Carter another assignment: the new governor would need an address that would stun the nation and garner headlines throughout the world. Harper and Wallace talked. They spent hours together during the Christmas season. "I'm gonna be more than just governor of Alabama," Wallace told his friend. "I'm gonna be the savior of the Southern way of life. I've met and talked with all the big Southerners: judge Leander Perez of Louisiana, Ross Barnett of Mississippi, J. B. Stoner of Georgia, and they're all gonna be in Montgomery on January fourteenth to hear me. I've promised 'em I'm gonna say what they want to hear. Now, put your boy to work and make me some words."

On the day before the inauguration, Ace Carter delivered the words. Late that night, John Peter Kohn pored over the speech. Grover Hall Jr., editor of the *Advertiser* and a valued friend, read over each word and made a few changes. Both approved the text.

In the winter afternoon sunlight, Wallace raised his hand and took the oath. Then he spoke to the thousands gathered on the capitol steps. He spoke to the hundreds of thousands who watched on statewide television and the millions who watched on national network television that night.

"Today I have stood where Jefferson Davis stood and took an oath to my people," he said. "It is very appropriate then that from this cradle of the Confederacy, this very heart of the great Anglo-Saxon southland, that today we sound the drum for freedom as have our generation of forebears before us time and again down through history.

"Let us rise to the call of freedom-loving blood that is in us and send our answer to the tyranny that clanks its chains upon the South.

"In the name of the greatest people that ever trod this earth, I draw the line in the dust and toss the gauntlet before the feet of tyranny.

"And I say: Segregation now! Segregation tomorrow! Segregation forever!"

In the pages of the *Advertiser* the next morning, Grover Hall quoted secessionist politician William Lowndes Yancey's introduction of Confederate president Jefferson Davis a century earlier, when Yancey said, "The man and the hour have met!" on the eve of Davis's inauguration. Like the government that rebelled from the Union in 1861, Hall predicted, the Wallace era would "snub its nose at the potentates of federal power and all of its grandiose snobbery and its willingness to push sovereign states asunder. Under Wallace's leadership, Alabama will show the nation that it can indeed exist and prevail without being under the thumb of Washington."

Wallace already knew he was going to do everything within his power to stop integration in Alabama. He had already let the Ku Klux Klan know that as governor he would allow them to get away with any kind of violence they found it necessary to commit to keep blacks down. Wallace had already talked it over with Oscar Harper and Seymore Trammel. In one meeting, Trammel later recalled, "Asa Carter said, 'We've got to do everything possible to keep the nigger communists from taking over.'"

Within days of taking office in 1963, Wallace called public safety director Al Lingo and said he would create an agency to investigate "all known integrationists and subversives." By the end of January, Wallace's people, including Trammel and Carter, proposed the Alabama Commission to Preserve the Peace. One of the governor's legislative floor leaders, senator Alton Turner of Luverne, began drawing up plans. Patterned after the U.S. House Un-American Activities Committee, which had been a powerful tool in the hands of U.S. senator Joe McCarthy, the

Peace Commission would have broad subpoena power, the authority to issue contempt citations, the state's investigative team of the Department of Public Safety at its beck and call, and the ability to hold hearings anywhere in the state. In the legislature, the governor's bill was said to "hold a new club over race agitators." Although Bill Number 9 had slight opposition because it gave Wallace the authority to bypass the attorney general's office, it passed. The newly formed commission was headed by state representative John Hawkins of Birmingham, who stated that Martin Luther King Jr. "is, and has been for ten years, closely advised by communists if not actually controlled by them." Thus began a long reign of intimidation by Wallace forces against desegregation.

Not satisfied with having only one such agency, Wallace began to plan the Alabama Sovereignty Commission, which he created by executive order. It too would be used basically for intimidation, and it was given much the same power as the Peace Commission. Operating with state funds, the Sovereignty Commission's professional staff visited every county seat and talked with every registrar, instructing them about how to impede black voter registration. They devised literacy tests, requiring the person wishing to register to interpret various sections of the state constitution. In some instances, it was reported that Sovereignty Commission staffers had copies of the constitution written in various foreign languages that they asked the registering person to interpret. All the while, white people were not required to pass any type of test.

Wallace's next move was to fulfill his campaign promise to keep black students from integrating public schools in Alabama. In every speech he had made in the previous two years, he promised to stand in the schoolhouse door. When young black students planned to enter the University of Alabama in May, the governor would stand in the entrance to Foster Auditorium, where students registered for class.

"If his refusal to turn over voting records to the Civil Rights Commission was soap opera," as Trammell said years later, "his stand in the schoolhouse door was Keystone Kops comedy. Every detail was planned in advance. Each move was choreographed, right down to every pause and phrase. Ace Carter proved he was a master. Of course, Wallace took it all very seriously. No one laughed."

For Wallace, this was the next building block in the foundation of his career. After he made a big show by standing in the schoolhouse door, again shaking his fist in the face of the federal government and its court, he would have a recognizable stump to stand on in 1964, when he would star in another show, running for the presidency. In essence, he was becoming the P. T. Barnum of American politics.

In the spring, James Alexander Hood of Gadsden, where he had been a halfback on the George Washington Carver High School football team, and Vivian Malone, who had grown up in Monroeville, prepared to register at the University of Alabama. Malone had graduated from high school in Mobile and was presently enrolled in Alabama A&M, an all-black college near Huntsville. Both were nineteen. Wallace prepared to stand in their way.

In Montgomery, Wallace ordered his director of the Department of Public Safety to send investigators to Gadsden and Mobile and dig up any dirt they could find on the students or their parents. Days later, the detectives reported that Hood and Malone and their parents were squeaky clean.

In Birmingham, attorneys for the NAACP filed a suit in the Northern District of Alabama on behalf of the two students. After a single hearing, chief judge Seybourn H. Lynne ordered the state university desegregated. He also issued an order enjoining Wallace from interfering with the admission.

As Wallace had done previously, he called Trammell into his office, and they began to look for ways Wallace could make a big show but not go to jail for defying the court order.

As the time neared, Wallace spoke several times with U.S. attorney general Robert F. Kennedy, who ultimately had the responsibility to ensure that the federal court order was carried out.

Finally, Kennedy flew to Montgomery to meet personally with the governor.

During a taped conversation, Kennedy asked, "You think it would be so horrifying to have a Negro attend the University of Alabama, Governor?"

Wallace snapped back, "I think it's horrifying for the federal courts and the central governments to rewrite all the laws and force upon the people that which they don't want, yes. I will never myself submit voluntarily to any integration of any school system in Alabama. And I feel it is in the best interests of the country and Alabama, and everybody concerned, that these matters ought to be—attempts ought to be—at least delayed. In fact, there is no time in my judgment when we will be ready for it—in my lifetime, at least. Certainly not at this time."

After Wallace and Kennedy bantered for a few minutes, Wallace stated, "I will never submit to an order of the federal courts ordering the integration of the school system."

In the weeks that followed, the two spoke several times by phone. A plan was mapped out: Wallace would stand in the doorway and make a short speech, President Kennedy would nationalize the Alabama National Guardsmen, Wallace would move aside, and the students would register.

Three days before registration, dozens of Confederate-gray state trooper cars with uniformed troopers moved onto the sleepy campus and set up roadblocks to divert traffic off University Avenue. Nearly a hundred years earlier, in the spring of 1865, Union general John T. Croxton's raiders burned most of the buildings of the school only days before general Robert E. Lee surrendered at Appomattox. Now it looked as though troops were once again preparing for battle beneath the famous oaks on the campus.

On the night of June 9, the chaplain of a Ku Klux Klan klavern, who identified himself only as a Baptist minister, led the speakers at a ballpark in Tuscaloosa. Following the preacher at the podium was grand cyclops Bobby Shelton in his scarlet gown, telling the crowd of several hundred, "We support Governor Wallace 100 percent. He's the only politician with guts enough to stand up for us and keep the niggers out of our schools."

On the evening of June 10, Wallace, Trammell, and other key officials from the administration flew from Montgomery to Tuscaloosa and set up headquarters in the Stafford Hotel downtown. With them was Winton "Red" Blount, a Montgomery millionaire businessman who would become president Richard Nixon's postmaster general. On this occasion, as chairman of the University of Alabama's board of trustees, Blount kept communications open with the university's president,

Frank Rose. Later, Blount confided, "It was all orchestrated. Everybody had a role to play, and they played it perfectly."

Also in the governor's suite was his friend and attorney, John Peter Kohn. Like he had with the inaugural speech, Kohn studied every word that Ace Carter had written. Kohn added legal language before returning it to Wallace.

Early on the morning of June 12, while James Hood and Vivian Malone were leaving Birmingham for Tuscaloosa, television cameras from the three major networks were being set up in front of Foster Auditorium. In Washington, D.C., President Kennedy was meeting with House Speaker John W. McCormack, Senate Majority Leader Mike Mansfield, and GOP Senate Leader Everett M. Dirksen. The four were discussing pending civil rights legislation.

In Tuscaloosa, Hood and Malone were taken to W. W. Brandon Armory about a mile from the campus, which had been completely sealed off by state troopers.

At 11:00 A.M. eastern daylight time, President Kennedy signed a proclamation assailing Wallace's action to "oppose and obstruct the orders of the U.S. District Court relating to the enrollment and attendance of Negro students at the University of Alabama."

Twenty-two minutes later, Wallace arrived at the doorway to the auditorium where registration would take place. In his entourage were his two brothers, Jack and Gerald, Seymore Trammell, and several others.

A caravan of black cars stopped within a hundred yards of the entrance. Hood and Malone remained in a car with John Doar, director of the civil rights division of the U.S. Justice Department. A decade later Doar became general counsel to the House Judiciary Committee to present Watergate evidence in the impeachment proceedings against President Nixon.

Leaving the car and marching toward the doorway where Wallace stood was forty-one-year-old deputy attorney general Nicholas Katzenbach. The six-foot-two, poker-faced former law professor and World War II prisoner of war stopped when Wallace raised his left hand. In a low voice, Katzenbach asked, "Will you move aside?"

Standing with his feet apart, Wallace did not move.

Katzenbach said, "I have here President Kennedy's proclamation. I have come to ask you for unequivocal assurance that you or anyone under your control will not bar these students."

"No," Wallace said.

"If you do not move aside, the consequences of your stand must rest with you," Katzenbach said.

Wallace lifted a paper and started reading words written by Ace Carter and edited by John Kohn.

"As governor and chief magistrate of the state of Alabama, I deem it my solemn obligation and duty to stand before you representing the rights and sovereignty of this state and its peoples.

"The unwelcomed, unwanted, unwarranted, and force-induced intrusion upon the campus of the University of Alabama today of the might of the central government offers a frightful example of the oppression of the rights, privileges, and sovereignty of this state by officers of the federal government.

"This intrusion results solely from force, or threat of force, undignified by any reasonable application of the principle of law, reason, and justice.

"It is important that the people of this state and nation understand that this action is in violation of rights reserved to the state by the Constitution of the United States and the Constitution of the state of Alabama.

"While some few may applaud these acts, millions of Americans will gaze in sorrow upon the situation existing at this great institution of learning.

"Only the Congress makes the law of the United States. To this date no statutory authority can be cited to the people of this country which authorizes the central government to ignore the sovereignty of this state in an attempt to subordinate the rights of Alabama and millions of Americans. There has been no legislative action by Congress justifying this intrusion.

"When the Constitution of the United States was enacted, a government was formed upon the promise that people, as individuals, are endowed with the rights of life, liberty, and property, and with the right of self-government."

Cocking his head sidewise, he continued his lecture on the right of self-government while Katzenbach and the nation watched and listened. Citing the Tenth Amendment of the U.S. Constitution, reserving to the states powers not delegated to the United States nor prohibited to the states, and stating that the public school system fell into that category, Wallace began his conclusion: "Therefore, I, George C. Wallace, as governor of the state of Alabama, have by my action raised issues between the central government and the sovereign state of Alabama, which said issues should be adjudicated in the manner prescribed by the Constitution of the United States, and now being mindful of my duties and responsibilities under the Constitution of the United States, the Constitution of Alabama, and seeking to preserve and maintain the peace and dignity of this state, and the individual freedoms of citizens thereof, do hereby denounce and forbid this illegal and unwarranted action by the central government."

Wallace folded his papers, clasped his hands behind his back, and looked as determined as ever.

Katzenbach turned, strode to his car, and rode away.

Wallace turned, disappeared into the building, and ordered the doors and windows barred. In a small air-conditioned office, he ate lunch sent by a local restaurant: a medium-rare steak and French fried potatoes he drenched with ketchup.

In Washington, President Kennedy signed an executive order nationalizing the Alabama Guard. Momentarily, secretary of defense Robert S. McNamara called Alabama's seventeen thousand guardsmen into active federal service and directed the 31st Infantry Division to proceed to Tuscaloosa.

U.S. marshals took Hood and Malone to their dormitories. Once there, according to the Justice Department, they would be considered full-fledged students.

However, by midafternoon, state troopers stood at parade rest in front of Foster Auditorium. Six trucks filled with federalized guardsmen arrived and stopped nearby. As brigadier general Henry V. Graham arrived with Hood and Malone, Wallace took his stance again. Graham stepped forward, saluted, and said, "It is my sad duty to ask you to step aside."

Not moving, Wallace once again read a prepared statement: "But for the unwarranted federalization of the National Guard, I would be your commander in chief. It is a bitter pill to swallow. I am grateful to the people of Alabama for the restraint which they have shown. I ask the people of Alabama to remain calm, to help us in this fight. We must have no violence. The guardsmen are our brothers. The trend toward military dictatorship continues. But this is a constitutional fight, and we are winning. God bless the people of Alabama, white and black."

Wallace then saluted Graham and stepped aside.

Hood and Malone were escorted into the building.

Wallace, his brothers, and his aides were whisked away in an awaiting state trooper car. As the car slowed to turn onto Tenth Street, a crowd gathered on the southern curb cheered. Wallace smiled and waved.

On the edge of the campus that night, troopers stopped a car with a Jefferson County tag. In the car, law enforcement officers found a box filled with dynamite, two rifles, and a box of ammunition. Three men, Robert Chambliss, Joe Pritchett, and Jesse Mabry, were taken to the Tuscaloosa police headquarters. All three admitted to being members of the Ku Klux Klan but claimed they were simply driving through the town on their way to Mississippi.

Several hours after Wallace finished his stand in the schoolhouse door, thirty-seven-year-old Medgar W. Evers, Mississippi field secretary for the NAACP, stepped from his car in front of his home in Jackson. He was returning from a late-night session of civil rights activists who had discussed the positive prospects of a national civil rights law being proposed by President Kennedy. At last things were looking up for him and his fellow workers. As he strode toward the front door, a fertilizer salesman named Byron de la Beckwith, a known member of the White Citizens Council, sighted down the barrel of his deer rifle. The bullet pierced Evers's back, and he fell onto the lawn. Fifteen minutes later, while police were attempting to load him into a vehicle, Evers said, "Turn me loose!" and died.

Byron de la Beckwith was charged and tried twice for murder. Each of the first two trials resulted in hung juries. Finally, in 1994, he was tried and convicted.

✮

By late summer, after the Peace Commission had already begun hearings to root out the communists in the civil rights movement, Wallace had created the Alabama Sovereignty Commission with former newsman Ed Strickland as its director. Strickland had been a member of governor John Patterson's administration after he wrote numerous news accounts about Phenix City and the assassination of Patterson's father.

Within days, Wallace and Strickland called to Montgomery leaders of every civic club in the state, thirty directors of local chambers of commerce, forty prominent lawyers, officials of every labor union, many businessmen, and lobbyists for forty trade and professional associations. Among them was AFL-CIO representative Earl Pippin. "Right off the bat, Wallace told us in no uncertain terms that it was our duty to strangle the communist movement before it gained momentum through the civil rights movement. We all have to stay together, the governor warned. If we didn't, the federal juggernaut will take control over our government and our lives. 'They want every little white school child to turn to communism,' he said. Listening, it chilled me to the bone. It was *that* frightening."

9

EDUCATION OF A LIBERAL

During the fall of 1962, after George Wallace campaigned successfully for governor, numerous bombings punctuated the night hours in Birmingham, already called Bombingham by some pundits.

Early in 1963, after Wallace was sworn in and promised "Segregation forever!" the Reverend Fred Lee Shuttlesworth and his Alabama Christian Movement for Human Rights joined with Dr. Martin Luther King Jr. and the Southern Christian Leadership Conference to fight back. Shuttlesworth and King were determined to bring peaceful desegregation to Birmingham. Copying the sit-in movement that started in Greensboro, North Carolina, and Nashville, Tennessee, black students from Miles and Daniel Payne colleges prepared to do the same at downtown "whites-only" lunch counters.

At first, the confrontations were mild. Few students actually sat at the counters of a diner on Fifth Avenue North. Those who did were quietly arrested and charged with violating the city's segregation ordinances. When a protester was attacked by Birmingham police commissioner Eugene "Bull" Connor's snarling German shepherd police dogs, local white attorney Charles Morgan Jr. telephoned his friends in the media. The incident, caught on camera by a local television crew, was magnified across the six o'clock news. The national network news picked it up. Soon, crews from the national networks were sent to Birmingham.

It was not long before they became thoroughly familiar with Connor's tactics.

Within days, Shuttlesworth led the first protest march to city hall. As they walked peacefully and orderly, a squadron of white police led by Connor turned fire hoses on the marchers, including children, knocking many off their feet and washing them down sidewalks against store-fronts. "My skin was burned by the sudden pressure of the water," recalled Janeece Langham, who was fourteen when she became a demonstrator. "I was knocked back against a brick building. My body hurt, but my brained seethed," said Langham, who was born and raised in north Birmingham. What had been basically an apathetic black population turned from hurt to anger. White leaders claimed, "The rioters are outside agitators." Bull Connor, who rode his closed white tank through black neighborhoods, told the press, "Most of our niggers aren't like this. These niggers are from up North."

Page one photographs and six o'clock news reports convinced president John Kennedy to send assistant attorney general Burke Marshall to Birmingham in an attempt to negotiate between black leaders and white authorities. Before this move, the federal government took a hands-off attitude, leaving enforcement of local laws up to local officials. First, Marshall convinced King to call off protests. But Shuttlesworth saw no immediate results. He demanded concessions from the city. If not, the demonstrations would continue. Although King was head of SCLC, he did not control the local leaders, and Shuttlesworth would not be stopped. Stubbornly he called for more demonstrations.

Within hours of Shuttlesworth's decision, journalists from NBC, CBS, and ABC national network news were in Birmingham, ready to shoot the big story. Charles Morgan called friends with the *New York Times*, *Los Angeles Times*, *Time*, and *Newsweek*. All came as fast as airplanes could bring them.

Dr. King and Shuttlesworth huddled with Morgan, who was one of the few white lawyers who would sit and listen to African American attorneys Arthur Davis Shores and Peter Hall. He knew they were vastly more learned and experienced than he was. "Arthur Shores had joined the NAACP back in the thirties," Morgan said. "He was a brilliant man, an exceptional lawyer. Peter Hall was a distinguished if arrogant man. I loved him. He once told Fred Shuttlesworth, 'You may be crazy as hell, but you are my kind of mad.'" In 1963, along with his good friend Orzell Billingsley Jr., Morgan offered legal advice to King and Shuttlesworth as well as ideas for their public relations battle in the nation's media. In Shuttlesworth's living room, Morgan penned a brief but powerful statement for the minister to read to the press, saying it was time for all black people to step forward and be counted in the struggle for justice.

Back in 1945, fifteen-year-old Charles Morgan had moved to Birmingham from Kentucky. He soon learned the town's history. Although the first European settlers entered the area as early as 1815, they did not find a rich, fertile soil like that of the Black Belt. Here, the area that became known as Jones Valley nestled between Red Mountain and the coal-rich hills to the north that later became mining country. During antebellum times, the population grew slowly. Little more than two hundred slaves were brought into the entire valley to help with farming. The only industry was blacksmithing; African Americans made horseshoes from iron dug from Red Mountain. Several munitions plants flourished during the Civil War.

It was not until December 1871 that the first lots were put up for sale in the newly chartered town of Birmingham. By 1878, Oxmoor Furnaces made coke from local coal, and pig iron from the coke. Hundreds of freed slaves from the Black Belt migrated to the town to work in the new industries. Soon railroads were completed to furnish transportation, and numerous blacks worked to lay the tracks and tend the railroad beds. In 1886, Union Station was built to handle the Louisville and Nashville, Alabama Great Southern, Georgia Pacific, and other lines.

Called the Magic City because it grew rapidly in the last decades of the nineteenth century, Birmingham's economy centered around coal and iron. United States Steel Corporation of Pennsylvania bought Tennessee Coal and Iron. A year later the United Mine Workers organized. Within days, twenty thousand black and white workers went on strike. They camped near the plant in northwest Birmingham in tents. By day, they blocked the entrance to the plant. By night, they sang protest songs around their fires. With no running water or sewage, the camp soon became a stinking area filled with disease and death. In the sweltering

August heat, governor Braxton Bragg Comer, an industrialist million-aire, sent the state militia to smash the camp, cutting down the tents with machetes, killing and injuring hundreds of blacks and whites. Immediately, the UMW stopped the strike. But the city was left with wounds that still ached and festered in the late 1940s.

As a teenager, Charles Morgan read about Comer, who developed Avondale Mills, a Birmingham textile company, to process the state's vast cotton crop. Later he expanded his cotton mills to a dozen Alabama communities. None welcomed labor unions. As governor, Comer initiated the passage of a child labor act that outlawed the hiring of any child under twelve. However, numerous twelve- and thirteen-year-olds worked double shifts in Comer's cotton mills, even while the industrialist was governor. Comer was representative of the kind of paranoid politics that filled the pages of twentieth-century Alabama history.

Still a teenager in 1946, Morgan became infatuated with a six-foot-eight-inch giant who wore size 18 shoes. Gubernatorial candidate James Elisha "Big Jim" Folsom, a former insurance salesman who had been defeated in 1942 in his first try for the governor's chair, was running again. Campaigning that spring, Folsom stood on courthouse steps in every county in the state. "When I was a boy down in the Wiregrass [southeast Alabama] I breathed the clean, fresh, green breeze that comes across the fields." In his big hands he held a mop and a suds bucket. He lifted them high for everyone to see. "Now, I'm gonna go down there to Montgomery and mop out the statehouse where all the corruption has left a mess. I'm gonna mop it out until what you got is a clean, fresh, green breeze." And when he called the owners of the steel mills and cotton mills in Birmingham "Got Rocks" and "Big Mules," saying they had been running the state too long with greed and malice, young Morgan knew instinctively that Folsom was right. In Morgan's eyes, Folsom was the only politician in the state who would step up to a Negro man on the street and shake his hand and ask for his vote. That took guts, Morgan figured. To Morgan, it was also the right thing to do.

A few weeks later, Folsom won. For Morgan, the victory amounted to a personal triumph for the average person with whom Folsom identified. By now Folsom was called by some pundits "the little man's big friend." Later, as a student at the University of Alabama in Tuscaloosa,

Morgan would campaign for Folsom when he ran for a second term in 1954.

One of Morgan's acquaintances on campus was Nelle Harper Lee, a young woman from Monroeville in southwest Alabama who wrote occasional columns for the campus newspaper, the *Crimson White*. They would see each other from time to time in the University Supply Store, or Supe Store, as it was called by students, drinking coffee and reading last-minute lessons. Years later her novel *To Kill a Mockingbird*, written in a Manhattan apartment, would have a profound influence on Morgan's life. He remembered the shy young woman from south Alabama, and she remembered the brash and brilliant young man from Birmingham.

Morgan was chairman of the school's homecoming activities. As such, he visited the law office of Marc Ray "Foots" Clement in downtown Tuscaloosa and asked Clement to volunteer as a judge of the homecoming queen contest. "I'd like to help you," Clement said, "but I know too many of the fathers involved. No matter whose daughter I helped select, ten others would be mad at me for life."

Morgan nodded. He understood. Then he added that all had not been lost. He said he had heard a lot about Clement and he had wanted to meet the man who was the intimate friend and adviser of Alabama's U.S. senators, several congressmen, and a number of other statewide politicians, including Folsom.

True to his nickname, Clement coupled his hands behind his head and put his big feet up onto his huge, crowded desk. He began a long dissertation of his personal political beliefs. He explained that he was a loyal Democrat and a true believer in Franklin D. Roosevelt, the New Deal, and the Tennessee Valley Authority, which provided cheap electricity in north Alabama, and that he had been a behind-the-scenes political mover-and-shaker since his student days at UA. He didn't mince words. He was the close friend of both Senators Hill and Sparkman, who called him daily.

"Loyalty is the most important thing you'll learn in life and in politics," Clement told Morgan. "Loyalty to principles and loyalty to friends. If you want to be successful in politics, tie yourself to your principles and your friends, and if you're for the right things, you and the principles you believe in will scale the mountain."

Before Morgan left his new friend's office, the two men shook hands. Clement said, "And one more thing: don't ever agree to be a judge in a college beauty contest."

In law school, Morgan took every course taught by a slight-built, soft-spoken professor from Illinois, Jay W. Murphy, who taught the Constitution, labor law, and jurisprudence. Murphy had worked in FDR's New Deal as administrator of the Puerto Rico Reconstruction Administration after he graduated from George Washington University. His wife, Alberta, was also an attorney, and they welcomed young Morgan and other students into their home. Morgan found the home an interesting and mind-expanding place where conversation was never dull. On the walls were samples of Jay Murphy's art: abstract paintings of Caribbean sunsets, deceptively simple but illuminating the atmosphere with wonder. It was here that he discovered like-minded people, such as fellow student George W. Dean Jr. from Montgomery and George Peach Taylor, also from Birmingham. In his quiet manner, Jay Murphy would throw out topics and listen to the young people discuss the issue. Afterward, he would explain the various aspects of the law determining such matters.

"Chuck Morgan and George Dean were among my favorites in the early 1950s," Professor Murphy said. "You could see the wheels turning when they tackled difficult, complex ideas. It was a delight. It made teaching fun and personally profitable."

An early director of the Tuscaloosa chapter of the American Civil Liberties Union, Murphy let it be known that he and his wife were civil rights advocates and enjoyed socializing with bright young African Americans. For Morgan, "Jay Murphy gave us a role model to pattern our lives after. He was not only a splendid teacher who made the law live for us, he was a great and gentle man who was a guiding light in his community. When you visited Jay and Alberta Murphy's house, every person was viewed on a level playing field. There, Negro leaders sat shoulder-to-shoulder with white counterparts. The only trouble was, the white leaders in Tuscaloosa would not visit the Murphys, whom they viewed as terrible radicals, if not worse. But those of us who were privileged to be their friends were just that: privileged."

✶

In September 1953, Charles Morgan and his sweetheart, Camille Walpole, whom he had known and dated since high school in Birmingham, married in Canterbury Episcopal Chapel in Tuscaloosa.

The following spring Morgan campaigned for Folsom, who had had to sit out a term because the Alabama Constitution forbade a governor from succeeding himself. Chuck and Camille traveled to Birmingham to see the candidate's final rally on the front steps of the Jefferson County courthouse.

Three days later, Folsom won handily.

Three weeks later, the U.S. Supreme Court ruled in *Brown v. Board of Education* that separate but equal was no longer the law of the land. Public education throughout the United States would be integrated. Alabama and the South could no longer discriminate legally against their Negro citizens. The state and the region would change forever.

In the first years of Folsom's second administration, Morgan traveled numerous times to Montgomery, where he was a guest upon occasion at the governor's mansion on Perry Street. He met Folsom's chauffeur, Winston Craig, whom he learned was the governor's number one adviser on Negro affairs. It was not unusual for Folsom to ask Craig's advice on any number of problems. From Gould Beech, a Folsom speechwriter, Morgan learned that many times Folsom would send Craig out to rural districts to meet with black people whom he taught how to register to vote. Often, Beech told the young man, Folsom would furnish Craig with cash for the poor black farmers who could not afford the poll tax. And now and then, Governor Folsom would send Craig to important meetings of black leaders to represent him and to report back what he learned. "One of the most rewarding things about working with Jim Folsom was being with these brilliant young people like Chuck Morgan," Beech said years later. "They made life extraordinarily interesting. Their minds worked fast and furious. None worked better and with more agility than Chuck Morgan's."

Within a year after the *Brown* decision, Morgan heard that a young Negro named Autherine Lucy had applied to the University of Alabama for admission. He watched from Alabama as Negro students were admitted to Louisiana State University and the University of North Carolina without violent incident. Believing that the same orderly change could happen on the UA campus, Morgan sought an audience with the school's president, Dr. Oliver Cromwell Carmichael. After Morgan explained his beliefs, outlining the way it could happen peacefully, Dr. Carmichael thanked him politely and said he would be in touch.

Morgan never heard a word from him. When Lucy was ordered by the federal court to be admitted to UA, neither the school nor the government was ready. She arrived on campus on Friday, February 3, 1956, riding in a Cadillac with a hundred-dollar bill for her registration fee, given to her by black Birmingham businessman A. G. Gaston. She wore a new dress, hose, and high heels. That night, after she attended classes without incident, crowds packed onto University Avenue. In front of the empty president's mansion—Carmichael having already left for a weekend out of town—the mob called out, "Keep 'Bama white!" and "Hey, hey, ho, ho, Autherine's got to go!" Morgan and a few other like-minded students met the following morning and came to the conclusion that the Friday night scene would not be repeated. They figured the hotheads had vented their steam and had gotten it out of their system.

On Saturday night they were proven wrong. One of the leaders of the previous night's mob, Leonard Wilson, a sophomore from Selma, led a bigger crowd up University Avenue. A car filled with a Negro family was beaten and rocked. By Sunday night, the mob that gathered on campus was twice the size of the original Friday night bunch. A carload of white men from Birmingham arrived on campus armed with explosives, preparing to do whatever they wished to keep the school lily-white. In that car was Robert "Dynamite Bob" Chambliss, who had been working with the Birmingham KKK since the late 1940s. He and his friends from the Birmingham klavern were stopped by state troopers and questioned by state investigators with the Department of Public Safety. After several hours, they were freed with their explosives.

Finally, on Monday morning, when Lucy arrived on campus for a class at Bibb Graves Hall, more than three thousand white protesters, including Chambliss and his Birmingham group and Leonard Wilson, were there to greet her. As she rode up, eggs were thrown at the car. A brick smashed a rear window. When she ran for the front door, an egg hit her squarely in the back. The crowd shouted, "Let's kill her! Let's kill her!" As she disappeared inside, they chanted, "Hey, hey, ho, ho, where in hell did the nigger go?" For the next three hours she remained locked inside while the crowd continued its hateful chants.

Outside, four white men were arrested. One was Chambliss, who was soon released. Another picked up by police but quickly turned loose was Asa Earl Carter.

"Despite ingrained Alabama attitudes toward segregation," Morgan wrote, "the Lucy Riots of 1956 were not inevitable. As a matter of fact, only an incredible series of oversights, miscalculations, and blunders in Washington, Montgomery, and Tuscaloosa made it possible for a small minority of university students—joined by a ragtail group of off-campus toughs—to successfully thwart orders of a federal court."

In the aftermath of the four nights of rioting, the school's administration and its board of trustees suspended Lucy as a student "for her protection and for the protection of other students and staff members."

Morgan later wrote, "The lesson seemed clear enough and its message flashed across the South: Violence works.

"As they would so many times in future years, the decent, law-abiding people of the state settled upon a comfortable explanation of how the Lucy Riots had come about: everything would have been all right, they told each other, if the NAACP hadn't driven her down to Tuscaloosa dressed fit to kill—and in a big black Cadillac.

"When she finally left Alabama, Autherine Lucy told the press that her one moment of hope had come some time before her violent entry on campus, while her case was still pending. A student leader had called and told her he would try his best to help prepare her way onto campus. I read her farewell comment with interest and a degree of regret for a battle lost. I had been the caller," he wrote in his 1963 memoir, *A Time to Speak.*

At the time of the riots, the Alabama Legislature passed what it called "a nullification resolution" and declared the *Brown* decision "null, void, and of no effect." The state would not follow the law of the United States.

The *New York Times* wrote, "Because of the Lucy case and the Montgomery bus boycott, Alabama stands today as a symbol of Southern resistance to desegregation."

On February 10, 1956, one week after the first mob gathered on the streets of Tuscaloosa, ten thousand white people packed the new state-owned Garrett Coliseum in Montgomery for the nation's largest rally of the White Citizens Council. U.S. senator James Eastland of Mississippi told the crowd, "Thank God the state of Alabama has started the offense. From this day, the direction is forward."

In Tuscaloosa, Chuck and Camille Morgan sat at their kitchen table and wondered what they should do about their new life together. Both were born and raised in the South. "We decided then and there that we must move forward and do the best we could for ourselves and for this place we called home," Morgan said.

After law school, Morgan and his bride headed back home to Birmingham, where they hoped to spend the rest of their lives, raise a family with their son Charles III, practice law, and enter the world of politics. At first, Morgan joined the highly respected firm of Dumas, O'Neal, and Hayes, practicing corporate and municipal-bond law. If he stayed with the firm, life would be easy and secure. It promised a remarkably bright future.

But the strong emotional riptides—courtroom drama that excited his imagination and the magical world of politics—called to him. The thoughts of these possibilities pulled constantly at his conscience and his pulsating imagination. He was far from an ordinary young attorney. He wanted more than a good job and a hefty weekly paycheck.

In January 1958, Morgan opened his own law office with a friend from school. Almost immediately, he hit the campaign trail for his friend and fellow Folsom supporter, state senator George Hawkins, in whom he found the same kind of progressive spirit he had discovered in Jim Folsom. However, it was not long before the practical side of Morgan realized that the young son of the slain attorney general-elect would be leading the field of fourteen candidates for governor. Morgan came home to Birmingham to watch the runoff election between Patterson and the Fightin' Little Judge, as the press called George Wallace.

Morgan got an up-close view of the legal system as it operated in Birmingham. He saw the all-white juries sentencing Negro defendants, paying little attention to the facts of cases. He saw the bring-the-guilty-bastard-in syndrome in the city's courtrooms. As a resident of upper-class Mountain Brook, where no Negroes lived in 1960, he watched as whites fled downtown. And when the Big Mules and Got Rocks pressed for a new Dixiecrat movement, he contacted his old friend in Tuscaloosa, Marc Ray "Foots" Clement, who continued to lead Loyalist Democrats. Following Clement's lead, Morgan assisted daily at the office of the state Democratic Party downtown to keep the progressives afloat.

When twenty-year-old Thomas C. Reeves, who was studying for the ministry at Birmingham-Southern College, had brought white Methodist students together with black students from Miles and Daniel Payne colleges to discuss mutual problems, he had been arrested and jailed.

After Reeves was released from jail, alumni went to Birmingham-Southern president Henry King Stanford and demanded the young man be expelled. Stanford refused. That night, hooded Ku Klux Klansmen burned a cross on the campus. But Dr. Stanford decided to fight the hotheads. He called several attorneys before one suggested Morgan, who took the case.

In court, Morgan had the case continued. After several more continuances, a dismissal was granted. Reeves graduated with Phi Beta Kappa honors.

In April 1960, Morgan read Pulitzer Prize–winning journalist Harrison Salisbury's two-part series about Birmingham in the *New York Times.* As he read Salisbury's words—"Every channel of communication, every medium of mutual interest, every reasoned approach, every inch of middle ground has been fragmented by the emotional dynamite of racism"—he realized that local criticism of the racist atmosphere had been "almost nonexistent." Now, Salisbury's articles had become "one of the most newsworthy events in Birmingham's history." And soon Morgan became a part of the story.

Not only did the citizens of Birmingham express shock at the Northern reporter's articles, a prosecuting attorney in nearby Bessemer called a grand jury into session for the purpose of determining whether the

New York Times was guilty of libel under state law. In its investigation, the jury issued a subpoena to the Reverend Robert E. "Bob" Hughes, a Methodist minister who was director of the Alabama Council on Human Relations, an affiliate of the Southern Regional Council in Atlanta, assigned to maintain and disseminate information about racial problems. In its search through telephone records from reporter Salisbury's hotel room, it had been determined that Hughes was one of Salisbury's primary sources. Hughes refused the grand jury's order that he appear and answer questions. He also refused to turn over ACHR records. In taking such a controversial stand, he needed an attorney. Once again, a number of lawyers refused. Finally, Morgan was asked and agreed.

The subpoena ordered Hughes to appear with council records within forty-eight hours. Morgan threw himself into his work wholeheartedly. Chuck and Camille worked through the night. He found several cases he believed pertinent: a U.S. Supreme Court holding that the National Association for the Advancement of Colored People did not have to surrender its records in the Daisy Bates case in Arkansas and a similar ruling when Alabama attorney general John Patterson tried to obtain NAACP records. Finally, Morgan decided to use the Bill of Rights: freedom of press, speech, worship, and assembly. In the early morning, Morgan and his team started out for the Bessemer courthouse about five miles west of downtown Birmingham. When Hughes asked what might happen, Morgan replied, "That's for the court and the Lord to decide, Bob. I'll do my best in court. The Lord is your jurisdiction."

After hearing the motion to quash the subpoena, the circuit judge denied the request and ordered Hughes to testify the next morning. Morgan then asked for a one-day delay to appeal. The judge again denied.

Morgan telephoned the State Supreme Court. A hearing was set for 8:00 A.M. the next day, only an hour before his client had been ordered to appear in Bessemer.

Again, Morgan, Camille, and Morgan's partner, Jim Shores, worked late. In the wee hours of the morning, Shores left for Montgomery, ninety miles south of Birmingham, where he would argue before the high court. Hughes and Morgan drove to the Bessemer courthouse, where only a few months before hooded Ku Klux Klansmen attacked a defendant in a civil rights case on the front steps and beat him with clubs.

Inside the courtroom, Morgan and Hughes waited.

Other witnesses waited. These included lawyers, rabbis, newsmen, and businessmen, all subpoenaed to testify.

When Morgan discovered that they had been turned down in Montgomery, he telephoned an associate in Washington, D.C., who filed a motion with the U.S. Supreme Court. Morgan and Hughes continued to wait.

Finally, on the following morning, September 2, Hughes was called. Alone and empty-handed, he walked into the grand jury room, where attorneys were not allowed to accompany their clients.

Minutes later, the door opened. The grand jury filed out. After them, the circuit solicitor and Hughes stepped into the courtroom. Morgan moved to his client's side.

Circuit judge Gardner F. Goodwyn Jr. was told the witness would not testify. Morgan told the judge that his client would be glad to tell what he said to Harrison Salisbury but would not furnish a membership list of the council, which he considered privileged information.

Judge Goodwyn told the solicitor to try again. The jurors, solicitor, and Hughes went back behind closed doors, only to return minutes later.

Asked if he still refused, Hughes answered, "Yes, sir."

The judge ruled Hughes in contempt of court and ordered confinement "until you purge yourself of contempt."

Hughes was taken to jail.

On the Tuesday after Labor Day, Morgan was visiting Hughes in jail when his name was called. The grand jury had issued a new subpoena. Now he was required only to appear before the body. It did not mention records.

Hughes appeared and told them what he had said to Salisbury, who was indicted by the jury on forty-two counts of criminal libel. However, the *Times* reporter was never served. Until the end of his life, the indictments against Harrison Salisbury remained outstanding, and he did not return to the state where he might have been prosecuted and imprisoned.

In the aftermath of his courageous stand, Bob Hughes was told by the North Alabama Conference of the Methodist Church to resign from the

Council on Human Relations or be dismissed from the ministry. At the last minute, it received a wire from the bishop in Southern Rhodesia, saying Hughes's services were needed in Africa. His transfer was approved.

Morgan reflected to friends that his experiences in the Reeves and Hughes cases fundamentally changed his perspective on the community in which he lived. They touched his conscience and changed his role as a Birmingham attorney. Now Morgan followed the example of his old professor Jay Murphy. Murphy had become involved not simply as a lawyer but as a member of the community. He became involved as a person who had a share of responsibility for the things that were happening to his home and to his client.

Years later, Morgan looked back on that time of change when he told me: "I could have turned my back on Reeves and Hughes. It would have been easy to do. Other lawyers did it every day. But I wouldn't be Chuck Morgan if I'd done that. I wouldn't be me. I discovered that it was part of my world, my conscience, to look these people in the face, then step up to the bench and fight their cause for them. *Their* cause became *my* cause."

In July 1960, Morgan read the novel *To Kill a Mockingbird* for the first time. "When I read my old classmate's words, I was knocked out by the gorgeous simplicity, the slender thread of decency that runs from page one to page three-hundred-and-twenty-something, the classic battle of good versus evil, and the ultimate victory of good. To me, Atticus Finch was the personification of everything I ever wanted to be. Not only does he stand up for Tom Robinson, the poor black man falsely accused and ultimately declared guilty by the white hypocrites, Atticus finds mercy and goodness for the poor white, mistreated, severely retarded white man who'd been abused all of his pitiful life. The moment I finished reading that book I knew I would read it over and over again. It was my destiny," Morgan told me.

In early May 1961, a bus carrying Freedom Riders on their symbolic ride through the South left Washington, D.C. In two weeks it would arrive in Birmingham, where Klan leader Hubert Page outlined the schedule to a meeting of the Eastview klavern.

KKK imperial wizard Bobby Shelton ordered that sixty men be selected to meet the buses when they arrived in Birmingham. Thirty would be stationed at the bus depot and thirty nearby at the Molton Hotel, ready to attack if needed. Hubert Page told the action squads that Bull Connor sent a special message: "By God, if you are going to do this thing, do it right."

Squad leaders from klaverns throughout Alabama gathered at the Eastview Klan headquarters in Woodlawn on Saturday, May 13, to plan what they would do when the Freedom Riders arrived the next morning. Among them was Gary Thomas Rowe, who had been planted in the Klan by the FBI and who informed his handlers of the meeting. At the gathering, he reported, Police Commissioner Connor told the Klansmen that they would have fifteen to twenty minutes to beat the riders until they "looked like a bulldog got a hold of them." And if the riders went to the restroom, the Klan was to take their clothes and make them enter the depot naked, where they would be arrested and sent to jail. If a Klansman was arrested by mistake, he said, he was to tell the police that the Negroes started it. He then warned them not to carry their KKK membership cards or pistols, unless they had permits.

Concerned about the possible violence that might befall the Freedom Riders, U.S. attorney general Robert F. Kennedy telephoned Chuck Morgan. He had gotten Morgan's name from Marc Ray Clement, who had recommended Morgan to senator John Sparkman as a bright young Democrat. Kennedy said he had heard Morgan was "a true Democrat." At the time Morgan had already met with Reverend Shuttlesworth, who told him and Orzell Billingsley, "I'm afraid for those young people." Morgan assured him, "If they're arrested, you call me and Orzell, and we'll do everything we can to get 'em out of jail as quickly as possible." He also assured Kennedy that he would be ready to provide any legal help he could give.

In Atlanta, the Freedom Riders were welcomed by King and the SCLC's executive director, Wyatt Tee Walker. After lunch, the bus left Atlanta, headed for Alabama.

By midafternoon, the bus carrying the Freedom Riders arrived in Anniston in northeast Alabama. Kenneth Adams, a former Ace Carter associate who had accompanied Carter in the attack on Nat King Cole, showed up at the depot with his group of Klansmen. A local policeman approached them and spoke with Adams. A few minutes later, Adams left with his men.

As the bus moved out of Anniston, fifty cars followed. Five miles out, a tire on the bus blew. It was later determined that it had been slashed. As the driver jumped off, about two hundred men surrounded the bus. Beating the bus with chains and clubs, some shouted, "Sieg heil!" as a firebomb was thrown through a window.

To ensure order, Governor Patterson had ordered a plainclothes investigator with the Alabama Department of Public Safety to board the bus in Atlanta. Now the armed agent pushed open the door, stepped off with his gun drawn, and told the mob to "get back and let these people off, or some of you are going to die." At the last minute, the riders left the bus as the state policeman fired into the air.

When several carloads of laughing state troopers arrived on the scene, the mob moved to their cars and rode away.

Soon, another bus arrived. Within an hour, the riders were moving westward again.

That night in Birmingham, Billingsley called Morgan and told him about the firebomb and said, "It looks like there will be plenty of trouble waiting for them here." Morgan said he had heard the news reports. He would be on standby.

When the bus arrived at the Birmingham bus station, it was immediately surrounded by Klansmen wielding clubs. The men beat their clubs against the bus. Some hit and broke windows. Two riders were jerked from the bus and beaten until blood ran down the front of their shirts. Across the street, uniformed policemen stood, waiting for orders from the police commissioner.

Throughout the afternoon, Howard K. Smith and his crew from CBS, in town shooting a documentary entitled *Who Speaks for Birmingham?*, filmed the entire violent incident that showed on the Sunday night news throughout the nation.

One of the bloodied riders, Jim Peck, was taken to University Hospital, where doctors sewed up five gashes on his head and face. At 2:15 A.M., Peck called the Reverend Fred Shuttlesworth, who had rescued other Freedom Riders and taken them to his house for safekeeping.

When Shuttlesworth arrived at the emergency room, he said Peck "looked like a mummy."

At the city jail Billingsley, Peter Hall, and Morgan worked to release the jailed Freedom Riders. However, several remained behind bars until they were freed the following week, when a judge heard the pleas of the attorneys.

On Saturday morning, a bus filled with Freedom Riders left Birmingham, heading south toward Montgomery.

With attorney general Robert Kennedy's special assistant, John Seigenthaler, a former reporter for the Nashville *Tennessean*, following in a rental car, the bus was scheduled to arrive in the capital city at 10:30 A.M. At ten, public safety director Floyd Mann went to police commissioner L. B. Sullivan's office to confirm that city police were waiting at the station. Just before the scheduled time of arrival, policemen left the Greyhound station on Court Street unattended. Only a handful of journalists remained. There was no security patrol.

As the bus pulled into the station and parked, riders began to step off onto a concrete loading dock. A mob of about a hundred men carrying metal pipes, baseball bats, and large sticks moved into the parking area and through the station. In the mob were the three Ku Klux Klansmen who had given Willie Edwards Jr. his last ride less than five years earlier.

"Filthy commies! Nigger lovers!" the crowd chanted.

More than two dozen white men waded into the group of riders who were trying to hide in the bus depot. They grabbed several men, both black and white, and pulled them out onto Court Street and beat them. Some were bleeding from their mouths and their heads.

The mob of whites hit anyone who got in its way. When John Lewis, a Student Nonviolent Coordinating Committee leader who had led student demonstrations in Nashville, ran for cover in the restroom, a white man with an iron bar struck him across the head. Lewis fell to his knees.

Although photographer Don Urbrock was smashed in the face with his own camera, he managed to catch Klansman Sonny Kyle Livingston in action. A series of photos later published in *Life* showed Livingston beating a black woman with a baseball bat and hitting her again after she had fallen to the sidewalk.

When Public Safety Director Mann found Seigenthaler bleeding on the sidewalk next to Washington Avenue, where he had been beaten by a man wielding a pipe after Seigenthaler had tried to rescue a female Freedom Rider, Mann drew his pistol. He demanded that the mob back away. He then flagged down a police car to take Seigenthaler to the hospital.

By the time police arrived and shot tear gas bombs into the crowd, more than a dozen people had been carried away to St. Margaret's Hospital, where they waited in the emergency room to be treated.

That night, Chuck and Camille Morgan watched the Montgomery massacre on national television. "It was a bloody sight that immediately sickened us," Morgan said later. For him, it was one more incident that darkened Alabama's name.

Morgan joined the newly organized Young Men's Business Club of Birmingham, which was made up of progressive-minded young people who wanted to change the image of their town. With another member, Morgan filed a lawsuit to join the suburb of Mountain Brook with nearby Homewood and Birmingham. They believed a unified community could grow and become more progressive. "We thought that we could manage to beat back the Ku Klux Klan violence if we all stuck together," Morgan said. He smiled wryly. "But everybody didn't think like we did. The conservatives wanted to escape the problems they saw growing larger and larger, more and more violent. They wanted to hide under a rock."

In the spring of 1963, after Wallace's angry cry of "Segregation forever!", Morgan met with his friends King and Shuttlesworth as they prepared to peacefully integrate Birmingham. "We will do it as nonviolent protesters," King told him. "But we *will* do it."

When a group of white Alabama religious leaders issued a public statement that questioned the timing and the methods of the Birmingham demonstrations, particularly the use of children, Morgan warned that these men of the cloth were laying a public relations foundation. Daily, the protesters grew in number and diminished in average age.

"These were some of the bravest people I'd ever seen in action," Morgan recalled. "They were not outside agitators as the local white establishment portrayed them. They were local people who were acting out their demands for a thing called freedom. They were young people who knew their parents, their grandparents, and their distant ancestors had never known freedom. They barely knew what the word meant, but they wanted some. They wanted to touch it and taste it. They were bound and determined to have it."

On Good Friday, April 12, King was arrested and charged with violating a court injunction prohibiting public civil rights demonstrations. Also arrested was Reverend Ralph David Abernathy, who had participated actively with King in the bus boycott eight years earlier in Montgomery.

In the city jail, King sat in his tiny cell and wrote a letter answering the white clergy's criticism. It began: "My dear fellow clergymen." It continued for twenty-one pages, describing Birmingham's "ugly record of brutality," stating, "I have almost reached the regrettable conclusion that the Negro's great stumbling block in his stride toward freedom is not the White Citizens Counciler or the Ku Klux Klanner, but the white moderate, who is more devoted to 'order' than to justice, who prefers a negative peace which is the absence of tension to a positive peace which is the presence of justice; who constantly says: 'I agree with you in the goal you seek, but I cannot agree with your methods of direct action.'" The letter ended, "Yours for the cause of peace and brotherhood." As Wyatt Tee Walker handed out copies to national journalists, he declared, "This is going to be one of the historic documents of the movement."

Soon after his release from jail, city fathers and civil rights leaders reached a settlement through peace talks led by Burke Marshall. King prepared to make a statement from the courtyard of the Gaston Motel, where more than a hundred reporters and a dozen television cameras waited. Inside King's room, Chuck Morgan and New York attorney Clarence Jones were revising his statement while King talked on the telephone with Harry Belafonte. When the singer told King he had three thousand people waiting to march on Washington, the preacher said he would need at least a hundred thousand. Minutes later, King read his statement: "Birmingham reached an accord with its conscience today. The acceptance of responsibility by local whites and Negro leadership offers an example of a free people uniting to meet and solve their problems. Birmingham may well offer for twentieth-century America an example of progressive race relations and for all mankind a dawn of a new day, a promise for all men, a day of opportunity and a new sense of freedom for all America."

On May 16, Len Holt wrote in the *National Guardian*, "Coming from the airport May 6, we drove past the A. G. Gaston Motel, integration headquarters. Then we saw why the downtown area was 'cop-less.' On the roofs of the three or four story buildings surrounding Kelly Ingram Park were clusters of policemen with shortwave radios over their shoulders. At the four intersections surrounding the park were dozens of white-helmeted officers."

Accompanying Birmingham police were reinforcements from the nearby towns of Bessemer, Fairfield, and Leeds. Jefferson County deputy sheriffs and a few state troopers stood with them. To Len Holt, "The officers seemed fearful. This fear was expressed in marathon chatter and forced joviality as they waited for the ordeal that was to come: another mass demonstration."

Nearby, four thousand African-American women, men, boys, girls, and mothers with babies watched from porches, lawns, cars, and streets around the park. As the scene became more and more tense, the police and the spectators looked toward the Sixteenth Street Baptist Church, where more than two thousand persons sat inside and three hundred stood outside. Most of these were grammar and high school students, who sang "We Shall Overcome" and other freedom songs.

A black minister standing near Holt said, "At any moment those cops expect three hundred years of hate to spew forth from that church."

Within minutes, four fire engines rolled up. High-powered hoses were attached to nozzle mounts on the streets. Nozzles were aimed toward the blacks in front of the church. Water shot through such nozzles would tumble grown men at a hundred feet. Holt was told it would strip bark from trees and tear bricks from walls.

Later that night, when the demonstrators walked toward the center of town, the hoses were turned on, pinning young blacks against the sides of buildings as Holt and other reporters looked on.

Two nights later, Morgan was hosting some journalists, including Claude Sitton of the *New York Times*, *Time*'s Dudley Morris, and Karl Fleming of *Newsweek*, for a celebratory drink and steak dinner. After a few stiff bourbons, Morgan was holding forth in his most cordial and sophisticated manner when he was called to the phone. The caller told him the Gaston Motel had just been bombed.

That night, the Klan was on the move. Undercover Klansman Gary Thomas Rowe told his FBI handler the Klan had enough dynamite to blow up half the town. Outside the motel, where no one was killed in the blast, a Negro mob gathered. They were ready to riot. It was the beginning of a long, hot summer.

★

While the daily demonstrations were happening in Birmingham and Governor Wallace was planning to stand in the schoolhouse door, Morgan visited Huntsville in northeast Alabama. In the living room of the new, modern home of Dr. John Cashin Jr., an African American dentist, Morgan was introduced to two young black men, Dave McGlathery, a twenty-six-year-old native of Huntsville who had graduated magna cum laude from Alabama A&M, a local public black college, and Marvin P. Carroll, a graduate of Howard University in Washington, D.C. McGlathery worked in the research projects division at NASA's Marshall Space Flight Center, and Carroll was employed in the electromagnetics laboratory at Redstone Arsenal. Both wanted to attend the University of Alabama's extension center at Huntsville. They did not wish to make a spectacle of their admission. This was not ideological or political. They simply wished to advance their professional careers. "All they wanted was to enroll and go to classes—and they thought that a white lawyer, a University of Alabama graduate, and someone who knew the state and its officials could accomplish their end," Morgan wrote. Would he guide them through enrollment without fanfare and, if possible, without a lawsuit?

Representing these clients, Morgan knew, would have been dangerous for a Birmingham lawyer. At the time, no white lawyer in the South had ever successfully brought suit to integrate a public school. Guardedly, Morgan agreed to advise and help them become students at the previously all-white school. Both men applied for admission. At first, both were rejected on technicalities.

Although Morgan hesitated in the beginning, on May 8 he filed a lawsuit in federal court asking his clients be admitted in June for summer study. Ultimately, after Carroll decided to withdraw his request, the court ordered McGlathery admitted.

On the morning of June 13, two days after Governor Wallace stood in the schoolhouse door in Tuscaloosa, McGlathery drove to the extension center and quietly registered.

Governor Wallace never said a word opposing the registration of McGlathery nor did he stand in the doorway at Huntsville. "It was typical George Wallace," Morgan said later. "He lied to his constituents from the moment he started running for statewide office back in the late fifties. He used their bitter racism, their complete insecurity, their childish need to be led like sheep to the slaughterhouse. His words were as empty as a goat's blathering. He snapped at the air. He thrust his chin forward, like he was going to bite. But his bite was pitiful, just as his words were pitiful, but the Ku Klux Klan took his words and acted out with their violence, riding through the night, blowing up poor people's houses and churches. Their innate meanness rose to the surface as his words echoed through the air of Dixie."

In August, King's March on Washington climaxed with 250,000 people crowded around the Reflecting Pool on the Mall. After songs by Joan Baez, Bob Dylan, Odetta, Peter, Paul, and Mary, and Pete Seeger, Roy Wilkins, director of the NAACP, announced that the previous night W. E. B. Du Bois had died in his sleep at age ninety-five in his home in Ghana. King stood on the stage at the base of the Washington monument. "I have a dream," he told the gathered masses.

"I have a dream that one day on the red hills of Georgia, the sons of former slaves and the sons of former slave owners will be able to sit down together at the table of brotherhood. I have a dream that one day even the state of Mississippi, a state sweltering with the heat of injustice, sweltering with the heat of oppression, will be transformed into an oasis of freedom and justice. I have a dream that my four little children will one day live in a nation where they will not be judged by the color of their skin but by the content of their character.

"I have a dream today!

"I have a dream that one day, down in Alabama, with its vicious racists, with its governor having his lips dripping with the words of 'interposition' and 'nullification'—one day right there in Alabama little black boys and black girls will be able to join hands with little white boys and white girls as sisters and brothers.

"I have a dream today!"

Speaking out in his powerful baritone voice, his words echoed through the muggy air of Washington, D.C. They were repeated over and over for television audiences across America and throughout the world. In the coming days, weeks, months, and years, Chuck Morgan would quote the words again and again.

On Sunday morning, September 15, 1963, four hundred people were milling around inside the Sixteenth Street Baptist Church in Birmingham, where many of the demonstrators had met daily before marching through downtown or going to a diner for a sit-in. In the basement of the church, children moved into their Sunday school classes.

Fourteen-year-old Cynthia Wesley was wearing a frilly white dress with a red sweater over her shoulders as she stepped from her father Claude's black Mercury. Claude Wesley, principal of a Negro school, drove away to fill up his tank. He planned to meet Cynthia later, after Sunday school.

At 9:22 A.M., he heard an explosion from two blocks away. Immediately, he drove back to the church, where he found mass confusion.

A bomb had blown a hole in the side of the red-brick building. Twelve-year-old Sarah Jean Collins stumbled out of the hole. Her hands covered her bloodied face.

Wesley searched through the debris for his daughter.

People stood around dumbfounded. They gazed unseeing into the smoky air. An ambulance and a fire truck arrived.

Among the glass and rubble, blood-splotched copies of the prayer of the day read: "Dear God, we are sorry for the times we were so unkind."

At a hospital, Claude Wesley was asked if his daughter was wearing a ring. "I said yes, she was, and they pulled her little hand out, and the little ring was there."

As Denise McNair's mother searched for her daughter in the wreckage of the church basement, she came upon her own father, M. W. Pippin. Staring through a film of tears, she uttered, "Daddy, I can't find Denise."

"She's dead, baby," he managed. "I've got one of her shoes in here. I'd like to blow the whole town up."

The bodies of four girls were found: Cynthia Wesley, Denise McNair, Carol Robertson, and Addie Mae Collins.

In Mountain Brook, the Morgans did not hear the explosion. When they heard about it, they were shocked to the core. Chuck Morgan remembered holding his wife and son close. After church, they heard people crying. White people mourned.

Throughout Sunday afternoon and early Monday morning, Morgan thought about what had happened. Pictures flashed through his brain. Recollections of the past years appeared like a newsreel at a Saturday afternoon double feature. He relived his own transformation during the years at the University of Alabama and since those days. Close-up profiles of Autherine Lucy, Tom Reeves, Bob Hughes, David Baker, and Dave McGlathery were remembered like flashbacks in a movie. By now, Morgan had read Harper Lee's Pulitzer Prize–winning novel, *To Kill a Mockingbird*, three times. To him, it was the best novel he had ever read, and Atticus Finch was by far the best character in literature. Over good bourbon in the evenings he would quote courtroom scenes verbatim. "It's the best," he judged. "There's no other work that comes even close. It captures the essence of the South, and it creates a true lawyer with a conscience." Atticus Finch's words to his young daughter, Scout, resonated like an echo in his brain: "You don't know a man until you've walked in his shoes." "I read it over and over again. Each time I read it I learn something new, find new meanings, a new depth of understanding I had not had before."

Early on Monday morning, Morgan sat at his desk. His hefty shoulders hunched forward, and he wrote. He remembered the *News* had boasted that Birmingham was a city of churches with more than seven hundred churches and temples.

As the police chief pledged to find, arrest, and prosecute the guilty party or parties, Morgan continued to think and write.

Then he walked. He strolled through the lobby of the Redmont Hotel, where several dozen uniformed state troopers stood around talking and laughing. He took the elevator to the second floor and marched into the meeting of the Young Men's Business Club.

After a short business discussion, Morgan was introduced as the club's speaker.

"Four little girls were killed in Birmingham yesterday," he began. He looked solemnly into the sea of white faces. "A mad, remorseful, worried community asks, 'Who did it? Who threw that bomb? Was it a Negro or a white?' The answer should be, 'We all did it.' Every last one of us is condemned for that crime and the bombing before it and the ones last month, last year, a decade ago. We all did it."

His refrain, "Who did it?" roared through the hall. "The 'who' is every little individual who talks about the 'niggers' and spreads the seeds of his hate to his neighbor and his son. The 'who' is every governor who ever shouted for lawlessness and became a law violator. It is every senator and every representative who in the halls of Congress stands and with mock humility tells the world that things back home aren't really like they are. It is courts that move ever so slowly and newspapers that timorously defend the law. It is all the Christians and all their ministers who spoke too late in anguished cries against violence. It is the coward in each of us who clucks admonitions."

Morgan continued, challenging the city and its population to look into the mirror and see the guilty. His familiar baritone rose above their heads and hit down upon their conscience.

"And who is really guilty? Each of us. Each citizen who has not consciously attempted to bring about peaceful compliance with the decisions of the Supreme Court of the United States, each citizen who has ever said, 'They ought to kill that nigger,' every citizen who votes for the candidate with the bloody flag.

"What's it like living in Birmingham? No one ever really has, and no one will until this city becomes a part of the United States.

"Birmingham is not a dying city. It is dead."

Applause was light. Then one member rose. Recognized, he suggested the club admit a Negro to its membership. After several moments of silence, the motion died without a second.

In the days ahead, the threatening calls and letters increased. Several promised to kill Morgan and his family. One asked if he had seen a mortician. When he said he knew no mortician, the caller said that he would soon know one.

Soon, Chuck and Camille Morgan decided they had had enough. They didn't want to raise their son in this environment. They moved to Alexandria, Virginia, where Chuck taught and wrote a book about their ordeal.

Soon, the American Civil Liberties Union called and made an offer. He would be a lone lawyer in the Atlanta office. For the first time, the ACLU would have a legal warrior in the South to fight for American Justice. To Morgan, those two words had to be capitalized. It was his goal to bring American Justice to the South.

10

COUNTRY-BOY LAWYER

When he first heard about the tragedy at the Sixteenth Street Baptist Church, Morris Seligman Dees Jr. was a young lawyer living in Mount Meigs, a rural community east of Montgomery. He and his wife, Beverly, were listening to the radio in the car. With their baby son between them, they were riding home from church.

At home, Dees drew a mental picture of the church wreckage. As he heard the cooing sound of his son, he thought about the parents of the children. As the thought remained, he hugged his young wife and son, Morris III, whom they called Scooter. Later Dees sat in his favorite chair and watched television. The screen showed the aftermath of the bombing ninety miles to the north in Birmingham. For the first time in his twenty-six years, he thought long and hard about the race problem.

Throughout the following week, his mind wandered over the other Birmingham bombings: preachers' homes blown up in the middle of the night, a motel owned by a black businessman smashed by explosives, and churches destroyed by dynamite. In his thoughts, none of those bombings was as evil or as devastating as the killing of children during Sunday school. During the week he read that a white supremacist told a meeting of the Ku Klux Klan that the terrorists deserved medals. The four little girls, he said, "weren't children. Children are little people, little human beings, and that means white people. . . . They're just little niggers . . . and if there's four less niggers tonight, then I say, 'Good for whoever planted the bomb.'" Reading the words, Dees felt a cold chill knot in his stomach, "a complete feeling of helplessness and then an anger at myself for not being able to do something about it at that moment in time," he said in a 1978 interview.

Dees watched on television as Dr. King spoke to eight thousand mourners at the joint funeral of three of the victims at Sixteenth Street Baptist, telling them, "The innocent blood of these little girls may well serve as the redemptive force that will bring new light to this dark city. Indeed, this tragic event may cause the white South to come to terms with its conscience."

As he thought about the situation throughout the week, a refrain kept coming back to him: what can I do?

As Dr. King prophesied, Dees came to terms with his conscience. Sitting in the comfort of his home, he thought about his own community. If he would lead, he thought, these people he had known all of his life would follow. Early in life he had thought seriously about someday becoming a preacher. Although he had followed his father's advice and become a lawyer, he still felt a strong love for the church and for the Holy Bible. In his heart of hearts, he felt he could be a lawyer and a preacher. He knew deep down that the people in central Alabama were good folks who did not hate. They were his neighbors.

Dees had grown up in the cotton fields and farmland east of Montgomery. He was well known in his community as Bubba Dees, the towheaded son of a hardworking farm family. After he and his wife and baby returned after he graduated from the University of Alabama Law School, he was named superintendent of the Sunday school at the Pike Road Baptist Church. While his mother and father had always been tolerant people who often displayed their personal affection to Negro neighbors, his most beloved uncle, his father's brother, was an outspoken racist. Still, Dees felt that most of the people here, even his uncle, did not hate.

Born and raised in a segregated world, Dees had known no other. However, on Sunday, September 22, 1963, he stepped in front of the congregation and looked out at all of the white faces. Throughout the previous week his thoughts had weighed heavily upon his conscience. He thought about what he was about to say. He had gone over the words in his mind, considering each. "Brothers and sisters, there's another Baptist church that needs our help," he said.

"Tell us, Bubba," the congregation said.

"It's a church that has had a tragedy."

His neighbors nodded. As he had thought, they were good, understanding folks.

"It's the Sixteenth Street Church in Birmingham, where four little girls were killed last Sunday and the church was destroyed."

Later, he wrote, "The blood drained from my friends' faces, the nodding stopped. The members of the Pike Road Baptist Church quickly fell into two camps—those who were angered by the suggestion and those who were too shocked to be angry. I couldn't make out their whispers, but I could read their expressions."

Dees pulled a check from his pocket. "I'm giving this to help the church rebuild," he told them. "I hope you all will either write a check of your own or give what cash you can."

In the back of the room, an old woman stood. "This ain't none of our business, Morris Jr. This ain't nothing we want to get involved in."

As she spoke, the congregation began nodding again.

Dees said, "I'd like for you all to join me in a little prayer for the girls before we go to our classes."

With lips clamped, he looked out over the faces that glared back at him in silence. He had always been a serious young man. Now he wanted to show his seriousness as never before. He wanted to reach out and touch his neighbors.

"Please," he said, "won't you join me in a prayer? We all have children of our own. No matter how you feel."

He shut his eyes and bowed his head. He prayed silently. In a brief moment, he heard shuffling and footfalls. Looking up, he saw that his wife, Beverly, was standing beside him. They prayed together.

When he finished praying, he looked up again. As his eyes scanned the room, he saw that no one else remained in the sanctuary. They were standing alone, looking out at the empty seats.

Dees and his wife would look back on that day and remember it vividly. From that moment, their lives changed. In his own way, he would do whatever it would take to bring out the best in these white Southerners whom he believed had forsaken him. The preacher in his soul would again rise to the surface.

To Dees, his suggestion that the people of Mount Meigs make a contribution to help rebuild a church was a tiny thing. His asking them to pray for the souls of little girls killed in the explosion did not seem extraordinary. "Just a silent prayer, an act consistent with Christian teachings, praying for the souls of other Christians. *Children.* And yet my good friends and neighbors could not free themselves from the slavery of the Southern tradition and, forgetting about color, do the Christian thing."

From the time he was old enough to lift a hoe or push a wheelbarrow, Morris Dees worked in the fields near the old Federal Road where more than a century earlier the first European settlers followed the ancient Indian trade routes southwest into the wilderness. They were tough people who came into the new territory and cleared the land, plowed, and planted. In the early years of the nineteenth century they settled Montgomery, which became a shipping hub where steamboats were loaded with cotton picked on farms like those Dees's grandfather worked in the twentieth century. For generation after generation, his kin had been farmers or country storekeepers, but his father, Morris Seligman Dees Sr., named for a Jewish merchant his father admired, wanted to break the cycle, telling young Bubba that he would become a lawyer when he grew up. The father was a tenant farmer who often found himself in debt at the end of harvest, when the cash crops were brought in.

"Watching him grow up, we always knew Morris would be a success," said a neighbor, Marlin Pinkston, whose uncle operated a country store. "He was a serious-minded young man, always the first to get into something that made money or got him recognition. When he stood up in front of the church, folks in the community wondered about him. They thought that maybe he'd gone off to the university and had fallen under the influence of some liberal professors."

When Bubba was nine, his father took him to Montgomery to governor Big Jim Folsom's first inauguration. Not unlike Chuck Morgan, Dees was impressed by the huge man who spoke out "for the little man." All the way home to Mount Meigs, Morris Sr. told his son about "my great friend, the governor." He talked about how, when Morris Jr. became a lawyer, he too would meet and know important men like Folsom.

From the beginning, Bubba was industrious. At eleven he had a newspaper route, riding his bicycle to deliver the *Montgomery Advertiser* to neighbors. He picked up Coca-Cola bottles along the roadside and sold them for a penny each to Marlin Pinkston's uncle. Rawboned, blond, and blue-eyed, he picked cotton alongside black workers who lived nearby. Soon he grew his own cotton and watermelons. While in high school, he bought a calf for fifteen dollars. A year later, he bred his calf with one of his father's bulls. He went to stockyards and bargained for more cattle. He bought a pig that weighed 80 pounds for five dollars. After he fattened it to 210 pounds with scraps from the high school lunchroom, he sold it for forty-five. When he added chickens, he awakened at five thirty every morning to feed them and gather eggs. By his senior year, he was harvesting 250 chickens a week, icing them down and selling them to country stores.

When he was a teenager his father asked him to help one of their African American neighbors, Clarence Williams, who had been stopped for driving while intoxicated. A state trooper had also charged him with resisting arrest. With his wife and nine children, Williams lived in a two-room shanty and eked out a living picking cotton for $3.50 a day and doing any other job he could find.

After Williams climbed into the cab of his truck, Dees asked him to tell what happened. "Bubba, you know my car ain't nothin' . . . and I was driving along there, and this tire rod came loose, and it ran off and hit that concrete median up there on the road, and it knocked me dizzy, and I was there, dizzy, and the state trooper came along, and he opened the door of my car and he pulled me out and he said, 'Nigger, what you doing drunk?' And I said, 'Boss, I ain't drunk.' And I got out and staggered 'round, and next thing I know that state trooper shoved me in the back of the car and hit me upside my head with a blackjack and took me on up to jail in Tuskegee."

Dees drove to the country store on U.S. 80 where judge Metcalf Letcher, a justice of the peace, operated his courtroom between floor-to-ceiling shelves packed with canned goods, hardware, snuff, and Prince Albert tobacco. With a Coca-Cola sign behind him, Judge Letcher stood next to a cash register and asked Dees what he wanted. When he said he had come to represent Williams, saying it was obvious that the older black man was not guilty, the judge asked the trooper to tell what had happened. The trooper said "the boy" had been drunk.

Dees said, "Judge, you know that's not right," and asked Williams to tell what had happened. When Williams finished, Judge Letcher hit the counter with his gavel and said, "Guilty. One-hundred-and-fifty-dollar fine. Bubba, you tell your daddy he can send three dollars a week up here. That'll be all."

Back home, Dees angrily told his father, "I know Clarence, and Clarence is not guilty. Can't you call the judge up there and do something about it?"

His father shook his head. "Judge Letcher's kind of tough. Besides, story is he keeps two sets of books, one for the state and one for himself, and that he makes a pretty penny on these fines."

"Well, that's not fair," Dees said. "It's not fair."

His father smiled and said, "Well, if you don't like it, why don't you go to law school."

In his senior year of high school, Dees was named Star Farmer of the Year by the Future Farmers of America and was awarded a scholarship to Auburn University. But his father remained steadfast in his wish for his son's future, telling him, "You be a lawyer, Bubba. No boll weevil ever ruined a law book."

Early that school year, Dees met Beverly Crum, a pretty brunette sophomore with a ponytail. He took her to Mount Meigs, showed her his animals, took her on a picnic, and talked excitedly about someday owning a farm. As the daughter of an air force officer, she had lived in many places around the world. Six months after they met, she told Dees that her father would soon be transferred to Germany.

On the spot, they agreed to elope. He borrowed his father's car to attend a Future Farmers of America hog-judging contest in Dothan in southeast Alabama. Instead, he drove Beverly eighty miles west to Meridian, Mississippi, where they were married, had dinner, went to a Western movie, and spent the night in the town's finest hotel.

Afraid of what his father would say or do, they kept the marriage secret for several weeks. Soon, however, his mother, in whom he had confided, told Morris Sr., who exploded, "You have ruined your life." When his son said, "I'm going to farm," his father spat, "Where?" When Dees said, "Right here," his father replied, "You ain't farming this farm." Ultimately, Morris Sr. told his son he would help him financially if he would go to college and law school. Bubba already had five thousand dollars in the bank. He also owned fifty head of cattle and two hundred hogs ready to be sold.

Dees started classes at the University of Alabama in the summer of 1955. That fall, Beverly attended Tuscaloosa High, where she finished a year later. In 1956, after the federal court ordered the university to admit Autherine Lucy as a student, Dees watched as "all hell broke loose." When he watched from a distance, it "was the first time I had ever seen Klansmen in action, the first time I had ever seen a mob. As it surged, retreated, and surged again like some monster, I felt frightened and disgusted. Many of these people were good, rational folks when they didn't have to think about integration, but once they became part of the crowd, they were swept up in the frenzy and turned into mean, dangerous aggressors."

On the Sunday following the Autherine Lucy riots, Dees stood before the congregation at the Baptist Student Union, where he was superintendent of the Sunday school for married couples. He read from First John: "If a man says, I love God, but hateth his brother, he is a liar: for he who loveth not his brother whom he hath seen, how can he love God whom he hath not seen." Putting aside the Bible, he looked out over the class. "Something really disturbs me," he said. "How can we profess to be Christians and really hate our brothers?

"Autherine Lucy tried to get on this campus. We don't know her, and we might not have been out there opposing her, but I think all of us didn't want her to be there. So how can we be good Christians? Do you remember when Jesus gave the Pharisee woman the 'water of life'? What are we to think of the courthouse here in Tuscaloosa, where there's one drinking fountain for white folks and one for colored? Were Jesus here, would he not say to a black woman, as he said to the Pharisee woman, 'Here, drink from the same water'?"

As he said the words, he remembered a time at Mount Meigs in the middle of a broiling hot cotton field when his father shared a water-drinking dipper with a tired, sweating black worker. It had astounded him then, just as his own words stunned his audience now. During the next week, the Baptist minister told him that some changes would be made. He said he needed someone with more experience as superintendent for married students.

When his mother sent him a fruitcake for his birthday, she sparked a fire in the young man's imagination. That night, he and Beverly talked. As such a fire would rage within him from time to time in his life, when ideas for various enterprises would come to him, he talked excitedly, his brain working full force as the thoughts poured out. He would write to mothers of students. For three dollars, they could send their children personalized, homemade birthday cakes. Who would not go for such a deal?

Bama Birthday Cake Service was born. He talked with a friend in the admissions office. He copied lists of students and parents and their addresses. He wrote letters to parents. More than 20 percent responded favorably, sending their checks in the return mail. As he learned more and more about the art of marketing, he discovered that such a response was phenomenal.

Joining him in the rapidly growing business was fellow law student Millard Fuller, whose background was similar. Fuller had grown up in rural east Alabama, where his father was a farmer and ran a country store. The two had met at a Young Democrats get-together.

By the time Dees and Fuller finished law school, Bama Birthday Cake Service was selling more than 350 cakes a month. Their business was so successful that they owned several pieces of property near the campus. Deciding to go into law practice together in Montgomery, they sold their holdings. With the profit, Dees bought a new Ford and a three-bedroom home in Mount Meigs.

*

After the Freedom Riders were attacked in downtown Montgomery in 1963, Klansman Claude Henley, a thirty-five-year-old used-car salesman accused of attacking a television reporter during the riot, walked into Dees's office. He was a defendant in a civil suit brought by the federal government and a criminal charge brought by the city. A photo published in *Life* showed Henley kicking a newsman. Henley told Dees that the well-known local attorney John Blue Hill had asked fifteen thousand dollars to represent him. Dees said he would defend him for five thousand. That was a great sum of money to the young man freshly out of law school. At the time, he didn't think about it as tainted money; it was simply a good-sized fee that would help the new partnership get started. Henley agreed.

While Dees knew the photo would not help in the assault case, it showed that Henley was not among the gang of attackers at the bus station. He was at least a block away, kicking a newsman.

As he sat in federal court several weeks later, Dees listened to Ku Klux Klansmen, including Bobby Shelton, making racist jokes. When judge Frank Johnson entered, he heard Dees's plea and immediately dropped Henley from the federal suit while enjoining him from future outbursts of violence.

Leaving, Dees was approached by two young Freedom Riders. The two black men gazed directly into the eyes of the blond-haired young lawyer. Their vision was extraordinarily intense. "How can you represent people like that?" one asked. "Don't you think black people have rights?"

"Yes, I do," Dees said. He added, "I agree with you 100 percent."

As he walked away, Dees continued thinking. His thoughts loomed larger and larger. He too felt the anger that the man had been feeling when he heard the racist language and when he experienced the violent hatred.

*

Not long after Dees and Fuller started their firm in Montgomery, a young high school girl entered their office. She was selling a book of favorite recipes to raise money for her local Future Homemakers of America club. As he viewed the exuberance expressed by the young salesperson, the idea struck Dees that he and Fuller could take the direct-mail skills they had learned in the cake business and sell similar products to the world at large.

Dees composed a letter and sent it to home economics teachers across the nation. Within three months, the partners had collected hundreds of recipes. Soon, they published *Favorite Recipes of Home Economics Teachers*. They sent a paperback book to every teacher with simple instructions about how their Future Homemakers of America club could sell the book for three dollars each and earn a dollar profit from each sale. Fuller & Dees Publishing would profit a dollar from each. At the end of another three months, students around America had sold a quarter million copies. It was the beginning of very profitable business that he would use in the future as a civil rights attorney.

In the meantime, Dees and Fuller began talking aloud to each other about their inner selves. Both were beginning to feel the tides of their consciences pulling them in the direction of doing more for their black brethren. Fuller had been raised a Congregationalist and had begun to wonder, *What am I going to do with my life?*

"Morris was a hungry guy," Fuller said. "He was hungrier than I was. Oh, I had a drive too, but not as insatiable as his. During this time, we talked a lot. We had similar feelings about our fellow man. We both wanted to help."

During the Selma-to-Montgomery March, they watched and talked. They didn't march, but they were sympathetic to the cause. They let their sympathies be known and were given the chance to do something. As a result, when marchers came to town after Judge Johnson ruled that the march could take place on a federal highway, both Dees and Fuller drove carloads of young people from Montgomery to Selma. Later, they watched from a grassy hillside near the capitol as thousands gathered to hear King's speech. Dees's uncle approached them as they watched. He stared into his nephew's face and said, "Nigger lover!", and then he turned and walked away.

⋆

Morris discovered the Unitarian Fellowship and found the people there more tolerant than the Baptists. "In the beginning, I'm not sure we would have ever succeeded with the Unitarian Fellowship, if it hadn't been for Morris," said Earl Pippin, one of the founders. "Morris brought a quality and gave freely to make it happen. Most of us believed as Morris believed: that Negro people deserved the rights of all people."

When the local chapter of the American Civil Liberties Union took up the cause of a campus newspaper editor at Troy State University, ACLU board members who knew Dees from the Fellowship asked if he would take the case. Gary Dickey was a Vietnam veteran who had written an editorial critical of Governor Wallace. After the editorial was published, Troy State president Ralph Adams, an old-time friend of the governor, suspended Dickey. Dees filed suit in federal court, where Judge Johnson ruled, "A state cannot force a college student to forfeit his constitutionally protected right of freedom of expression as a condition to his attending a state-supported institution."

During this time, Dees and his first wife were divorced. Beverly moved to Louisville to pursue graduate studies while their sons stayed on the ranch with their father. Not long after, he married a young woman who had worked for years as an editor at Fuller & Dees, Maureene Buck, an attractive brunette who had been a Maid of Cotton in Georgia.

By 1967, Fuller & Dees Publishing was selling more than three million cookbooks a year. As their success grew, Fuller continued to reevaluate his life. Wishing "to serve God," he sold his interest in the company to Dees. Soon after, Fuller started the organization that became Habitat for Humanity, moving eventually to Americus, Georgia, where he made friends with future president Jimmy Carter. "I took what Morris and I learned together and applied it to Habitat," Fuller said. "One thing about Morris: he will always be number one. That's his nature. He listens, he hears, and he acts. If he does something, it's never halfway."

That year, Dees was named by the National Jaycees as one of ten Outstanding Young Men in America, along with Ralph Nader and Joseph Califano.

Early in 1968, stranded in an airport overnight, he browsed a newsstand and found a paperback book, *The Story of My Life*, by famed attorney Clarence Darrow. Dees read through the night. By dawn, he felt the strength of a religious conversion fill his body and his soul. As a boy, Darrow wrote, "not only could I put myself in the other person's place, but I could not avoid doing so. My sympathies always went out to the weak, the suffering and the poor."

Reading the words, Dees felt an instant kinship. He knew those feelings and felt that his own struggle had been articulated. Darrow's words, ideas, and ideals mirrored Dees's own.

"My instinct was to doubt the majority view," Darrow wrote. Dees thought of his own view, standing before the congregation of his church, speaking out on behalf of the victims of the bombing, speaking out in favor of Autherine Lucy, standing up against the actions of the Ku Klux Klan. It was the same feeling he had had as a teenager trying to help the family's neighbor, Clarence Williams, with the stubborn justice of the peace. As his plane took off the next morning, Dees reread the words, "I have lived my life and I have fought my battles, not against the weak and poor—but against power, injustice, against oppression."

By the end of the trip, Morris Dees was a new person. "I would sell the company as soon as possible," he decided. From that moment forward, he would "specialize in civil rights law. All the things in my life had brought me to this point, all the pulls and tugs of my conscience, found a singular peace. It did not matter what my neighbors would think, or the judges, the bankers, or even my relatives."

Back home in Montgomery, African American attorney Fred Gray called and asked if Dees would assist him in representing the Alabama State Teachers Association, an all-black group, in an attempt to keep Auburn from locating a campus in the capital city. It was ASTA's position that such a school would promote a separate-but-unequal dual education system. An Auburn campus in Montgomery, where all-black Alabama State University was located, would become an all-white institution. When Gray called, Dees agreed to join him. "I didn't have to think about it that much," Dees said. "The words of Clarence Darrow's autobiography were fresh in my head. Besides, I liked Fred Gray very much. He was one of the true heroes to come out of the bus boycott of the middle 1950s. He is deceptively brilliant. He is so soft-spoken, you might not think of him as an intellect, but he is one of the smartest and most effective lawyers I have ever known. And he is a good man with great moral strength."

In 1969, when the Reverend William Sloane Coffin, an outspoken opponent of the Vietnam War, was refused permission to speak to a student group at Auburn University, Dees filed suit on behalf of students in federal court. Once again, judge Frank Johnson ruled that Coffin's First Amendment right could not be breached.

The morning after Coffin's speech, Dees found huge letters, KKK, marked on the walls of his office, which had been wrecked by vandals. Furious, he called his former client whom he had gotten out of trouble after the Freedom Riders riot. He told Claude Henley what he had found and asked if he would come to his office.

Sitting in his office with his former client who had been charged with kicking a television cameraman, Dees telephoned Bobby Shelton, imperial wizard of the United Klans of America. On the speakerphone, Dees described what had happened and told him that his friend was sitting across the desk. As Shelton began to speak, Dees brought an automatic shotgun from beneath his desk and aimed it at Henley.

"Tell Bobby what I'm doing," Dees said.

Nervously, Henley told him.

As Dees pushed a shell into the chamber, he said, "Tell him now."

As the man spoke, Dees said, "I'm going to blow this son of a bitch's head right off of his goddamn neck. You don't fuck with me now."

Shelton told Henley, "If you can talk to somebody down there and find out what's going on, you tell him to let Morris alone. Just leave him alone."

In the next few months, Dees sold his company to the Times Mirror Corporation. With the money invested, he began the next step in his conversion: filing suit on behalf of two young black clients who had been refused admission to the Montgomery YMCA. The case, *Smith*

v. Montgomery YMCA, shook the city more than any other since the bus boycott litigation more than thirteen years earlier.

Members of the white establishment met in private caucus at the Montgomery Country Club. Ku Klux Klansmen gathered in backrooms of cafés and juke joints and at their clubhouse in north Montgomery. *What are we going to do?* they asked one another.

They were stymied. They were afraid of the local white lawyer who knew them and knew their world. They were afraid because they knew Dees was not afraid. He had money. He was not a black lawyer, like Fred Gray, who had filed *Browder v. Gayle*. Back then, the town fathers explained that it was the Negro lawyer operating for his Negro clients. Now they were also afraid because they knew segregated life in Alabama's capital city would never be the same again. If they couldn't keep the YMCA segregated, what institution would be the next to integrate?

In the end, Judge Johnson enjoined the YMCA from denying blacks membership in any branches or excluding them from any programs, stopping them from building new branches if the site perpetuated segregation policies of the past, halting their recruiting only in all-white schools without recruiting equally in predominantly black schools, and excluding blacks from its board of directors or other governing bodies.

On appeal, Johnson's order was upheld.

Morris Dees had made the first difficult decisions to confront the segregated society in which he grew up. He stepped out of the crowd and shook his fist in the face of the racist enemy, and now he wanted to go beyond mere symbolic gestures. He wanted to do something stronger and develop something long-lasting. Soon, he was joined by Joe Levin Jr., a young Jewish lawyer who had returned to Montgomery after a year in New York and had worked a year with his father, a well-known and respected collections attorney with a thriving practice. But after a year, Levin knew he was not cut out for this brand of law. He yearned for the courtroom. In him, Dees recognized "a natural-born trial lawyer with great promise and great talent."

Like Dees, Levin had been raised in a Southern family and taught respect and reverence for the "Southern way of life." A student at the

University of Alabama when Governor Wallace was standing in the schoolhouse door, he witnessed a fraternity brother being persecuted for expressing an unpopular view. When Melvin Meyer, editor of the *Crimson White* campus newspaper, wrote an editorial in favor of integration, fellow students taunted him. Early one morning, Levin and other members of the Jewish fraternity awakened to find a twelve-foot burning cross in their front yard. "Over time, that one incident forced me to reevaluate the traditional Southern attitude I'd grown up with," he said. "Prior to that time, I saw myself as a white Southerner. I had not experienced that kind of naked hatred. Once my eyes were opened, I couldn't ignore others who were persecuted around me."

Among the early pro bono cases the two young lawyers handled was *Parducci v. Rutland*. They represented an English teacher who had been fired from Jefferson Davis High School for teaching "Welcome to the Monkey House," a short story by Kurt Vonnegut. Again, the court ruled in favor of the teacher's First Amendment right to academic freedom.

Soon the law firm of Levin & Dees became the Southern Poverty Law Center. Again, the rapid wheels of Dees's brain turned toward creating a nonprofit organization without equal in the South or the nation. He knew what he wanted. He found a great friend and fellow courtroom fighter in Levin. Together, they would fight for the downtrodden underdog throughout the South and across the nation.

As far as Morris Dees was concerned, he and Levin were fulfilling the promise begun long ago by Clarence Darrow.

11

THE ALABAMA STORY

After his firebrand inaugural address in 1963, George Wallace was the poster child for every big-shot segregationist from Leander Perez to J. B. Stoner, all of whom praised Wallace for his verbal candor and his courage to stand up against the big federal government. When the Ku Klux Klan held rallies and burned crosses, they displayed Wallace's photo and waved Wallace banners in the air.

After Wallace's "Segregation Forever!" speech in January and Dr. King's "I Have a Dream" speech in August, word spread that President John F. Kennedy and a majority of congressmen in Washington were writing a civil rights act that would expand integration. It would totally outlaw segregation in schools, public places, and employment. It would enforce the constitutional right to vote and would expand the jurisdiction of federal district courts, giving them the power to provide relief against discrimination in all public accommodations.

As he heard more and more details, Wallace became infuriated. He knew that this law would give his nemesis, judge Frank Johnson, more power. To Wallace, this was not only a shame, it was a terrible sin. All of the talk proved to him and his people that the Commission to Preserve the Peace and the Sovereignty Commission were necessary for the state to uphold its laws against integration. He asked his floor leaders in both houses of the Alabama Legislature if these agencies should be given more power. A few lawmakers answered affirmatively. State senator Alton Turner of Crenshaw County told the governor that he would support whatever increase in power he thought necessary.

In the governor's office on Goat Hill in Montgomery, Wallace paced the floor, his fist balled, his slicked-down hair shining in the light of the antebellum chandelier, and his leather-soled shoes snapping out a rhythm on the marble floor. "I will carry the Alabama story to the people of the North and to the people of our entire nation," he declared to the men sitting at the conference table, his friend and attorney John Kohn, *Advertiser* reporter Bob Ingram, friend and supporter Oscar Harper, and press secretary Bill Jones.

In the days to come, Asa Earl Carter, who had been working quietly in the rear office of Harper's publishing company, would bring forth diatribes that pleased Wallace immensely. His compositions would ring out over the land. Furthermore, in advance of Wallace's tour, Carter accompanied his friend Bobby Shelton, grand dragon and imperial wizard of the United Klans of America, to the Midwest, where they fanned the flames in klaverns in southern Illinois, Indiana, and Ohio, and readied the right-wing audiences for the Wallace bandwagon. Shelton said that Carter "got the crowds all churned up. He was really good at doing that."

Beginning first up East, where the governor would speak on Ivy League college campuses, the Wallace entourage included his press secretary, his attorney, and a couple of good old boys, including Harper and Dave Silverman, a Montgomery businessman whom Wallace referred to as "my Jew."

The first stop was the oldest and most revered institution of all the Ivy League schools, Harvard, where he spoke in Sanders Auditorium. As he entered, strutting like a bantam rooster with his head thrust high and his chin jutted forward, students hissed. He smiled. "When we speak of the Negro in the South," he said in a patronizing tone, "the image in our minds is that great residue of easygoing, basically happy, unambitious African who constitutes 40 percent of our population, and who the white man of the South, in addition to educating his own children, has attempted to educate, to furnish public health and civil protection.

"Let me pass now to the cold, stark, realistic, political reason why the racial issue has been so violently precipitated on the American scene at this time." As he spoke, he gained a rhythm. He rocked back and forth on his heels. His words were patronizing, his stance confrontational.

"Let us look at the 1954 school case, *Brown vs. Topeka*, the lawyers call it. It did not, I assure you, as some seem to think, spring instantly into existence full-grown and ready for action equipped with injunctive process, preferred appeal, set bayonets, and all its accouterments like Botticelli would have us believe Venus came to the shores of Greece full-grown and full-blown on the breath of Boreas." As he read the words written by Asa Carter, Wallace jutted his chin as high as he could thrust it.

Brown, he said, was not the first "ultraliberal, socialist, collectivist, maverick decision of the Supreme Court to jump over the fence of the doctrine of *stare decisis* into the field theretofore protected by the Constitution and begin honing down the pillars of our governmental home which we thought was a structure of laws—and not of men, of defined and restrictive powers—and not of centralized and autocratic competence."

Wallace went on and on, finally stating that "this court of causes was purely political as it wantonly destroyed another principle of law."

Wallace basically repeated the same speech at Dartmouth, Brown, and Smith. Later, he spoke to crowds across the Midwest, where he encountered homemade signs of encouragement carried by hooded and gowned Ku Klux Klansmen. When the word of the assassination of President John F. Kennedy in Dallas stunned people throughout the world on November 22, Wallace went home to Alabama. He would sit tight until the emotional uproar over Kennedy's death settled.

During the spring of 1964, Wallace traveled to the West. In Denver, Los Angeles, Seattle, and Portland, Oregon, Wallace continued to tell what he called "the true story of segregation and civil rights." When Wallace swept through the South making similar speeches, his aides called it Operation Dixie. When he arrived in New Orleans, he was met at the airport by white supremacists waving the Confederate Stars and Bars led by judge Leander Perez from Plaquemines Parish and Willie Rainach, who had been engineering Louisiana's massive resistance against what he called "federal intervention."

Back in Montgomery, state senator Alton Turner, a staunch Wallace floor leader, was joined by Black Belt senators Walter C. Givhan of Dallas County and Roland Cooper of Wilcox County to give the Commission to Preserve the Peace broader powers to not only subpoena witnesses but to have them immediately confined to jail for contempt if they did not comply. Opposing the bill were progressive senators led by Bob Gilchrist of Morgan County and Finus St. John of Cullman County. The latter group managed to fight off a vote through an entire legislative session.

★

In Georgia on July 4, Wallace was the special guest of Lester Maddox, who had wielded an ax handle to drive black and white demonstrators from the parking lot of his Atlanta restaurant. With them in Atlanta's Lakewood Park was former Mississippi governor Ross Barnett, another true believer in the "Southern way of life."

Once again, Asa Carter had written Wallace's speech for the Patriots Rally Against Tyranny. With many of Carter's KKK friends and associates in the audience of more than eleven thousand, Wallace was ready to talk.

On July 3, when president Lyndon Johnson signed the Civil Rights Act, Wallace had ranted to his friends gathered in his office in the Alabama capitol. Oscar Harper and Asa Carter had brought a freshly typed copy of his speech. As he first read it, he knew it would resonate with the Georgia crowd.

As he was being introduced, three black men rose in protest. As they booed, two white factory workers "picked up their folding chairs and began beating the men about the head and shoulders," according to historian Dan Carter. "Within seconds, they were joined by a half dozen other white spectators who continued to kick and pommel the protestors even after they fell to the ground. The surrounding crowd shouted 'Kill 'em!' 'Hit 'em!' and 'We want Wallace!'"

Wallace began, outlining the actions of the patriots of July 4, 1776, who "pledged their lives, their fortunes, and their sacred honor to establish and defend the proposition that governments are created by the people, empowered by the people . . . and must forever remain subservient to the will of the people."

The people were silent, listening, as he said it was "a cruel irony" that only the day before President Johnson signed "the most monstrous piece of legislation ever enacted by the United States Congress.

"It is a fraud, a sham, and a hoax."

The people jumped to their feet. They screamed rebel yells. They shouted, "Tell 'em, George!"

"This bill will live in infamy," he said. "To sign it into law at any time is tragic. To do so upon the eve of the celebration of our independence insults the intelligence of the American people."

Again, they applauded loudly.

"This bill is fraudulent in intent, in design, and in execution. It is misnamed. Each and every provision is mistitled. It was rammed through the Congress on the wave of ballyhoo, promotions, and publicity stunts reminiscent of P. T. Barnum."

To Wallace, the Civil Rights Act would "enslave the nation."

Wallace told his audience that U.S. senator Hubert Humphrey had suggested that President Johnson "call the fifty state governors together to work out ways and means to enforce this rotten measure.

"There is no need for him to call on me. I am not about to be a party to anything having to do with the law that is going to destroy individual freedom and liberty in this country."

He said emphatically that he would not enforce "a law that will destroy our free enterprise system . . . neighborhood schools . . . the rights of private property . . . your right—and my right—to choose my neighbors or to sell my house to whomever I choose."

After each statement, the audience clapped and shouted. Some jumped to their feet and stomped.

According to Wallace, the people of the South would never learn the truth from its newspapers that "are run and operated by left-wing liberals, communist sympathizers, and members of the Americans for Democratic Action." He pointed toward reporters standing nearby, taking notes. "Newspapers will never tell the people the truth," he said, "because the truth is simple: The Civil Rights Act of 1964 is communist inspired."

He continued to talk long into the blazing hot July afternoon. At the end of each sentence, the people shouted, "George! George! George!"

As he strutted back and forth across the stage, he delivered one of his most powerful racist speeches. The governor never uttered the word "nigger" but used code phrases like "the boot of tyranny," "the power to dictate," and "the framework of our priceless freedoms." *Whose priceless freedoms?* Indeed, the "priceless freedoms" of white members of a collapsing social order.

At the end of the speech, KKK grand dragon Calvin Craig, who sat on the stage with the other segregationist leaders, remarked that it was "the finest speech I've ever heard presented."

By the end of the decade, Steven Brill, writing in *New York* magazine, called Wallace's nemesis, judge Frank Johnson, "the real governor of Alabama."

On May 12, 1967, *Time* featured the judge on its cover. Recalling Alabama's course through the decade, it flashed through the scenes of Wallace, his fist upraised, declaring "Segregation forever!" and his stand in the schoolhouse door and blacks standing in line to vote for the first time. "Millions of Americans know these names and remember these scenes," the magazine stated. "Yet few know the name of the man central to them all, Frank Minis Johnson, the U.S. district judge for Alabama's twenty-three southeastern counties. At forty-eight, Johnson has established an impressive record of calm and considered judgment that has stamped him as one of the most important men in America. In eleven and a half years of interpreting and enforcing the U.S. Constitution, he has wrought social and political changes that affect all of Alabama, all of the South, and all of the nation."

When he read the words, it was reported, Wallace threatened, "I'll show the son of a bitch who is important!"

In the early 1960s, an investigator for the Ku Klux Klan, Ralph R. Roton, who had dropped out of school in the tenth grade, signed with the Peace Commission as an undercover operative. A good friend of Robert Shelton, Roton had worked with Number 1,638 of Confederate Lodge 11 of the United Klans of America, directly under Shelton's guidance.

With the Peace Commission, Roton worked directly with Al Lingo in the Department of Public Safety. With a press card from the *Birmingham Independent*, known as a right-wing weekly, Roton photographed and recorded what he said were "communists in the March on Washington."

In the meantime, Wallace's Star Chamber–styled Peace Commission and Sovereignty Commission held hearings and issued statements. From Sovereignty Commission director Ed Strickland, Alabama's chiefs of police were warned that "lawless bands of Negro toughs roam the jungles of New York and other major cities, openly beating, robbing, raping, and killing whites in a wave of terror reminiscent of the Mau Mau." If drastic measures were not taken soon, he warned, these gangs would soon come south to continue their terror. In September, Peace Commission director John Hawkins warned that "a special brand of revolution will bring havoc. Black Power revolutionaries will burn and pillage rural areas where homes are widely separated and law enforcement is spread thin. We do not consider it merely a threat. We must consider this a certainty, based upon the evidence we now have."

Strickland and Hawkins issued directives to law enforcement agencies across Alabama to be on the lookout for such "bands of renegade outsiders as the black-based Student Nonviolent Coordinating Committee (SNCC) members out of Atlanta, led by known communists, who will soon be infiltrating our state and attempting to influence our young people as the outside agitators did in Birmingham in the recent past."

12

REQUIEM FOR JIMMIE LEE JACKSON

After the Freedom Riders moved on and the demonstrations in Birmingham climaxed and diminished, Alabama's Black Belt became the scene for upheaval and change. Through the late 1950s and early '60s, while J. L. Chestnut and Orzell Billingsley and Peter Hall tried cases in the courthouses, few local blacks had the gumption or the imagination of Sam Boynton, who stood up for William Earl Fikes when he was charged with multiple rapes. It was Boynton who called Hall and persuaded him to come to Selma and represent Fikes.

Boynton would not bow to the economic intimidation that most African Americans experienced with the white landlords and storeowners. Boynton and his wife, Amelia, both graduates of Tuskegee Institute, wanted to reach out and help their black brothers and sisters. Through these years, Boynton encouraged young blacks throughout the west-central counties of Alabama's Black Belt, admonishing them to study hard, complete their education, register to vote, and become solid citizens. "That is the way we make ourselves known and make ourselves felt by everybody. It is the way we make our communities worthwhile," he told young people in Perry, Marengo, Dallas, and Wilcox counties.

Lawton Hughes, who grew up on a farm west of Selma, remembered Boynton visiting his father and sitting on the front porch and talking about what might happen if children like Lawton and his two sisters got a good education. "I believe it was Mr. Boynton who influenced my father to send me and the girls to school," he remembered. Now a retired high school teacher, he said that every time Boynton visited he always told Lawton's father to register and vote.

As her husband began suffering from high blood pressure that slowed his activities in the early 1960s, Amelia Boynton picked up the pace for herself. She and her female friends held impromptu classes in how to register to vote, the necessity of the NAACP, and how to organize in their local communities. Although he suffered a number of small strokes, Sam Boynton continued as president of the Dallas County Voters League he had started in the late 1940s, when he was joined by his friends, Ernest Doyle and J. D. Hunter, veterans of World War II who had come home and started the local chapter of the NAACP.

In the years after the *Brown* decision and the bus boycott decision, Selma whites reacted with moderate concern. The white power structure, including probate judge Bernard Reynolds, mayor Chris Heinz, circuit judge James Hare, and state senator Walter Givhan, formed the White Citizens Council, met regularly in the high school football stadium, and offered encouragement to the legislature and its move to separate itself from federal law. "I was always steadfast in my stance," said Givhan, who was a floor leader for Wallace. "I never wavered. I was for the white men and women of Alabama. I didn't think the nigger would ever get the vote. I was opposed to that every inch of the way. As long as we could keep the nigger from voting in the Black Belt, the white folks had the power that they had held since slavery days. If we let them vote, we would lose power. It was as simple as that."

In spite of the racial divide, Boynton called regular meetings of the Voters League. Although it consisted of only a handful of black people, Boynton considered it a beginning. He counted among his closest friends J. L. Chestnut Jr., who had come back home in the late fifties to practice as Selma's only black attorney. Also part of the inside circle was Frederick Reese, a contemporary of Chestnut who had graduated from Alabama State College in Montgomery, returned to Selma, and taught science at Hudson High School. He was soon elected president of the black teachers' association and urged teachers to register to vote.

One of Amelia Boynton's closest friends was Marie Foster, a widow who worked as a dental hygienist in her brother's office, which occupied the first floor under Boynton's upstairs office on Franklin Street. At the Voters League meetings, Foster taught an occasional class in citizenship. For nearly a decade she walked downtown to the courthouse, waited her turn, took the registration test, and was rejected. "She knew more about the history of our country, the state of Alabama, Dallas County, and Selma than just about anyone I ever met," remembered Kathryn Tucker Windham, a local writer and historian.

During the time of frustration, Marie Foster never gave up. Each time she was rejected, she told Amelia Boynton and others that she would succeed the next time. She knew she had not failed the test. But the white registrar took her test, disappeared into another room, and came out minutes later with red marks covering the test sheet. The registrar waved the sheet in front of Foster's face, not allowing her to read it. "You've failed again," she was told. Foster would walk away from the courthouse telling herself that there would come a time when the racist white registrars would give up. After several years of trying, she was finally given a passing grade and was allowed to register. Years later, she said, "I practically had to recite the U.S. and the Alabama constitutions, but they gave in to my persistence." After her acceptance, she was reinvigorated in her pursuit to educate the black populace of Dallas County. Often she said the biggest problem was the reluctance of the people to attempt to register over and over again as she had. And after those who attempted failed, many did not return to try again. Then Foster would push harder than ever, telling them her personal story and showing them the results.

More than once she worked with adult students, teaching them not only the facts of history and government but the simple tasks of writing their names and addresses.

For his own experience, J. L. Chestnut Jr. remembered entering the registrar's office after returning home in 1958. He fully expected to be turned down. As a new black lawyer, he saw himself as the "perfect test case—a law-school graduate who knew a lot more about the Constitution than the people giving the test. Here was something to put my name on the map in a hurry, help me build a clientele."

"When I went in," Chestnut wrote in *Black in Selma*, "this old fella—who I later saw on every other jury (they called near the same group of white men as jurors every time)—gave me a questionnaire and a look of curious disdain. I was delighted with his attitude. I thought, This ignorant old coot will make the best possible witness. Hell, he may become the unwitting father of black voting in Dallas County. On the space for employment on the application blank, I wrote *Soon*. I didn't have an office yet. I completed the written questionnaire pertaining to government. Then the old fella asked me some questions about the Constitution. The one I remember is: 'How are the constitution of the United States and Alabama the same?'

"I said, 'They both remain unenforced and floating in the same sea of hypocrisy.' I think he liked the roll of the words. He looked at me and smiled. 'Professor, you qualify.' I was so taken aback and dejected I didn't know what to do."

By the early 1960s, according to Chestnut and others, no such attitude existed in the registrar's office of Dallas County. The tests were much more difficult. There were a number of different tests. When an applicant came in more than once, he or she could expect a different set of questions each time. In Dallas County in 1962 fewer than 5 percent of voting-age blacks were registered to vote. Statewide, only 13.2 percent were registered.

Chestnut wrote that if anyone had told him the group of people who met in Boynton's office "was in a sense the genesis of a movement that would win the right to vote for blacks all over America, I would have said not just 'You're dreaming' but 'You're crazy.' I did not foresee that at all, though I attended virtually every meeting."

Like Marie Foster, Chestnut was confounded, frustrated, and disillusioned. When he first came home, he had been hopeful. Now, "I'd tried this and tried that and my efforts weren't amounting to much. Even Martin Luther King was a disappointment. I'd been so excited about him busting loose in Montgomery, but he moved back home to Atlanta. I thought, Goddamn!"

After Freedom Summer in Mississippi, a SNCC worker returning to Atlanta stopped in Selma. He spent an afternoon talking with young African Americans he knew there. They told him basically that Selma,

Dallas County, and the Black Belt were impossible. While the KKK wasn't burning houses and churches, the white bosses worked steadily and surely, keeping the blacks down. The power structure kept its invisible thumb heavy on the black population. Back in Atlanta at SNCC headquarters, the field worker stepped up to the map of the South and marked a black X over Selma. The young men and women of SNCC were told the black X meant it was dangerous and community organizing impossible. This is the place, the young people were told, where sheriff James G. "Jim" Clark Jr. had put out the word in 1963 that he wanted to deputize some white men to accompany him to Birmingham to put out the fire started by King and Shuttlesworth. The next morning three hundred men showed up on the steps of the Dallas County courthouse. The sheriff, decked out in his two-tone brown and tan uniform, snakeskin cowboy boots, wide-brimmed black hat, and wraparound shades, deputized the men en masse. He then led them eighty miles northeast to Birmingham, where they were led into downtown streets by police commissioner Bull Connor. They stood guard behind Connor while his firemen aimed their water hoses at the orderly demonstrators marching single file down the sidewalk from the Sixteenth Street Baptist Church toward city hall.

When he heard the warnings, Bernard LaFayette, a divinity student on leave from American Baptist Theological Seminary in Nashville, was intrigued. He had ridden the bus from Washington, D.C., to Jackson, Mississippi, encountering Anniston, Birmingham, and Montgomery along the way. He had been one of many who integrated the food counters in several Southern states. He went door-to-door teaching citizenship classes across the Delta during Freedom Summer. Surely, he thought, Selma could not be worse than those places.

Although fellow SNCC workers warned against it, LaFayette took off for Selma. He would make an exploratory trip, question local black leaders, and listen to their responses. Then he would make up his mind whether to return and work full-time for voter registration. He found a handful of interesting and interested black people there. Other than the Boyntons, he sat down with J. L. Chestnut Jr., Marie Foster, Ernest Doyle, and F. D. Reese. They saw a fresh-faced, idealistic young man who had already been arrested and beaten, preached to and sworn at, but he got back up and dusted himself off and headed back into the fray. That was what he was doing in Selma, he told them. He was looking for another place to spread the glory of freedom. The older blacks were impressed.

Back in Atlanta, twenty-two-year-old LaFayette talked excitedly about the challenge he found in the Alabama Black Belt. More determined than ever, he talked with passion to his wife, Colia, who quickly fell into the rhythm of his enthusiasm. Also listening was John Robert Lewis, another SNCC field worker who had been side by side with LaFayette at the American Baptist Theological Seminary and at the Woolworth lunch counters in Greensboro and Nashville. Born and raised in rural Pike County in southeast Alabama, Lewis knew early in life that he wanted to get as far away from cotton picking as he could. And he knew that rural and small town Alabama would be hard to conquer for civil rights. After all, when the Freedom Riders' bus pulled into the station in Montgomery, young Lewis had been beaten across the head with a Kluxer's club. Bleeding profusely, he had been taken to St. Margaret's Hospital to be sewn up before moving on across Alabama, through Selma and the Black Belt, and finally arriving at their destination in Jackson, Mississippi. As for now, Lewis decided he would not return to Selma. He would go later, if needed, he promised his friends.

But Bernard and Colia LaFayette took off southwest in their 1948 Chevrolet, heading into the place some of his peers likened unto hell.

When he arrived, he told Chestnut, "I'm here to help." After the young lawyer showed him around town, LaFayette spoke to a meeting of the Elks but was met with general apathy. At Selma University, several students took to him and his ideas quickly and began helping him recruit other students to assist him in his quest to educate black people to register to vote. Chestnut was impressed with LaFayette's even-tempered intellectual arguments, particularly with older blacks to whom Chestnut might likely reply, "That's the biggest Uncle Tom crap I ever heard."

After LaFayette left a barbershop, Chestnut heard a man say, "It's not gonna come to a damn thing. Somebody'll get their brains blown out. Somebody'll lose their job, and they're not gonna get anybody to register anyway. Remember those people who signed the petition to integrate the schools? Got run out of town and nothin' came of it."

At the same time, black minister Claude Brown was working to help blacks by organizing the Ralph Bunche Club to build a black YMCA. He led a fund drive to help Selma University to educate poor black students. He bought books for the school's library. But he was not impressed with LaFayette and his ideas, and Brown said as much.

While LaFayette organized meetings of twenty to forty blacks, gathering them together and preaching the necessity of voter registration, hoping they would not only line up at the courthouse but go back into the community and repeat his words, Brown told his friend Chestnut that Bernard and his followers were advocating the theory of "burning down the barn to kill the rats." Brown said, "Not one black college would exist had it not been for white people, and they didn't do that because they hated us. They did it because they were Christian and felt for all people. To jump up now and denounce white people as racists is to ignore a hundred years of help and support."

The Reform Presbyterian minister's argument was the same Chestnut had heard from well-meaning middle-class black people all of his life. His mother, a teacher, told him over and over again that the white superintendent of schools was her friend and she counted on him for her secure position in education.

The tall, slender LaFayette took to the elderly and sickly Sam Boynton, gravitating to his bed, leaning over the ailing leader and listening to his words. Before he passed away in May, Boynton told Chestnut that Bernard's visits gave him a feeling that he was passing the torch to a younger generation. Upon Boynton's death, the Reverend Lewis Lloyd Anderson made his Tabernacle Baptist Church available for the funeral. In essence, it would become Selma's first mass meeting. Anderson was a powerful speaker who often worked hellfire and damnation against the white power structure into his spiritual sermons.

When the young minister first came to Selma's Tabernacle Baptist, the middle-aged, middle-class congregation did not know what they had found in a preacher. Anderson was not only a powerful speaker; he had a mind of his own. When he spoke out in 1956 in favor of his friend Martin Luther King Jr. and the bus boycott, a group of deacons in the church opposed him. They even got a court injunction barring him from the sanctuary. However, a splinter group led by Dr. William Dinkins, who was to become Anderson's father-in-law, prevailed to keep him as their minister.

Soon after, Anderson was driving a car that hit and killed a black pedestrian. Charged with manslaughter, he was convicted and sentenced to ten years. His was the same case described earlier, when Peter Hall, Orzell Billingsley, and Fred Gray defended him and appealed his case to the U.S. Supreme Court, where the conviction was overturned.

Now, against the wishes of Dinkins and church leaders who had rallied to keep him through all of the trouble, Anderson agreed to allow the church to be used for the cause. It was one thing for the older, conservative black church leaders to allow their minister to speak in favor of a cause fifty miles away, but it was another thing altogether when it became local. As the large church began filling, Sheriff Clark rushed down the central aisle. With several deputies, he waved a court order from circuit judge James Hare saying the sheriff and his men needed to be present to preserve public safety. Ernest Doyle asked them to leave their firearms outside, but the sheriff ignored his request. He and his men stood against a wall and watched as more than three hundred blacks entered and sat.

Taking the pulpit was SNCC chairman James Forman, a former journalist who had reported for the *Chicago Defender* before he came south and became a civil rights activist. Responding to LaFayette's call, he told the crowd that included more than a hundred teenagers that black people were tired of kowtowing to the wishes of the white powers. Pointing toward Clark and his deputies, Forman said, "They stand by with their loaded guns and try to intimidate us. I say to you tonight: Go downtown next week and step up to the desk and register to vote." The crowd responded, "Amen, brother!"

After Forman, the Reverend C. C. Hunter, an older member of the Voters League, responded, saying the blacks should not blame everything on the white man. "We had a lot to do with it ourselves," he said. He said black people had to take responsibility for their actions.

Clark and his men wrote names and car tag numbers in their notebooks, glared at the attendees as they filed out, and even told some of the older blacks that everyone knew who they were. On the following Monday, in barber and beauty shops, at the Elks and in the hallways of Selma University, the number one topic of conversation was the mass meeting and Forman's message.

Bernard LaFayette began organizing weekly mass meetings. He met with groups at country churches throughout Dallas County and the Black Belt. One night a carload of whites stopped him, pulled him from his car, and beat him bloody, blacking his eyes. On another occasion he was arrested for vagrancy.

While Bernard was organizing, Colia LaFayette worked with Marie Foster and other women. She too met with students at the university and talked to them about voting.

One of the guest speakers at a mass meeting was James Bevel, an officer in SNCC who found Tabernacle Baptist packed with people standing in the aisles. When the people responded enthusiastically, he promised to return.

After Bernard and Colia LaFayette left Selma to return to college, the organizing efforts were picked up by SNCC field secretary Worth Long, who began his civil rights work in his native Arkansas, and Prathia Hall, who had worked alongside future NAACP chairman Julian Bond in SNCC's Atlanta office. Soon, daily demonstrations took place on downtown streets, where sometimes hundreds of black people lined up to register to vote. They stood in single file down the halls of the county courthouse and spilled out onto the sidewalk. Each day, when the registrars denied each person, the lines grew longer. As they stood in line, Sheriff Clark and his deputies walked from one end to the other, taking names and making notes.

By now, word spread that Selma was the new battleground. Because the African Americans had come alive with a sense of pride in themselves and a sense of worth as human beings, and because the white power structure had steeled its backbone against any change whatsoever, here was the ideal place for the civil rights revolution to continue: where governor George Wallace was sacred to the white leaders who believed in his Alabama story.

In the aftermath of the passage of the Civil Rights Act in July 1964, a group of teenagers marched downtown to test the new law. They stepped up to the ticket booth of a segregated movie theater and put their money through the slot. Behind them, Sheriff Clark and his deputies moved in rapidly and arrested them for trespassing. Another group stepped into segregated restrooms in the courthouse and were arrested for trespassing. Among these was fifteen-year-old Vivian Webb, whose mother sewed shirts for the Selma Apparel Company. Discovering her child had been arrested, Mrs. Webb begged Probate Judge Reynolds to let her go free, promising him she would never demonstrate again. After her release, Vivian left Selma for New York, where she would live with relatives.

Later in the week a group gathered in an empty lot, protesting the earlier arrests. Sheriff Clark and his men shot tear gas into the crowd. Within seconds, deputies began beating the people indiscriminately. Photographs of the beatings were published throughout the United States and around the world.

By December, little more than three hundred black citizens of Dallas County had registered to vote. About half of these were residents of Selma. That was an increase of about one-third since Bernard LaFayette arrived.

On Saturday, January 2, 1965, Dr. King arrived in Selma to speak at the Brown Chapel African Methodist Episcopal Church. With him was John Lewis, who had been arrested in Selma by Sheriff Clark back in the summer when he arrived to help his friends, Worth Long and Prathia Hall, in their organizing efforts. It was one of many times he had arrived in this town that reminded him so much of his own hometown of Troy in Alabama's Wiregrass region. He knew its sleepy, segregated streets like the back of his hand. He knew that white law enforcement watched his every move.

As he listened to Dr. King, Lewis knew the fight for freedom had just begun. If Governor Wallace and the Alabama Legislature would not force Dallas County registrars to register its black citizens to vote, "we will seek to arouse the federal government by marching by the thousands," he said. He promised a great outpouring of people and a full-force support by SCLC. Then he said, "We must be willing to go to jail by the thousands."

In the congregation that day was nine-year-old Sheyann Webb, Vivian Webb's little sister. Looking back, Sheyann wrote, "You had to *hear*

Dr. King to really get his message. It wasn't just *what* he said, but *how* he said it. When he said that about be willing to go to jail by the thousands, the word 'thousands' wasn't said, it was more like a quivery vibration in a loud and urgent stage whisper, and part of the word, *thouuu*, just rolled through the church. Without really thinking about it in so many terms, I just became, that day, a part of the movement to gain our freedom. Before there could be those thousands, there had to be one of us at a time."

Demonstrations, Dr. King said, would begin in two weeks. Meanwhile, John Lewis and others, a coalition of SCLC, SNCC, and the Dallas County Voters League, would plan and organize out of SNCC offices on the corner of Alabama and Franklin avenues that had once been Sam Boynton's headquarters.

As promised, demonstrations began two weeks later. As the march arrived at the courthouse, Sheriff Clark and his deputies surrounded the group. With billy clubs in hand, the officers pushed into the midst of the demonstrators. Then Clark ordered the marchers into an alley. They refused. When Mrs. Boynton didn't move quickly, Clark stepped to her side and, as John Herbers wrote in the *New York Times* the next day, "grabbed her by the back of her collar and pushed her roughly for half a block into a patrol car." She and thirty-six other marchers were taken to jail.

The next day, Clark ordered demonstrators to line up down the alley and enter the courthouse through the side door. Lewis told him they wished to enter through the front door. A minute later, Lewis and others were arrested and locked in a fenced outdoor area next to the jail that was already full.

Several days later, when Sheriff Clark approached the marchers, Annie Lee Cooper, a heavyset maid at the town's only black motel, was wrestled to the ground by three deputies. Clark stood over her with his billy club raised. In the *Times*, Herbers wrote, "'I wish you would hit me, you scum,' she snapped at the sheriff. He then brought his billy club down on her head with a whack that was heard throughout the crowd gathered in the street." Again, photos by news photographers were published across America and the world. She was taken away, shackled in two pairs of handcuffs, her head still bleeding.

Several days later, Dr. King arrived. Marching with him were more than 250 demonstrators. Confronted by Clark with his deputies and fifty state troopers, King refused to step aside. Singing "I ain't gonna let Jim Clark turn me 'round," they were taken to jail.

On the following day, February 4, Fred Shuttlesworth came down from Birmingham. Coretta Scott King, who was born and raised in Perry County in the Black Belt, arrived from Atlanta to appear at a rally for her husband, who sat in the city jail. And Malcolm X was shuttled into Selma from Montgomery's airport, where he had arrived from New York. All spoke. Malcolm X said, "I think that the people of this part of the world would do well to listen to Dr. Martin Luther King and give him what he's asking for and give it to him fast, before some other factions come along and try to do it another way."

Nine-year-old friends Sheyann Webb and Rachel West, who years later would write a memoir entitled *Selma, Lord, Selma*, were dwarfed by adults as they stood in church that evening and sang, "Ain't gonna let George Wallace turn me 'round, turn me 'round; ain't gonna let George Wallace turn me 'round; I'll keep a-walkin', I'll keep a-talkin', marching up to freedom land." For Sheyann, "singing at those meetings had a purpose; it wasn't just for entertainment. Those songs carried a message. They were different from Negro spirituals, which—as beautiful as they were—told of some distant hope while carrying the burdens of this life. Freedom songs cried out for justice right now, not later."

Like a tragic opera, every afternoon's march grew in intensity. Nearly two weeks after King was released from jail, his associate at SCLC, Reverend C. T. Vivian, led the demonstration. Vivian had increased his movement activity since his student days at Nashville. A Freedom Rider, he had been arrested in Jackson and taken to Parchman Prison. He had been with Shuttlesworth in Birmingham and spent the summer of '64 in the Mississippi Delta. When Sheriff Clark stopped the march, Vivian stepped up to face him. "You remind me of Nazis," Vivian said. "You're racists the same way Hitler was a racist." When the last word left Vivian's mouth, Clark balled his fist and swung. He hit Vivian in the mouth, knocking him off balance. He hit so hard, a middle finger broke. Two deputies took Vivian to jail while Clark, backed by state troopers, ordered the others to disperse.

Two nights later, after Vivian had been released from jail in Selma, several hundred demonstrators gathered at Marion, the seat of Perry

Attorney Fred Gray, Rosa Parks, and E. D. Nixon walk down Montgomery Street on Monday, December 5, 1955, on their way to city court on the first morning of the bus boycott. AUTHOR'S COLLECTION

Reverend Martin Luther King Jr. steps from a Montgomery city bus after the first legal desegregated ride at the end of the year-long boycott in December 1956.

AUTHOR'S COLLECTION

Johnnie Rebecca Carr became president of the Montgomery Improvement Association when Reverend King left Montgomery for Atlanta, where he became chairman of the Southern Christian Leadership Conference.
AUTHOR'S COLLECTION

Detective Jack Shows led early investigations by the Montgomery Police Department into the church bombings. Later he led the attorney general's investigation into the Sixteenth Street Baptist Church bombing in Birmingham.
AUTHOR'S COLLECTION

Alabama African American attorneys discuss a civil rights case with reporters outside the office of Montgomery circuit solicitor William Thetford. From left to right, they are Fred Gray, Orzell Billingsley, Charles Langford, Arthur Shores, and Peter Hall. ASSOCIATED PRESS

In August 1956, White Citizens Council leader Asa Carter speaks to a crowd denouncing school integration. ASSOCIATED PRESS

George C. Wallace speaks at a White Citizens Council rally in Alabama, stirring the emotional white audience to stand up for segregation. ALABAMA DEPARTMENT OF ARCHIVES AND HISTORY

In September 1958, governor James E. "Big Jim" Folsom called a press conference to commute the death sentence of a black man charged with stealing $1.95.
AUTHOR'S COLLECTION

Charles Morgan Jr. was a young attorney in Birmingham in 1963 when he spoke out against the terror of the Ku Klux Klan and the horrendous murder of four little black girls at the Sixteenth Street Baptist Church. AUTHOR'S COLLECTION

Author Wayne Greenhaw as a young reporter covering civil rights for the *Alabama Journal*, the afternoon newspaper in Montgomery, in the 1960s.

AUTHOR'S COLLECTION

Attorney Charles Morgan stands on the steps of the U.S. Supreme Court after arguing *Reynolds v. Sims* for one person, one vote.

Demonstrators for voting rights walk in the rain along U.S. 82 on the Selma-to-Montgomery March.

U.S. district judge Frank M. Johnson Jr. sits at his desk in the federal courthouse in Montgomery that is now named for him. PENNY WEAVER

Dr. Martin Luther King Jr. speaks at a rally for voter registration in Alabama's Black Belt. JIM PEPPLER

Grand cyclops of the United Klans of America Bobby Shelton smokes a cigarette while a cross burns in the background. ASSOCIATED PRESS

Robert Chambliss is booked at the Birmingham jail after being arrested and charged with the bombing of the Sixteenth Street Baptist Church. ALABAMA DEPARTMENT OF ARCHIVES AND HISTORY

Ku Klux Klansmen advertise for membership during a rally in front of the Alabama state capitol. JIM PEPPLER, ALABAMA DEPARTMENT OF ARCHIVES AND HISTORY

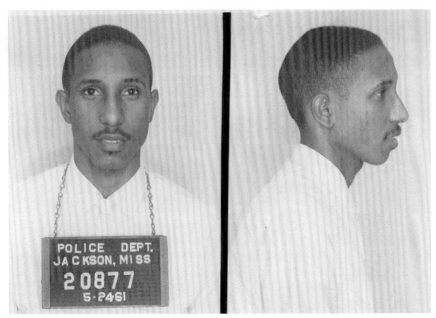

Bernard LaFayette, a young Student Nonviolent Coordinating Committee activist, defied odds and went to Selma to begin working on voter registration at a time when many activists had marked the town with a black "X" on the map in SNCC headquarters. AUTHOR'S COLLECTION

Klansmen carry flags during a rally in front of the Alabama state capitol in Montgomery.
JIM PEPPLER, ALABAMA DEPARTMENT OF ARCHIVES AND HISTORY

Southern Courier editor Robert Ellis "Bob" Smith works in the Montgomery office of the weekly newspaper that covered civil rights news in Alabama and Mississippi from the spring of 1965 through 1968. JIM PEPPLER

Southern Courier reporter Barbara Ann Flowers (nee Howard) interviews Stokely Carmichael in Prattville, where the civil rights activist was jailed. JIM PEPPLER

Barbara Ann Flowers enjoyed her corner of the *Southern Courier* offices in the Frank Leu Building in downtown Montgomery. She was watched over by posters of Stokely Carmichael and Sidney Poitier. JIM PEPPLER

Southern Courier photographer Jim Peppler poses with one of his favorite subjects in the rural Black Belt of Alabama. JIM PEPPLER

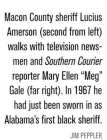

Macon County sheriff Lucius Amerson (second from left) walks with television news-men and *Southern Courier* reporter Mary Ellen "Meg" Gale (far right). In 1967 he had just been sworn in as Alabama's first black sheriff.
JIM PEPPLER

Southern Courier editor Mike Lottman takes notes at a civil rights event in Alabama's Black Belt. JIM PEPPLER

Reverend Ralph David Abernathy preaches at the funeral of Dr. King. Reverend Fred Shuttlesworth stands to the far right. ALABAMA DEPARTMENT OF ARCHIVES AND HISTORY

Activist John Hulett returned to his Lowndes County home, became an outspoken activist for voter registration, and was elected sheriff and later probate judge. JIM PEPPLER

Southern Poverty Law Center founders Morris Dees and Joe Levin put their heads together to file lawsuits against the Ku Klux Klan. PENNY WEAVER, SOUTHERN POVERTY LAW CENTER

Michael Donald was a young African American who was walking down a street in Mobile when two Ku Klux Klansmen forced him into their car and took him to a wooded area where they slit his throat.

SOUTHERN POVERTY LAW CENTER

Morris Dees stands with Beulah Mae Donald on the porch of the house she bought with Klan money won in a lawsuit after her son was murdered by Klansmen. JOANN CHANCELLOR, SOUTHERN POVERTY LAW CENTER

Alabama attorney general Bill Baxley, U.S. district judge Frank M. Johnson Jr., and former governor James E. "Big Jim" Folsom enjoy a moment of relaxation. AUTHOR'S COLLECTION

Segregationist J. B. Stoner on the day of his indictment in Birmingham, Alabama. ASSOCIATED PRESS

Governor George Wallace signs a bill supported by the first black representative elected in Alabama since Reconstruction, Fred Gray, on the right. Flanking Wallace to the left are state representatives Thomas Gilmore and Johnny Ford.
TOMMY GILES

Representing the Southern Poverty Law Center, Julian Bond speaks to a crowd gathered in Montgomery to dedicate the Civil Rights Memorial. THOMAS ENGLAND, SOUTHERN POVERTY LAW CENTER

Julian Bond shows Rosa Parks the circular fountain at the Civil Rights Memorial, where the names of forty activists who lost their lives in the struggle are etched. THOMAS ENGLAND, SOUTHERN POVERTY LAW CENTER

County, about twenty miles northwest of Selma. A tiny town in the midst of flat cotton fields, Marion was the home of an all-white military academy and an all-white female college and little else. By the time Vivian spoke at the Zion Methodist church, more than four hundred people had filled the church. More than a hundred others stood outside. After Vivian's talk, the people marched toward the jail where SCLC worker James Orange was being held after his arrest for organizing local demonstrations. The marchers planned to sing outside his cell. Sheriff Clark, a dozen deputies, and two dozen troopers stood nearby.

When the march proceeded down the main street, Clark and the law enforcement officers stepped out to halt the demonstrators. Onlookers stood three deep on the sides of the street. Near the front of the march were three television cameramen recording the event. Behind them were Richard Valeriani with NBC and John Herbers of the *New York Times*.

As Clark moved closer, a local black farmer named James Dobynes dropped to his knees. "Dear Lord God," Dobynes began, his voice quivering.

At that moment, the streetlights went black.

Like the sudden darkness was a dramatic cue, policemen with billy clubs began beating the marchers, who screamed and shouted. The next day, Herbers wrote in the *Times*, "Negroes could be heard screaming, and loud whacks rang through the square."

Twenty-six-year-old Jimmie Lee Jackson helped his ailing eighty-two-year-old grandfather, Cager Lee, into Mack's Café to escape the onslaught.

Following them into the café was a state trooper named James Bonard Fowler, who swung a long nightstick from side to side. When he raised the club and moved toward the old man, Jackson shouted, "Stop!" And when the trooper raised the club to hit Jackson's mother, Viola, Jackson put up his arms to stop the blow.

Since returning from a stint in the U.S. Army, Jackson had lived with his mother and his grandfather in the country near Marion. He worked with crews that cut pulpwood in the forests of west-central Alabama from before dawn until after dusk six days a week. As a cutter, he was on the lowest rung of the economic ladder. On Sundays, he was the youngest deacon in the small Baptist church he had attended all of his life.

When Jackson raised his hands and begged Fowler to stop, the trooper turned on him, drew his pistol, aimed it toward the young man's stomach, and fired.

As Jackson fell, Fowler kicked. His foot hit Jackson in the hip. Then he shoved Jackson, pushing him through the door. Outside, Jackson fell into a puddle of his own blood.

In the midst of the turmoil, Jackson was taken to the Good Samaritan Hospital in Selma. As doctors worked on him, Jackson lingered between life and death.

Fifty miles to the east in Montgomery, television spotlights glared down on governor George Wallace, who squared his shoulders behind his desk in the capitol. With cameras rolling and newsmen taking notes, he stated that he was outlawing all nighttime marches and demonstrations in the state. He said, "The tragedy in Marion was the work of professional agitators with pro-communist affiliations."

Forty-eight hours after Jimmie Lee Jackson had been shot, Malcolm X was shot to death in Harlem in New York City. Five days later, Jackson died.

Fowler was indicted for the murder of Jackson more than forty-two years after the young man died. Fired as a trooper in 1968 after he struck a supervisor, Fowler was living on a farm near Geneva in south Alabama when indicted. He claimed that he shot Jackson in self-defense. Two years after the indictment, he still had not been tried.

Jimmie Lee Jackson's flag-draped coffin was carried to Brown AME Chapel, where more than four hundred mourners pushed into the pews and more than six hundred stood outside in the rain beneath a banner that read in squared capital letters: RACISM KILLED OUR BROTHER.

At the funeral Dr. King's voice rang over the crowd. Then James Bevel, who had demonstrated by the side of Bernard LaFayette and John Lewis in Nashville, Birmingham, and in the state of Mississippi, spoke in his own inimitable voice.

Rachel West and Sheyann Webb stood with other children, all of whom held candles in remembrance of Jimmie Lee Jackson, while the words of the ministers rang around them. On the steps outside the church they sang, "O Freedom! O Freedom! And before I'll be a slave I'll be buried in my grave and go home to the Lord and be free." As they sang, the little girls cried.

Later, Sheyann Webb remembered: "I had met Jimmie Lee Jackson only once. It was one night at Brown Chapel, and he had come there with Albert Turner, one of the SCLC workers from Marion." At the funeral, she said, Reverend L. L. Anderson told them, "Jimmie Lee's earned his place in history beside John Brown, Abraham Lincoln, and Medgar Evers. When Jimmie Lee gets up to heaven, he won't find that God has one place for white people and another for black people, but just one place for all of us. Jimmie Lee Jackson's struggle is over, and he is free at last."

Following behind the hearse along a muddy dirt path toward the cemetery, walking shoulder to shoulder with Jackson's mourners, James Bevel said, "We ought to take his body all the way to Montgomery and put it on the steps of the capitol." He added, "We ought to give George Wallace the body of Jimmie Lee Jackson. Just put him right in ol' Wallace's hands."

Later, in the quietness and solitude of someone's living room, Dr. King said, "You know, Bevel's got a good idea."

All eyes turned to him.

"We ought to march from Selma to Montgomery to bring this thing to a head," he said. "We don't need any more Jimmie Lee Jacksons."

"We can do it in his memory," Bevel said.

"We can make his life really mean something," someone else said.

According to John Lewis, the meetings that followed were crammed with ideas about the centerpiece of the struggle: a Selma-to-Montgomery march to support the Voting Rights Act that was being proposed in Congress.

In Montgomery, Governor Wallace declared, "I'm not gonna have a bunch of niggers walking along a highway in this state as long as I'm governor."

In Atlanta, Lewis told his group at SNCC, who had been arguing about the need for such a march, "I'm a native Alabaman. I grew up in Alabama. I feel a deep kinship with the people there on a lot of levels. You know I've been to Selma many, many times. I've been arrested there.

I've been jailed there. If these people want to march, I'm going to march with them. You decide what you want to do, but I'm going to march."

On the afternoon of Sunday, March 7, several hundred men, women, and teenagers, many still in their church clothes, met in a baseball field near downtown Selma. Leading the march were John Lewis, James Bevel, and SCLC's Andrew Young and Hosea Williams. Behind them were the older women of the Dallas County Voters League, Amelia Boynton and Marie Foster.

That morning, after they put on their finest dresses, both Sheyann Webb and Rachel West said they were afraid. Still, they decided to march. When Sheyann told her mother, "she nodded, and all of a sudden she hugged me close to her, then turned away. 'Momma,' I said, 'you gonna cry?' And she shook her head. 'No, I'm just proud of you.'" They remembered the details of the stories from Marion, where Jimmie Lee Jackson had been killed. Thinking about it, they shivered. But they fell into line, moving with the others.

As they walked past the county courthouse Lewis noticed that a number of black families parked their cars, got out, and joined in the march.

As the group grew larger and larger, Lewis and Bevel crossed over the high hump of the Edmund Pettus Bridge, named for a Confederate general who later became a U.S. senator.

The marchers knew they would not go far. No provisions had been made to feed, water, and care for hundreds on a four- or five-day hike to the capital city. At best, they would go three or four miles to Craig Air Force Base before turning back and having a prayer vigil.

On the southern side of the bridge, Trooper Major John Cloud stepped into the middle of the highway. Into a bullhorn, he said, "This is an unlawful assembly. Your march is not conducive to the public safety. You are ordered to disperse and go back to your church or your homes."

Hosea Williams asked if he could have a word with the major.

Cloud answered, "There is no word to be had." He said the group had two minutes to disperse.

The marchers did not move. Lewis suggested they pray. Word spread. As the marchers began to kneel, Major Cloud said, "Troopers! Advance!"

As public safety director Al Lingo watched from a nearby car, troopers waded into the marchers. A trooper swung his billy club at Lewis, hitting the left side of his head. Another hit Williams.

Roy Reed wrote in the *New York Times*, "The troopers rushed forward, their blue uniforms and white helmets blurring into a flying wedge as they moved.

"The wedge moved with such force that it seemed almost to pass over the waiting column instead of through it.

"The first 10 or 20 Negroes were swept to the ground screaming, arms and legs flying, and packs and bags went skittering across the grassy divider strip and on to the pavement on both sides.

"Those still on their feet retreated.

"The troopers continued pushing, using both the force of their bodies and the prodding of their nightsticks.

"A cheer went up from the white spectators lining the south side of the highway."

As Clark and his mounted posse drove their horses into the crowd of blacks, whites on the sidelines cheered. Television cameras captured the ordeal as it unfolded. Someone shouted, "Tear gas!" and more blacks scurried back over the bridge toward Selma.

Later, Governor Wallace insisted, "I never authorized the troopers to attack the demonstrators. That damn Al Lingo acted on his own."

Sheyann Webb remembered, "I just turned and ran. And just as I was turning the tear gas got me; it burned my nose first and then got my eyes. I was blinded by tears. So I began running and not seeing where I was going." Later, at home, she began shaking and couldn't stop though both her mother and father were hugging her.

That night, Bloody Sunday was shown on national television. President Johnson watched. Governor Wallace watched. Dr. King watched. A stunned nation watched.

Attorney Fred Gray, representing King and SCLC, filed for an injunction against Wallace, Lingo, and Clark in U.S. District Court in Montgomery. On Monday, judge Frank Johnson issued two: one enjoining these men from interfering with peaceful demonstrations and another enjoining King and his followers from attempting further marches until after a hearing he set for March 11.

On Tuesday, King led two thousand marchers in Selma from Brown Chapel to the bridge, where they were stopped by a U.S. marshal who read Johnson's order forbidding further marches.

After the hearing, which lasted several days, Judge Johnson ruled that King and his followers had the constitutional right to demonstrate peacefully. If they marched along a federal highway, the governor and his law enforcement officers, including the National Guard, would be required to protect the demonstrators.

✮

On Saturday, March 13, 1965, while the hearing was taking place in Montgomery, Governor Wallace traveled to Washington, D.C., at the invitation of president Lyndon Johnson.

In the Oval Office, the two men sat down and talked like two old-time Southern politicians in small-town Texas or Alabama. Sitting nearby were presidential aides Richard Goodwin and Nicholas Katzenbach. With Wallace were finance director Seymore Trammell and press secretary Bill Jones.

Johnson: "George, you see all those demonstrators there in front of the White House?"

Wallace: "Yes, Mr. President, I saw them."

Johnson: "Those goddamn niggers have kept my daughters awake every night with their screaming and hollering night after night. Wouldn't it be just wonderful if we could put an end to all those demonstrations?"

Wallace: "Oh, yes, Mr. President, that would be wonderful."

Johnson: "Then why don't you let the niggers vote?"

Wallace: "They can vote, if they're registered."

Johnson: "Well, then, George, why don't you just tell them county registrars to register those niggers?"

Wallace: "I don't have that power, Mr. President. Under Alabama law, that belongs to the county registrars."

Johnson: "George, don't you shit me. Who runs Alabama? Don't shit me about your persuasive powers. I had on the TV this morning and I saw you and you were talking and you were attacking me, George."

Wallace: "Not you, Mr. President. I was speaking against federal intervention."

Johnson: "You was attacking me, George. And you know what? You were so damned persuasive that I almost changed my mind. George, you and I shouldn't be thinking about 1968. We should be thinking about 1988. We'll both be dead and gone then. What do you want left behind? You want a great big marble monument that says, GEORGE WALLACE: HE BUILT? Or do you want a little piece of scrawny pine laying there that says, GEORGE WALLACE: HE HATED?"

★

On Sunday, March 21, less than a month after Jimmie Lee Jackson died in his hospital room, four thousand people gathered in and around Brown Chapel. They heard Dr. King pray and followed him down the street, through downtown, over the Edmund Pettus Bridge, and out of town on U.S. 80 through a drizzling rain.

Only little more than a hundred continued on the trek that ended in Montgomery, where more than five thousand met them. On the night before the final day I stood with new friends from Ivy League colleges in a big field behind St. Jude Catholic Church, where many of the demonstrators camped under the stars. From a flatbed truck, singers Peter, Paul, and Mary sang "If I Had a Hammer," "Blowin' in the Wind," and "Tell It on the Mountain." After Pete Seeger did "This Land Is Your Land" and Joan Baez "Joe Hill," they all joined Harry Belafonte in singing "We Shall Overcome."

On the next afternoon in the drizzling rain, Dr. King stood on the steps of the Alabama capitol and said, "I know that some of you are asking, 'How long will it take?' I come to say to you this afternoon, however difficult the moment, however frustrating the hour, it will not be long, because truth pressed to earth will rise again. How long? Not long, because no lie can live forever. How long? Not long, because you still reap what you sow. How long? Not long, because the arc of the moral universe is long, but it bends toward justice."

Years later, Frank Johnson told journalist Frank Sikora, "If I had been a black person, I might have been there. If I had been black and been subjected to some of the laws they'd been subjected to, I might have had some serious questions about this democracy being the best politi-cal system.

"From the moment I issued the order permitting that march, I had been certain that I had done what was right according to the laws of this nation. As I watched those people—and some of them were mere chil-dren—I was absolutely convinced I had been right. I had never watched a march or demonstration before, but there was something special about the Selma-to-Montgomery march. I think the people demonstrated something about democracy: that it can never be taken for granted; they also showed that there is a way in this system to gain human rights. They followed the channel prescribed within the framework of the law. I think the march decision also showed some black people that valid complaints can be addressed within the system, according to the Con-stitution, and can be addressed without resorting to violence."

13

DON QUIXOTE OF THE SOUTH

When Charles Morgan Jr. met Roger N. Baldwin in 1964, the eighty-year-old who founded and was the first executive director of the American Civil Liberties Union said, "Oh, yes, you're the young man who's going south. We sent a man south in the 1930s. He lasted about six weeks, as I recall."

As ACLU's Southern director, Morgan would fight legal windmills. He opened an office at 5 Forsyth Street across from the *Atlanta Journal and Constitution* in the same building with the Southern Regional Council and Vernon Jordan's Voter Education Project.

Morgan's offices became a gathering place for newsmen, politicians, civil rights leaders, and other interested parties. Claude Sitton, Gene Roberts, and Roy Reed of the *New York Times*, Jack Nelson of the *Los Angeles Times*, Joe Cumming of *Time*, Karl Fleming of *Newsweek*, and others on the Southern beat regularly congregated around Morgan's desk in the late afternoons for sips of bourbon-and-branch and to hear the latest news about what was happening around the South. It was not unusual for Dr. King and his latest protégés to drop by and join in the conversation. Now and then Morgan would refer to the civil rights leader as "De Lawd," and King would grin widely in response.

To the ACLU office Morgan brought with him his old case, *Billingsley v. Clayton*, that he had filed with his friend Orzell Billingsley Jr. It was their ongoing struggle to desegregate the Alabama jury system, and it still lingered in Judge Johnson's U.S. District Court in Montgomery. At the time it was filed the court did not have the authority to rule. That would not come until after the Civil Rights Act of 1964 stood up to challenges from Governor Wallace and others on the far right. Soon, after those challenges were met and overcome, Morgan had the tools to apply his trade with a quiet vengeance in the name of Billingsley's father.

Sitting in a roomy apartment in an antebellum mansion on the edge of Montgomery's West End, Orzell Billingsley Jr., called Zellie X by his close friends, said, "Chuck Morgan is the movie star of the civil rights attorneys. Me and Fred Gray and Peter Hall and Arthur Shores and J. L. Chestnut, we do the dirty work, but Chuck gets the headlines. He knows what's newsworthy. Me, I file some stuff that gets attention, like making Freedom City, when they put up the tents on The Mall at the end of the Poor People's March on Washington, a municipality unto itself." Billingsley grinned toothily.

Billingsley was talking about his expertise in incorporating municipalities, which he did throughout the Black Belt, putting the small towns into a position to obtain waterworks and other public utilities through federal grants. "Chuck wouldn't ever do that, he's too serious-minded. Or the time I filed to incorporate Gee's Bend down in the Black Belt. I told 'em at the courthouse I was going to rename it King City and we were gonna have an Oklahoma sculptor build a sixty-foot-high statue of Dr. Martin Luther King Jr. in the town square, where all those plantation owners could look up in the sky and see him against the sunset." Everywhere Billingsley traveled in Alabama, he said, agents from the Peace Commission or Sovereignty Commission would follow with their cameras and recorders. "When they point their cameras at me, I just smile for 'em," Billingsley said.

On the afternoon of Saturday, August 25, 1965, only five months after he participated in the Selma-to-Montgomery March, twenty-five-year-old white seminarian Jonathan M. Daniels was looking for a cold Coca-Cola in the muggy heat of Lowndes County. He and eighteen protesters had been arrested for carrying signs reading EQUAL JUSTICE FOR ALL and NO

MORE BACK DOORS. For the past three days they had been jailed in the county seat of Hayneville. The old stone jailhouse constructed with slave labor more than a hundred years earlier was located on the south side of the small town. It towered over an area known as the race track, where slaves once rode their owners' horses in Saturday afternoon gentlemen's races. The two-storied rock structure was one of the many remnants of antebellum days in the rural county where blacks still outnumbered whites four to one. Shortly after noon the demonstrators had been released and ordered to leave the town. At a pay telephone booth outside the courthouse, they called Selma to ask friends to pick them up as soon as possible.

That afternoon, after playing a game of dominoes with friends on the portico of the courthouse, lifelong Lowndes County resident Thomas L. Coleman strolled across the lawn to the Cash Store with his twelve-gauge shotgun cradled in his hands. The lanky fifty-four-year-old white civilian deputy sheriff looked as casual as a cowboy in a western shoot-'em-up as he leaned against a cooler and enjoyed the cool, dark confines of the old store.

When Daniels opened the door of the store, he and his friends wanting to quench their jailhouse thirst, Coleman shouted, "Get out! The store is closed! I'll blow your goddamned heads off, you sons of bitches!"

Later, twenty-six-year-old Catholic priest Father Richard Morrisroe, who had also been arrested while demonstrating, said Daniels asked Coleman if he was threatening them, to which Coleman responded, "You damn right I am!"

Instantly, a shot rang out. Daniels clinched his stomach and fell onto the floor of the porch. A student at Episcopal Theological Seminary in Massachusetts, Daniels had taken leave from school to work in Alabama. He arrived in the Black Belt in time for the march to Montgomery. He remained to work with the Episcopal Society for Cultural and Racial Unity. For the past two weeks he had volunteered to expand organizing efforts to Lowndes County. Now he lay bleeding on the front stoop of the store.

While Coleman blasted again, he shouted, "Run! I'll kill all you niggers!" In the dust outside, Morrisroe, who had turned to flee, lay wounded, having been shot in the lower spine.

Down the hall from Morgan's office at 5 Forsyth Street, ESCRU executive director Reverend John M. Morris learned the details of the shooting before nightfall and strode to the ACLU office and repeated what he had heard. He was fresh off the phone with the U.S. Justice Department, whose representatives were doing nothing in Lowndes County but waiting for orders from Washington.

"We will do something," Morgan declared.

Five days after the shooting that left Daniels dead and Morrisroe paralyzed, Morgan arrived in Montgomery. When his friend, local attorney George W. Dean Jr., met him at the airport he had a briefcase filled with papers. Morgan and Dean went directly to the U.S. District Court, where Morgan filed *White v. Crook* on behalf of Gardenia White, Lillian S. McGill, Jesse W. Favor, Willie May Strickland, and John Hulett, whom he characterized as "five brave black people." Also listed as plaintiffs were Jonathan Daniels's mother and ESCRU's Reverend Morris. The suit against Bruce Crook and other white Lowndes County jury commissioners "brought the federal government into the struggle against the all-white, all-male juries of the Southern Justice System," Morgan wrote. "It also brought the Justice Department into the struggle for equal women's rights."

"That was the way Morgan worked," Dean said. "He didn't dally around. As soon as Morris told him the details, he was on the phone to me. He had his young associates pulled up to his desk, listening to his every word. He gave each a task to find a legal way to do what needed to be done. As he worked hurriedly he dotted every *i* and crossed every *t*. He talked with law professors at Harvard, Yale, North Carolina. He knew everybody. He sought advice from social psychologists. He assigned me research into the Alabama situation. He prepared to ride. When I picked him up at the airport he was talking like a whirlwind. His mind was going ninety-to-nothing. Steel trap. When he got like that, nothing stopped him."

While Morgan was preparing the suit, Alabama attorney general Richmond Flowers, the scion of a successful business family in Houston County in the southeastern Wiregrass, announced that his office would be prosecuting Tom Coleman for murder.

Less than two weeks prior to the shooting, Coleman had spoken to Flowers, who was watching while federal officials in Lowndes County had been registering blacks to vote. Coleman said, "You and Katzenbach ought to get off the Ku Klux Klan and get on these outfits down here trying to get these niggers registered. If you don't get off the Klan investigation, we'll get you off."

Morgan asked federal judges to enjoin all Lowndes County trials until the jury discrimination question was settled. Morgan argued, "All white juries drawn from all-white lists give killers a license to murder."

In Hayneville, deputy attorney general Joe Breck Gantt told circuit judge T. Werth Thagard that it would be "impossible for the State to obtain a fair trial" in the county.

On September 27, little more than a month after Daniels had been killed, Father Morrisroe lay in a Chicago hospital, "medically and physically unable to testify," Gantt told the court. "I can't prosecute this case without Morrisroe. The only reason he is not here now is because he is in danger of losing his life."

In the slave-constructed, two-story, whitewashed courthouse, Gantt stood before the judge and said, "The State has no alternative than to ask that this case be *nolle prosequi* [set aside temporarily]." At breaks in the proceedings, Gantt had told reporters that if he were allowed to drop the case he could later bring Coleman to trial, after Morrisroe recovered.

"I'm ordering you here and now to proceed with the prosecution of this case," Judge Thagard told Gantt.

With palms up and outstretched, Gantt answered, "Your honor, I don't want to be a part of putting perjured testimony on that witness stand. I can't proceed any further. I can't prosecute this case. I have no case whatsoever."

As Gantt's last word left his mouth, Thagard said that if he did not proceed, he would hold him in contempt.

Reporters, sitting near a six-by-six iron-barred cage where defendants had once been held during court proceedings, stopped writing. They glanced around the courtroom at white faces on one side of the center aisle and blacks on the other side. All watched in silence. Gantt was a lone figure in front of the high bench of justice. Quietly, he said, "No."

All eyes shifted to the judge, whose colorless lips were clinched as he said, "Mr. Gantt, you are hereby removed from this case."

The local district attorney was handed the case.

After a white male jury was chosen, a deputy sheriff testified that he had seen the entire incident. After Daniels was released from jail, he said, the Episcopal seminarian walked up a dirt road toward town. At Cash Store, he said, Daniels was carrying something in his hand that flashed in the afternoon sunlight. "We figured it was a gun or a switchblade knife."

According to a written statement from Morrisroe that was read to the jury, "When Daniels was shot, I turned to leave. I did not want to play hero. Another shot was fired, and I was struck by that shot in my lower spine, and I fell to the ground. To my knowledge, at the time of the threat and the first shot, Daniels did not have a knife, gun, stick, or other weapon in his hand. The only thing I had in mine was a dime."

Other testimony showed that Daniels was wearing a silver crucifix around his neck.

Deputy sheriff Joe Jackson testified that he watched Daniels after he was released from jail and "he kissed that nigger girl." Asked if Daniels kissed her on the cheek, he answered, "He kissed her right in the mouth." The spectators and some of the jury laughed heartily.

After deliberating an hour and twenty-nine minutes, the jury found Coleman not guilty.

To Morgan the words were a sting that would swell and ache.

In Atlanta, he met with the Southern Christian Leadership Conference's top guns: Dr. King, Andrew Young, Ralph Abernathy, and Hosea Williams. "As far as we're concerned," King said, "Southern courts have forfeited their right to administer justice." In answer, the SCLC planned marches on courthouses and sit-ins in jury boxes.

Morgan knew that during the past fifteen years the Justice Department had asked its ninety-two U.S. attorneys to report any instances of jury discrimination by federal courts. Each time it asked, no response was heard. "And when we urged the Justice Department to prosecute civil rights cases, they asked: 'Why prosecute?' Then answered themselves: 'All-white juries will turn the killers loose.'"

Soon, however, the Justice Department entered Morgan's suit, *White v. Crook*, and federal judges ordered the inclusion of blacks on jury rolls. The judges also applied the equal protection clause of the Fourteenth

Amendment to sex as well as race. The ruling struck down Alabama's law that excluded all women from jury service. It was a ruling that would grow in importance.

"Every time we filed a lawsuit in Alabama, a so-called investigator with the Peace Commission would take our picture," Morgan said. "I would pose for them, smile, and give them the finger. They were as sorry a lot as I ever saw.

"The same was true in Mississippi, South Carolina, or Georgia. They all had these groups named by the governors or the legislatures. They all said 'communist' every other word.

"It was all damned ridiculous, a waste of taxpayers' dollars, ineffective, and really hilarious, if it hadn't been so damn frightening. And it was frightening. The intimidation factor in Alabama was horrific. People quaked when the Peace Commission or the Sovereignty Commission sneaked around in the shadows."

In February 1966, Morgan and his old friend Orzell Billingsley Jr. filed a suit to desegregate the Alabama prison system. Caliph Washington had been convicted of murdering a Bessemer policeman, and Johnnie Coleman had been convicted of murdering a white man in Greene County. Both were black and testified at their trials that they were not guilty. Billingsley believed them.

In the Birmingham city jail, waiting trial on protesting charges, were two longtime friends of Morgan. Both were SCLC staffers and activists. Hosea L. Williams was black and Thomas E. Houck Jr., white. They were added to the suit to desegregate all Alabama state, county, and city prisons and jails. Frank Lee was the state commissioner of corrections. Morgan styled his suit *Washington v. Lee*.

Throughout the South, prisons were bad. Prisons for blacks were terrible. In many cases, black inmates were treated worse than slaves in the days before the Emancipation Proclamation. Morgan wrote: "In the Jefferson County, Alabama, courthouse I watched as bailiffs and deputy sheriffs kept back the mothers, daughters, wives, and friends of chained-together prison-garbed black men. Faltering and crying, their loved ones asked me or some other white lawyer, 'Please tell him that . . .'

"By then I knew that we would have annihilated blacks had they been more literate and less useful. In Hitler's Germany armbands identified Jews. Those with black skin could have been annihilated more easily. But they were the labor pool with which to break strikes. They served as the pickers of cotton, the diggers of ditches. They emptied bedpans and cleaned the outhouses of our lives. Uneducated, propertyless, disenfranchised, and excluded from justice, except as defendants, they were no threat to whites. While they remained useful and didn't get 'out of line,' their lives were assured, for no matter how worthless lower-class white folks said blacks were, the rich, well-born, and able upper-class whites knew that they and black folks were really the only people indispensably required by Our Southern Way of Life."

Again, Morgan challenged the constitutionality of segregation. As he and Camille talked about the case, as they discussed every case that he was preparing to argue, she gave him a phrase to use: "Integrated prisons should be a great deterrent to white crime."

Morgan was pleased that the case would be heard by a three-judge panel, including district judge Frank Johnson and circuit judge Richard T. Rives, both of whom, in Morgan's opinion, "really believed in the Constitution." The third was Birmingham's chief district judge Seybourn H. Lynne, who had also been the third and dissenting judge that heard the Montgomery bus boycott case ten years earlier.

At trial, Morgan called to the stand the director of the Southern Regional Council's study of Deep South prisons. Tall, heavy, soft-spoken, and black, John O. Boone was a graduate of Morehouse College and Atlanta University. After fourteen years working at the Atlanta Federal Penitentiary, he had been chief classification officer at the federal prison in Terre Haute, Indiana.

On cross-examination, Boone was asked by assistant attorney general Gordon Madison, "How long did it take to desegregate the Atlanta federal prison?" He answered, "Overnight."

Asked why the federal experience was applicable to state prisoners, he said, "I have met some of your ex-inmates. In fact, I have encountered hundreds and hundreds of them in federal prisons."

Asked if federal prisoners are different from state inmates, Boone replied, "No, sir."

After a state witness, Jefferson County sheriff Melvin Bailey, finished answering questions from attorneys, Judge Johnson leaned down from the bench and asked, "Is there any instance in your experience where it is necessary to classify solely because of race? In order to maintain and operate your prison properly?" Bailey answered, "I would have to say no."

The state then called its named defendant, state prison commissioner Frank Lee, who had been sheriff of Greene County in the Black Belt, where he and his brother Bill had been legendary lawmen for decades. When the state assistant attorney general asked if any inmate among Alabama's "vicious, violent, rebellious, and deadly inmates" had a gun, Lee testified that to his knowledge there was not one gun inside any of the state's penal institutions.

In the end, all three judges agreed that Alabama's law segregating its prisoners was unconstitutional.

After the state appealed, on November 7, 1967, Morgan argued the case before the U.S. Supreme Court. Morgan asked the court for "speed and a court order," while assistant attorney general Madison asked for "reasonableness and time." Morgan added, "It is a tragic reality that no man in Alabama in public office, subject to appointment by the governor, can, in fact, exercise his discretion and his duty without an order of the court."

During questioning, justice Hugo Black, a native of Clay County, Alabama, pondered Morgan's statement: "In Walker County there is no municipal jail of two rooms."

Justice Black asked Morgan: "Are these the ones they call calabooses?"

Morgan: "Yes, sir; they are the ones that are called calabooses."

Black: "What have they been doing in those places when they have a black and a white?"

Morgan: "Well, I reckon in those small towns they just haven't had a Negro and a white man get drunk on the same night. I don't know."

As the justices chuckled, they also exchanged knowing glances. On March 11, 1968, the Supreme Court upheld the ruling of the lower court that Alabama's law was unconstitutional.

A month later, in circuit court in Greene County, Alabama, after the jury rolls had been desegregated, Johnnie Coleman, one of the plaintiffs in *Washington v. Lee*, was retried. His attorneys, Orzell Billingsley and Peter Hall, struck all the white males on the jury roll. The prosecution struck all the white females. Twelve black jurors remained. On April 4, 1968, the jury found Coleman not guilty.

After Coleman was released, he, his family, and his lawyers celebrated until they heard that evening that Dr. King had been assassinated in Memphis.

The named plaintiff, Caliph Washington, remained on death row. Twice his murder conviction was reversed. On January 12, 1971, Alabama Court of Appeals judge Aubrey M. Cates set aside the conviction, saying that blacks had been systematically excluded from the grand jury that had indicted Washington in Bessemer in 1957.

Throughout the 1960s, when Morgan was in and out of Montgomery, filing suits in Judge Johnson's court, he associated with local attorney George Dean, whom he had met in law school. During the years they had become best friends, thinking alike on the issues of race and politics. "Chuck and I learned from the same great man, Jay Murphy, who was the finest legal mind teaching at the University of Alabama," Dean said. "He made you think about the law, not seeing it as a static thing but as a creative tool that could be used to mold ideas. From him, Chuck's imagination was teased. Most of the time he put together lawsuits like a damn good mystery novelist wove a story. He started with a premise and then began to put together the pieces, letting his imagination lead him from one law to the other through a complex forest of legalese. Put that together with his natural flare for the dramatic and you have one hell of fine attorney."

Morgan was given to long afternoons of drinking and talking and late nights of working prodigiously, law books open on his desk, phones in both hands. "To keep working like this, fighting the good fight day in and day out, week in and week out, year after year, you have to dream quixotic dreams. I fight with both fists flailing. I don't quit, no matter what. You can dream the dreams, but you've got to hunker down and fight the sons of bitches," he said more than once.

In 1967 Morgan met a young recent graduate of Vanderbilt Law School, Reber F. Boult Jr., at an ACLU lunch in Nashville. With his friend and classmate, Isaiah Thornton "Tony" Creswell Jr., Boult traveled to Atlanta to meet with Morgan, who enticed him by describing an organized legal assault Morgan termed Operation Southern Justice. On January 2, 1968, Morgan hired Boult as his associate.

"When a major brief needed writing," Boult remembered, "Chuck would do it at home. He lived in the Piedmont-Lindberg area, a few miles from Forsyth. He would send his drafts to us in a taxi, and we'd send the typed drafts back in a taxi. Basically, there would be a taxi going and coming all afternoon and night or until Chuck caught a plane to some speaking engagement, leaving me with a pile of penciled, tiny handwriting and a blizzard of little cutouts from copies of case reports, history books, and newspaper articles to put into whatever order I might think he'd want."

To Boult, Morgan was an original. "Chuck was the first—and maybe the only lawyer other than me—to use the Brandeis Brief. That is, he used a lot of stuff that had been published in places other than law books. Our brief in a case to desegregate the Georgia prisons, *Wilson v. Kelley,* had fifty or sixty pages of history of Georgia's jails and prisons as an outgrowth or extension of slavery." To George Dean: "Chuck Morgan was a helluva writer. Long before John Grisham, his briefs read like a novel. Chuck made law interesting. He brought out the dramatic. To him, the law was something real. It breathed."

In the late afternoon of April 4, 1968, Camille telephoned her husband with the news that his friend, Dr. King, had been shot and killed. He erupted into a fit of rage and despair. He ordered a case of whiskey and began to drink. All the while, tears flowed down his jowly cheeks.

Days later, Morgan joined other mourners as King's coffin was carried through the streets of Atlanta to his final burial place.

Sitting on a pier overlooking Choctawhatchee Bay in the panhandle of Florida, he told a friend, "We lost a great leader, a magnificent human being, and I lost one of the best friends and advisers I ever had. He did so much in so little time. You know, Bob Dylan had it right: the times they are a-changing. And Martin King did more than anyone I know to make them change."

In June 1972, after their son graduated from high school, the Morgans moved to Washington, D.C., where Chuck would become director of the national office of the ACLU.

From the national office, he defended not only poor blacks, antiwar demonstrators, and conscientious objectors, including the most famous of all, Muhammad Ali, but he also represented the Ku Klux Klan when it was refused the right to march in a Midwestern town. "Every person and organization in this country deserves the best representation possible. I don't care who they are or what they are," he stated. "In every case that I fought, I did so against great odds. I was not jumping out in front of the pack with a favorite cause. I was pushing against the grain. I was fighting the powers that be. And many, many people presumed my clients guilty before they had one day in court. It is my duty and my pleasure to serve my client's cause. As Clarence Darrow said when representing a wealthy defendant, 'I do not believe I need to tell this court or my friends that I would fight just as hard for the rich as for the poor.'"

In the spring of 1973, while attending Harvard under a Nieman Fellowship for midcareer journalists, Ed Williams and I hosted a seminar for the Kennedy Institute of Politics. Williams was a brilliant newsman who had trained under the tutelage of Hodding Carter III at the *Delta Democrat Times* in Greenville, Mississippi. As leaders of the seminar, we invited a number of Southern politicians, attorneys, and people responsible for the awakening South to take part in the program. When the word-of-mouth news spread around campus, our weekly seminar, which had started with about fifteen students, grew to more than a hundred regular attendees.

In one of our final programs, Chuck Morgan spoke without a note. As the chunky-built Morgan moved among the students sitting on the floor of Winthrop House on the banks of the Charles River, he spoke, his voice rising and falling, accentuating the drama of the past two decades.

"The people who were guarding our Southern way of life said, 'If we give 'em an inch, they will take a mile.'"

Morgan's voice halted. He gazed out into the sea of eager young faces. Then he nodded slightly. His eyes sparkled. "They gave us an inch, and we took a mile."

For two hours he outlined each of the cases that had meant so much to so many during the trying times of the 1950s and '60s in the American South.

In the final moments, he spoke to the students just as he might speak to the nine mighty justices of the U.S. Supreme Court. "I believe as Eugene Victor Debs believed. When he looked up into the face of the judge who would sentence him for activities during the Pullman strike, he declared, 'As long as an innocent man lingers behind bars, I will not be free.'"

There was silence. Then the students and professors who were watching and listening were moved to thunderous applause.

Later in 1973, after William O. Douglas became the justice with the longest tenure in Supreme Court history, Linda Charlton, who covered the court for the *New York Times*, asked which of his thousands of decisions had "had the most impact on the country and its citizens." After pondering the question for a few minutes, Justice Douglas answered, "The reapportionment case—*Reynolds v. Sims.*" That suit, filed by Morgan in 1961, made "one person, one vote" the law of the land.

14

THE *SOUTHERN COURIER*

In the spring of 1965, a group of dedicated college students and recent graduates from the North came south to establish a weekly nonprofit newspaper to report civil rights happenings and racial problems. Most, such as editors Robert Ellis Smith and Michael S. Lottman, had graduated from Harvard and were eager to make their names in journalism.

The young men and women of the *Southern Courier* came to watch and listen and write about the South and Southerners. Mike Lottman said, "Most of us discovered that both white and black Southerners were complex, multilayered individuals living in a complex, multilayered society. Life in the South was not as simple as most outsiders viewed it."

Bob Smith, who also served as president, viewed his "work on the *Southern Courier* as an act of patriotism. Not to save the black people, but to save my country. I was outraged that there were parts of the country where Americans were subjected to different rules," where "persons were denied the right to vote, sit on juries, get a decent job, live in good housing, stay in adequate travel accommodations, or eat in a restaurant of their choice.

"I went south to make sure these rights were available to *all* Americans. I was also motivated by the idea that my generation could be more effective using *our skills* and not merely march in demonstrations—which was not my style. This idea was fashioned after the Medical

Committee for Human Rights, doctors and interns who used their skills in the South. If I went, I told myself, I was going to get involved in the community and stay beyond the summer. I disapproved of 'drive-by' civil rights. Later I disparaged it as 'reform by jet plane.'"

A 1962 graduate of Harvard, where he was president of the *Crimson* undergraduate newspaper, Smith was a New Englander, born and raised in Providence, Rhode Island. He was working as a reporter for the *Detroit Free Press* when he was drafted into the U.S. Army. Several weeks into basic training at Fort Dix, New Jersey, he was on his way to mess hall on Monday morning, September 16, 1963, when his eye caught a headline about the killing of four little black girls in a church bombing in Birmingham. Later, learning more about the incident, he was shaken by the violent deaths. "That afternoon at bayonet training," Smith recalled, "I was asked to chant, 'Kill! Kill! Kill!' It was so incongruous. I thought, 'I don't belong here.' Several months later, we heard that President Kennedy had been shot in Dallas." When a fellow soldier whispered, "Who did it?" Smith said, "A Southern racist." After that violent incident, he had stronger feelings that he did not belong in a militaristic setting where killing was the primary goal.

"I am a political activist, but I'm not a rebel. I continued my army service until the completion of two years. About two months before my release, friends I respected and trusted at the *Harvard Crimson* told me about the *Southern Courier*. So I was not involved in the founding of the paper. I was in the second wave." When he arrived, he found the new paper "even looked like the original Cambridge version. Some of us called it the *Dixie Crimson*. We simply applied what we had learned about good journalism as undergraduate reporters and editors."

Mike Lottman dittoed his colleague's assessment. Born in Buffalo, New York, and raised in the Midwest, Lottman had seen how the people of Canton, Ohio, lived separate lives. In some subdivisions there, he said, "No Jews, much less blacks, would ever be allowed to own a home."

After graduating from Harvard, where he was managing editor of the *Crimson* when Smith was president, Lottman started his journalism career on the *Chicago Daily News*. In the spring of 1965, after vacationing in Florida during the Selma-to-Montgomery March, he received a call telling him about plans for the *Courier*. "The whole idea really appealed to me. I would not have been a good civil rights demonstrator, but this call gave me the opportunity to use what skills I had in something I belatedly thought I should be doing."

"The *Courier* was the brainchild of two rights-minded veterans of a summer in Mississippi," according to an article in the Summer News of the *Harvard Crimson* on July 21, 1967, by Stephen E. Cotton, who had been the Birmingham staff of the *Courier* in 1965–66. "The two, former *Crimson* editors Ellen Lake '66 and Peter Cummings '66, envisioned a network of five statewide weekly newspapers in five Deep South states. But that would have taken $75,000 to get going, and months of letter-writing, phone calls, and collections around Harvard produced only $35,000."

After Freedom Summer in Mississippi in 1964, Lake and Cummings returned to Harvard for their junior year. Later they drove down to Atlanta for a civil rights advocacy conference. "We stopped at a gas station," Lake said, "and were threatened and followed—pursued—by two white men in a truck who wouldn't sell us gas, and that made everything a lot more real." At Harvard, working on the *Crimson*, they decided to return to the South as journalists. They began to make plans, recruit friends to help, and raise money to fund the venture.

During the summer of 1965, the staff worked out of Atlanta, traveling the South and reporting what they found. At the end of the summer, when Lake and Cummings returned to Harvard, Smith and Lottman remained.

✶

James H. "Jim" Peppler, a graduate of Penn State, had grown up in the blue-collar neighborhood of South Philadelphia. He had recently begun training as a photographer. After he was accepted for graduate school, his faculty advisor saw an article in the *New York Times* about the journalistic experiment by young Harvard students to publish a weekly newspaper in the South covering civil rights. He showed the article to Peppler, who immediately became excited about the idea. A young married student and recent father, Peppler headed south to become the *Courier*'s photographer.

Geoffrey Cowan, who had been in Mississippi for Freedom Summer and was attending Yale Law School, was told about the project early in

1965. He worked to raise seed money in the beginning, then traveled with Peppler to Selma, where they were joined by several others.

Smith and Lottman determined that Atlanta was too far away from the true civil rights activities. In the fall, the *Courier* rented offices on the sixth floor of the Frank Leu Building on Commerce Street in the heart of downtown Montgomery. Soon, the *Courier* moved to the top floor. Lottman was told later the reason for the move was because white women who worked in other offices had complained to the building's management that they did not feel comfortable using the same restroom with black employees of the *Courier*.

Everyday life at the *Courier* was filled with little misadventures. Soon after moving into the Montgomery offices, Lieutenant Paul Dumas of the police department showed up, sat down with Lottman, and told him if he or his staff had any problems to call him. One day when the integrated group went to lunch at Morrison's cafeteria, some white men raised their voices and muttered threats. "One of the people in the serving line warned that we might get hurt when we left," Lottman remembered. "I called Dumas to get us out of there. As a result, nothing happened."

Peppler became photography editor. His wife, Amy, and their daughter, Robin, arrived in Montgomery, where they moved into an upstairs apartment at the corner of Court Street and Felder Avenue, where Cliff and Virginia Durr lived downstairs. Amy also worked at the *Courier* as layout editor while her husband roamed Alabama, shooting black-and-white images. Avoiding the usual cliché newspaper photographs, Peppler created full-page layouts of his work. Later, editor Lottman recalled, "The most popular component of the *Courier* was the remarkable photography of Jim Peppler. People were really delighted to see themselves or someone they knew or someone like them portrayed as they really were in the pages of a newspaper. Certainly they seldom saw much of that in the white press other than mug shots of people who got arrested."

Peppler remembered: "There were a lot of adventures for me in the three years I was with the *Courier*, from May 1965 to May 1968. I was arrested in Crenshaw County, beaten in Prattville, had a gun put to my head in Mount Meigs, totaled a car on the way to Selma, was encircled and lambasted by police and auxiliaries in Fort Deposit, discovered the communities of Newtown and Clayton Alley in Montgomery and Little Korea in Birmingham, learned the blues at the Laicos Club and Tom's Place in Montgomery, picked cotton with the Bracey family in Wetumpka, photographed King speaking and the Klan marching on the same day in Montgomery, was the only photographer allowed to photograph the swearing-in ceremony of Lucius Amerson in Macon County [the first black sheriff in the state's history]. It was three years of grand adventures every week and often every day."

"We often covered Dr. Martin Luther King's barnstorming tours through the South," Smith said. In September of 1965, *Courier* reporter Steve Cotton wrote about King's visit to Crawfordville, Georgia. In his first article, he wrote that the little town nearly doubled in size when "more than seven hundred Negroes and a handful of white civil rights workers packed the Friendship Baptist church to hear Dr. King. When there was no more room inside, latecomers had to huddle outside the doorways in order to hear.

"'There will be neither peace nor tranquility in this community until the Negro receives justice in Crawfordville,' Dr. King declared. He said his organization, SCLC, was 'here to stand by your side until freedom is yours.'

"The racial situation in Crawfordville, he said, 'left you with no choice but to demonstrate and left us with no choice but to support your demonstrations.'"

Cotton had just arrived in the South. On his way to Montgomery, he stopped in Crawfordville to cover King's appearance. A native of Chicago, Cotton grew up on the South Side in the integrated Hyde Park–Kenwood neighborhood, where he was among the small minority of whites attending Hyde Park High School. At Harvard he worked on the *Crimson*, a year behind Cummings and Lake, who recruited him for the *Courier*. Soon Cotton was assigned to Birmingham, where he was provided "a cheap red car that Ralph Nader would not have approved of," a one-bedroom bungalow, and "a weekly salary of twenty-two dollars and change." A year later he returned to Harvard, became chairman of the *Crimson* editorial board, and graduated from Harvard Law.

✶

In October 1965, when the *Courier* was barely six months old, Bob Smith began to think ahead. The first of December would be the tenth anniversary of the start of the Montgomery bus boycott. For Smith, it would be a splendid journalistic coup if the *Courier* could publish a special piece by King.

By mid-November, he still had not received the piece from King. At his office in Atlanta, King's secretary said he really wanted to do it but Smith must be patient.

While waiting, Smith talked with Rosa Parks in Detroit. She did not believe her story was significant, saying she had done nothing important. However, Smith jotted down her account of what happened on Thursday night, December 1, 1955. When he read it back to her, she approved. She did not consider herself a revolutionary, she said. She was tired from working all day and tired of being told to move to the back of the bus. When the driver demanded that she move, she decided on the spot to refuse.

As Smith waited nervously, he left space open at the top of page one. At the last minute, a Western Union telegram was delivered. Smith rushed to read the copy. To Smith, the words were as eloquent as good poetry. Across the top of page one, the headline, "Montgomery Sparked a Revolution," announced King's thousand-word sermon on the tenth anniversary.

In his customary flowery language, King evoked Greek historian Thucydides as saying, "The secret of happiness is freedom and the secret of freedom, courage." The preacher wrote, "We are now embarked upon a momentous movement for civil rights, a radical refurbishing of the former racist caste order of America. The movement has been labeled the Negro revolution. It is truly a revolution, but a revolution which can only be fully understood when looked upon in the light of history—and the fires of freedom which flickered then burned brightly in Montgomery, the Cradle of the Confederacy."

✶

With a weekly press run of about thirty thousand, the *Courier* sold for ten cents with a yearly subscription costing five dollars in the South and ten dollars elsewhere in the United States. In those days, before computers, there were numerous problems publishing a weekly newspaper. Most weeklies covered a specific neighborhood, town, or county, not an entire state or region, like the *Courier*.

Reporters in the field typed or handwrote copy they sent to Montgomery by bus. Mary Ellen "Meg" Gale drove fifty miles from Tuskegee on Wednesday afternoon, delivering her copy in person. Lottman remembered that Meg Gale "usually wrote about half the paper and never needed editing." After staying with a coworker for a day, she would return to Tuskegee on Friday mornings with bundles of the new issue in the trunk of her car.

On deadline day, the typesetting machines were operated by Barbara Flowers, a young woman from Montgomery whose "remarkable family knew everyone and everything involved in the local civil rights movement," Lottman said. She was fifteen or sixteen. "She set type for years, with a few minutes out to have two kids. She also covered some stories and wrote them up and in the end was the *Courier*'s associate editor, my right-hand person."

"One of Barbara's friends, Viola Bradford, was just getting out of high school and started out doing headlines. Later, she became the paper's all-time superstar when she began writing articles and demonstrated a gift for being able to make sense out of—and capture the truth of—any story we asked her to cover," Lottman recalled.

Barbara Flowers converted the words and headlines into justified columns. Then the copy was cut and pasted onto layout sheets by Amy Peppler, who worked until about 1:00 A.M. She was often helped by Gail Falk, who drove to Montgomery from Mississippi. "Paste-up in those days was a laborious process," according to Lottman, "but the finished product had to get to the printer by first thing Thursday morning, no matter what, or the printing and distribution schedules would be hopelessly screwed up."

Issues were printed in Montgomery by Paul Woolley, who had printed New Dealer Aubrey Williams's liberal-leaning *Southern Farmer* in the late 1940s and early '50s. The printers took bales of newspapers to the bus stations on Thursday night or Friday morning for distribution throughout Alabama and parts of Mississippi.

Times were often tough financially for the executive staff, paying rent, printing costs, payroll, and expense accounts. "At one point," Lottman said, "the folks up North sent me none other than Jim Fallows [who later wrote speeches for President Jimmy Carter and became national correspondent for *The Atlantic*], then on the *Crimson* business board, to help us sell advertising. I decided to give the kid a break and let him cover a story in Albany, Georgia, where the black kids, having no swimming pool and excluded from the white YMCA, went swimming in the local creek, where one of them drowned. Of course, he did a great job, and so a talented ad salesman was lost to the world."

"One *Courier* crusade that was ours alone was the persistent discrimination practiced by the YMCA in Montgomery and other places," Lottman pointed out. "When the YMCA sponsored a speed-reading class and then turned away the one or more black kids who showed up to take the class," the *Courier* reported what happened.

Lottman remembered: "The YMCA in Montgomery was a dazzling new building with a swimming pool. Its black counterpart was a dump. This was true elsewhere as well. I talked to Bill Chandler [executive director of the Montgomery Y] and got nothing but evasions and then to James Bunting at the National YMCA who provided more and dumber evasions. He described to me a process whereby local chapters got a certain number of warnings and a certain number of chances to correct themselves. If discrimination continued, the [local Y] could be decertified. I asked how many times had he warned the Montgomery chapter about the discriminations I had called him about, and, of course, he said none."

Throughout the mid-1960s, the *Courier* continued to report discriminations by the YMCA in Montgomery and its circulation area. Eventually, Morris Dees and Joe Levin filed a successful challenge to the segregation of the YMCA in Montgomery.

✦

A number of bright and talented young blacks contacted reporters and asked to work for the paper.

Mertis Rubin, Lottman said, "was really very, very good. She lived in a small Mississippi town, Mendenhall, and covered politics and always did an excellent job." In a September 1967 issue she produced two stories from Mississippi. The first was datelined Fayette: "The night before last Tuesday's Democratic primary run-off, Will T. Turner told about six hundred Negroes here, 'Make up your mind if you want to be black or white.' Evidently, a lot of them decided to be white.

"Turner, a Negro running for sheriff in Jefferson County, went down in defeat. So did all the other Negro candidates everywhere else in the state."

Mertis Rubin's second story on page one was datelined Jackson, the Mississippi capital. "Almost every Negro leader has been asked at one time or another, 'Where did the Negro vote go in the statewide races?' There have been no solid answers."

Rubin's political reportage was often compared favorably to other journalists, including the respected Bill Minor, who covered Mississippi for the New Orleans *Times-Picayune*. Later, she was rejected for a reporting job on a larger Northern newspaper because of spelling errors in her writing. She became a nurse, returned to Mississippi, and was shot to death by her husband in a domestic argument in 1999.

When a young African American veteran of Vietnam named Kenneth Lumpkin walked into the offices, he wanted to become a news photographer. He began following *Courier* photographer Jim Peppler, who took him under his wing and began teaching him. After Peppler left in May 1968, Lumpkin met the challenge of filling the void. Later, after a downward spiral into drugs, homelessness, and personal loss, he edited and published a paper of his own in the Midwest.

The *Southern Courier* "covered the federal antipoverty programs like no other news organization," Lottman said. "These articles covering what people and the antipoverty programs were actually doing in small, rural towns and communities were not always earth-shaking. But they meant something to the people in the small communities and the towns of Alabama and east Mississippi. The coverage by the *Courier* was just about the only way, at that time, that they could find out what people in other places were doing, what kind of issues the others were confronting, and letting them know that they were not alone."

In the *Courier*, Mary Ellen Gale wrote: "Why did half-a-dozen Community Action Program (CAP) directors from Alabama go to Washington last week?

"Members of the group said they went to ask the federal Office of Economic Opportunity for local control over antipoverty programs.

"But a leader of South East Alabama Self-Help Association (SEASHA) said the CAP directors were trying to block SEASHA before it has a chance to get started.

"This is their primary motive, charged Rufus C. Huffman, treasurer of SEASHA—a new, mostly Negro organization to fight poverty in twelve Alabama counties."

Mary Ellen Gale, who had been assistant managing editor of the *Crimson*, worked as a reporter for the *Philadelphia Bulletin* after graduating from Harvard.

When the *Bulletin* sent her to Birmingham to cover the demonstrations, it "was the first time I saw the Southern civil rights movement close up, and I was very profoundly affected by everything." She was especially moved by "the courage, grace, and dignity of the people, even little children, the way in which every virtue that I respected seemed to be reflected in the activities that black people were undertaking to try to get what seemed to me the most minimal of rights." These were rights, she said, "that they should automatically have had without question." On another occasion, "I saw some very well-dressed, prim-and-proper-looking black women with their white gloves and beautiful hats try to integrate a church in Birmingham and be turned away by white people, even though they said, 'We're Baptists too. We share your faith.' And then, 'No, you may not come in.'"

When her friends from Harvard called and told her about what they were doing in Alabama, Gale eagerly agreed to join them, thinking that it would give her a journalistic opportunity of a lifetime.

In the fall of 1965, Gale wrote numerous articles about twenty-one-year-old Sammy Younge Jr., who had attended Cornwall Academy in Massachusetts before serving a stint in the U.S. Navy. A recent graduate of Tuskegee Institute, Younge had been born into a well-to-do family in the same east Alabama college town. As a member of SNCC, Younge led a series of demonstrations to integrate local white churches.

On the night of January 3, 1966, after leaving SNCC offices, Younge stopped at a service station, where he sought to use the restroom. The owner, sixty-seven-year-old Marvin Segrest, pulled a revolver and told Younge to move on. After Younge found a piece of wood large enough to use as a weapon, he returned with it in his hand. As he approached, Segrest shot twice. The second gunshot hit Younge in the head.

Gale not only wrote about the shooting, she covered the trial in which Segrest testified that he shot in self-defense. After an all-white jury found Segrest not guilty, the small town filled with demonstrators. One night, when more than fifteen hundred marched, looted, and wrecked businesses, a yellow stripe was painted down the back of the Confederate statue in front of the Macon County courthouse. The statue's face was painted black. Whites reacted. Gun-toting men paraded around courthouse square and through black neighborhoods. Gale reported it all in the pages of the *Courier*.

In the fall of 1966, Gale was named executive editor of the paper. Later, after she left the *Courier*, she graduated from Yale Law School. She then worked in Washington, D.C., with Chuck Morgan. Today she is an attorney in California, where she also teaches law at Whittier College. For Gale, "The Southern civil rights movement was one of the great stories of its time, and I was immensely lucky and privileged to play a small part in it."

In 1967, Joan Clark Tornow, a student attending Antioch College in Ohio, returned to Birmingham, where she had graduated from all-white Shades Valley High School five years earlier. Tornow had grown up in Ohio before her father had accepted a position at the University of Alabama Medical Center in Birmingham in 1958. Now she was returning in order to work as a reporter for the *Southern Courier*.

Like her fellow reporters, she too had been affected by the violence of the late 1950s and early '60s in the South. She wanted to help.

When she heard about a young black man, James Small, being fatally shot by a police officer, she wanted to find out why and how. In the back pages of the *Birmingham News,* she read that he had been spotted near a school where, allegedly, break-ins had previously been attempted. She read in the article that a policeman had ordered Small to stop and then fired a "warning shot" into the air. Later, Small's body was found.

After acquiring the minimal police report, Tornow visited the victim's family at their home. Small's eighteen-year-old sister, Charlena, said that she and her brother had been talking late into the night when they ran out of cigarettes. Charlena convinced James to walk a few blocks to purchase more cigarettes from a vending machine. When he didn't return promptly, Charlena fell asleep. Mrs. Small, the victim's mother, said that she was awakened early the next morning by a phone call. A white officer asked if she had a son named James. Assuming her son was asleep in the next room, and wondering what the problem could be, she replied that she did have a son by that name. The officer said, "Well, you better come get him 'cause he's in the morgue." Mrs. Small added that when they went to identify the body, they were given James's possessions—his hat, his money clip, and an unopened pack of cigarettes.

Tornow went to the black funeral home where Small's body had been transferred. He lay on an embalming table. When the mortician uncovered the body, she could clearly see that the bullet entered his back, where it was lodged.

Tornow's article appeared in the *Southern Courier* on February 25, 1967. Her byline at the time was Joan Clark. The report was the only detailed coverage of the killing.

Several nights after Small was killed, Tornow sat next to Mrs. Small and Charlena in a pew at the Jackson Street Baptist Church, where Reverend Fred Shuttlesworth talked to an overflow crowd about the latest in a string of police shootings. Shuttlesworth said, "Every time you turn around, some Negro's being killed by some trigger-happy policeman in Birmingham." He asked Mrs. Small if she would speak, but she was too overcome with grief. She turned to Tornow, who felt "stunned by the responsibility." Years later, Tornow reflected, "The hunger for truth in that room was palpable, and it emboldened me."

Now in her sixties, Tornow said that her experience as a reporter for the *Southern Courier* was "a life-changing experience." She added, "I learned the tremendous importance in a democracy of investigative reporting, including that done by alternative presses, not just the mainstream press. I feel that my own part was small but that the role of the *Southern Courier* during the sixties was huge."

✳

In the spring of 1968, when word reached *Courier* offices that Dr. King had been shot and killed in Memphis, staffers were devastated. Shocked and dismayed, Jim Peppler, camera in hand, traveled to Atlanta for the funeral. His work during the massive funeral was stunning and remarkable. Through the years, he had taken many images of the man whose words he took to heart and whose work he admired. Back in Montgomery, Peppler decided to leave. Later, he explained, "I couldn't keep working on the *Courier* without knowing he was alive."

In the meantime, Bob Smith had moved to New York, where he worked on Long Island for *Newsday* and its publisher, Bill Moyers, who had been a reader and admirer of the *Southern Courier* when he was President Lyndon Johnson's press secretary. Soon Peppler was hired by *Newsday*, where he became an award-winning photojournalist.

✳

In the South, the *Courier* lost its Ford Foundation grant. Lottman tried to find other sources, but in the waning days of 1968 he knew the end was near. With the Vietnam War in the front of most minds, civil rights had become less and less popular, even among liberals. By the end of the year, Lottman scrambled to pay every bill that was owed. Looking back, Lottman, today an attorney in Tennessee, said that he still regrets giving up. "The kind of journalism practiced by the *Courier* hardly exists anywhere today, and the need is as great as ever."

Looking back after forty years, Bob Smith, speaking to the Southern Historical Association in Richmond, Virginia, said in his paper entitled "Reporting the Civil Rights Movement," "I came to love the separateness of the U.S. South—separate language, cuisine, music, folk-ways, economy. I also came to believe that with racial equality—not to mention interstate travel and network television—this separateness would disappear.

"Those of us who used our college educations to work in the civil rights movement were members of a transition generation in college, from the 'silent generation' of the Fifties to the 'activist generation' of the Sixties. Our generation never produced an elected President, but we were catalysts in a great social movement. Some of us were reporters in an epic transition in the civil rights movement, from the original church-based passive resistance growing out of Montgomery to the more assertive student-based movement generated around Black Power. That, too, originated in Alabama. And we were there."

15

THE RISE OF JOHN HULETT

Throughout the lifetime of the *Southern Courier*, an ongoing story was chronicling the rise of John Hulett as a civil rights leader in Lowndes County.

After high school in the late 1940s, Hulett left his family's farm in Gordonsville and headed to Birmingham, where he found a job in the furnace rooms of the Stove and Range Company. Never afraid of hard work, the tough young man who had walked miles behind a mule and plow in the Black Belt cotton fields worked the furnaces by day. At night and on weekends, Hulett listened to the preachings of W. C. Patton. Like E. D. Nixon in Montgomery, Patton was a true civil rights pioneer. In 1947, he became the third executive director of the Alabama NAACP after years of escorting his black neighbors to the Jefferson County courthouse to register to vote. On numerous occasions he was arrested just for telling his neighbors that voting was their right as citizens. "Even before we ever heard of Martin Luther King Jr.," Hulett said years later, "W. C. Patton talked to us about our rights as human beings and workers and people of this planet. I was threatened by white bosses over and over again for telling my fellow workers about Mr. Patton and about the NAACP.

"You talk about a hard town, I tell you Birmingham in the 1940s and '50s was a hard town. A man would work his hands to the bone and get next-to-nothing take-home pay. When I joined Local 1489 of the foundry workers' union, I figured I was there for good. And let me tell you, that wasn't a good feeling. It was like I was being held in a place worse than hell. But, dammit, I was going to make that hell the best hell I could make it." Hulett was deceptively slight and less than six feet tall. He looked small but was tough as nails physically and mentally.

And when he joined the NAACP, he said, "there was an enlightenment that came from 'do unto others.' In Pratt City, near the steel mills of north Birmingham, black folks were proud to have jobs. The big white bosses took advantage of the people who slaved for them. It was a rough existence, but I had it better than a lot of them. I stretched my muscles as best I could."

Following Patton's direction, Hulett worked to expand the NAACP. He went door to door in his neighborhood, repeating the rights talk he had heard from Patton, telling people they could register to vote, raising money to build a playground for black children, and creating general community support for the organization.

In 1956, Alabama attorney general John Patterson filed a lawsuit in circuit court in Montgomery. As part of the suit, Patterson asked that the NAACP turn over a list of members and their addresses. As membership chairman of the local NAACP, the Reverend Fred Shuttlesworth was holding a meeting at the headquarters on Fourth Avenue North in downtown Birmingham when a deputy appeared with an injunction. On the spot, Shuttlesworth refused. In Montgomery, the judge ruled the group in contempt and fined it ten thousand dollars. After the court's citation, the attorney general declared the NAACP outlawed and insinuated that it was communist inspired.

Early the morning after the ruling, Shuttlesworth sat straight up in bed, thinking that he would call a mass meeting and would preach against the court and its ruling. His friend, attorney Arthur Shores, warned him against such a demonstration. "It's an injunction," he said. "You could go to jail." Still, Shuttlesworth insisted. His friend, Reverend R. L. Alford, offered his large church, Sardis Baptist.

Two weeks after the NAACP was outlawed, Hulett attended the Sardis Baptist Church on Tuesday, June 5, 1956. As he listened to Shuttlesworth's fiery sermon denouncing the demons of Alabama's all-white law enforcement and legal system, Hulett was moved. "Hearing him, my heart beat heavy in my chest," Hulett remembered. "I'd heard a lot of firebrand country preachers. I'd listened to W. C. Patton's calm voice telling us what we needed to do to make ourselves upright citizens. But nothing moved me like Fred Shuttlesworth's voice shaking the rafters of Sardis Baptist. He was a tall man with a great, black, expressive face. He had long, long fingers that gripped that podium and looked like he was going to rip it out of its frame. He leaned so far forward, I thought he was surely coming off the pulpit. His voice shook as he said, 'We'll not rest until we walk the streets and ride the buses as free people. Freedom is what we're fighting for. Freedom is what we're going to gain, while we gain it by nonviolent means. We will march. We will hold our banners high. Not one white person will be harmed. Not one hair on the head of one white person will be harmed. If anyone gets arrested, it'll be me. If anybody goes to jail, it'll be me. If anyone suffers, it'll be me. If anybody gets killed, it'll be me.'"

Within days, Hulett joined Shuttlesworth's new organization, Alabama Christian Movement for Human Rights. "I had been in the presence of the reverend a few times. I'd heard him preach. I'd been caught up in his words. When he talked, lightning flashed in the minds of men and women and little children. It was a lightning that brought about a joy, a release, a feeling of warmth inside, but it also shook you to action. You wanted to jump up and holler out and go do something right then and there. When I sat at his feet and listened to him, when he looked into my face, I knew that some day soon I'd be going home to Lowndes County and carry his teachings with me.

"You talk about a man of courage, I tell you that the Reverend Shuttlesworth didn't have one ounce of scared in him. His bones were tough as iron girders. His heart was strong as leather. Even to this day, when I think about him, I know that I'll never be the man he was, but he gave me something to stride toward."

For two years the NAACP did not operate in Alabama. In 1958 justice John Harlan wrote a unanimous opinion for the U.S. Supreme Court, ruling that the Alabama court had violated the constitutional rights of the NAACP protected by the due process clause of the Fourth Amendment.

On Christmas night of 1956, as Shuttlesworth talked with a deacon of his church in the living room of his small house, a bomb exploded beneath him. Suddenly the preacher began to fall through the floor. Shuttlesworth later told Hulett, "The sons of bitches were after me; it was the Ku Klux Klan. For a while, we thought they were just down there in Montgomery. Now, all of a sudden, I knew they were everywhere. But I did not despair, even at that moment when I was falling. I understood that God was taking care of me. If there had ever been an ounce of fear in me, I lost it after that."

On the day after Shuttlesworth's living room was bombed, Hulett arrived at the Shuttlesworth home shortly before nightfall. In his hands Hulett carried his twelve-gauge shotgun. Seeing him, Shuttlesworth said there was no need for the gun. "Nonviolence," he said. "We're teaching nonviolence."

"I won't use it," Hulett said. "Unless absolutely necessary." That night he sat in his car parked at the curb outside the house. He kept the gun nearby. It was a quiet night.

When Shuttlesworth called another mass meeting, an unidentified caller said the Ku Klux Klan would blow the church "to kingdom come."

Hearing about the threat, Hulett said the intruders "will have to come through me to get to the reverend and his flock." Before the meeting, Hulett and several friends searched the sanctuary, the basement, and the grounds. Finding it safe, Hulett locked all of the entrances and exits. Although it violated the fire codes, he said later, he knew "no uninvited guests would be sneaking in." He planted himself in his car outside near the front door. Throughout the meeting, he kept watch.

Outside the home of African American attorney Arthur Shores, Hulett was keeping watch while Shores, Shuttlesworth, and others were meeting. As Hulett watched, a car with its lights off eased up to the curb. When he recognized the car as a police cruiser, Hulett nodded to the officer. "We were just checking on you," the policeman said. Hulett recalled, "What I thought was: Yeah, you're checking on me all right. You're checking to see what damage you can do. Back in those days, I wouldn't trust a white policeman two feet. As far as I was concerned in Bombingham, they were all Ku Klux."

✮

In 1959, Hulett returned home to Lowndes County. His father was sick. He needed help on the small farm. John's grandfather, Hilliard Hulett, was born a slave on a Black Belt plantation. After emancipation he had eked out a living and saved enough cash to purchase a small piece of land they now farmed.

Back home, Hulett hoped to put to work the teachings of W. C. Patton and Fred Shuttlesworth. As far as Hulett was concerned, it was time someone brought civil rights to Lowndes County in a meaningful way.

Through the early 1960s, Hulett and his black neighbors talked about civil rights, but John noticed that most of them were still afraid of local whites. Through the years, the white landowners had repeatedly threatened the blacks. To Hulett, as he watched and remembered, the threat of financial intimidation hung in the air like moisture on a muggy August night. The threats had become more frequent and more severe in recent years. Blacks told stories about the white men riding with the KKK. Those had been the tales that threaded gossip for years.

According to journalist Frye Gaillard in *Cradle of Freedom*, Hulett and several friends met one winter night in 1965 at the home of the Reverend J. C. Lawson. "There were five or six of them that night, an intrepid handful who talked about the power that went with the ballot. They lived in a county where 81 percent of the people were black, but every instrument of power, political and economic, was in the hands of the whites. The average black citizen subsisted on $985 a year, and if that reality was unlikely to change, the political system was a whole different issue."

As the men talked, Gaillard wrote, "John Hulett noticed a curious thing. The Reverend Lawson, who was elderly and blind, kept talking in a whisper, and Hulett realized after a while that the old man was terrified. With the nearest white person two miles away, he was still so afraid of being overheard that he could barely bring himself to speak aloud.

"It soon became apparent that his paranoia was not out of place. When they met the next time at a different location, a white man crept to a corner by the chimney, and they found him there when the meeting dispersed." Now, they surmised, there was no reason to meet in secret. Hulett called for a meeting of black citizens. It was agreed that they would all register to vote. At the courthouse, probate judge Harrell Hammonds, a landowner who had been friendly with many blacks, told them where to find the registrar, but they were still turned away. No reason was offered.

Two weeks later they tried again. With even more people wanting to register, the elderly preacher who had displayed fright, Lawson, led the way with Hulett by his side. Hulett and Lawson were registered. They became the first black voters in Lowndes County in more than sixty years.

After he registered, Hulett took it upon himself to act as a one-man team to educate his neighbors. In the late afternoons and early evenings, Hulett drove his old truck across the rolling hills of Lowndes County, stopping at every little unpainted shack or double-wide trailer or converted barn where people lived. He sat on front porches from the cotton fields near Fort Deposit to the bottomlands along the Alabama River. He talked about the power of the vote. "If we don't vote, we might as well stay in the clutches of white slaveowners," he said. "We do all the work on these farms, and the white folks have got all the power. It's because they've got the vote and they use it." When the people complained that they had been to Hayneville to the courthouse and had gone to the registrar but had been turned away, Hulett wrinkled his face and shook his head, looking pained. "You've got to keep on trying," he said. "When you're turned down, go back. Go back again and again. Let them know that you will not take no for an answer. At some point, they're going to get tired of it. They're going to give in. When they do, you'll have the vote. Then you'll use it."

When young Jonathan Daniels was murdered in broad daylight at the Cash Store in Hayneville and Thomas L. Coleman was found not guilty by an all-white jury, Hulett reckoned the local whites would think they had a license to kill. Quietly but effectively, keeping his twelve-gauge shotgun on the front seat of his pickup, Hulett put out the word: "Kill one of us, we'll kill three of you." And when the Ku Klux Klan saw him with his gun, "they knew what it meant," he said more than once.

"It's the one thing they understand. It doesn't take a real smart person not to want to get himself shot."

In the summer of 1965, when SNCC arrived, the group of student protestors was represented by Bob Mants, who had been in Dallas County with John Lewis, and Stokely Carmichael, a slender, well-spoken young man whose intensity had only heightened during the previous year in Mississippi. Although others, like a local black storekeeper and a local farmer, warned the young people to stay off the rural roads after dark, Hulett offered no advice. He believed they came to do a job. If it took moving about in dangerous places, so be it. When they needed to go to Fort Deposit or Hayneville at night, Hulett would often drive them or accompany them. By now, Hulett was instrumental in forming the Lowndes County Freedom Organization, patterned after his hero Shuttlesworth's group in Birmingham. "We thought of ourselves as the center for black power," Hulett said. "Not in the way Stokely came to see it, but believing in ourselves and our voting power as more and more of us were registered. We also believed in our money power when we sold our goods at market, when the merchants wanted us to buy from them. After all, we were by far the largest percent of the population of this part of the world. If they did not treat us right, we wouldn't buy."

In the years the *Courier* wrote about him, Hulett and the LCFO that became the Black Panther political party grew and became more and more important. The reporters described the voting education seminars that were often held in a tent near White Hall. At one time more than twenty tents were erected on a high ground that became known as Freedom City. In the months after Stokely Carmichael arrived on the scene, the persona of the LCFO changed in minds of some people. To some observers it became a group of armed militants wandering around the Black Belt looking for trouble. Freedom City was their hideout. Mike Lottman and others with the *Courier* knew better. And Hulett knew better as he watched them mature before his eyes. What he liked more than anything else about them was their effectiveness. They worked hard. They walked into the county courthouse with the citizens they had been teaching. They stood by while the men and women registered to vote.

After they were registered, the SNCC volunteers who had been sent to Lowndes County by the Atlanta office taught the citizens about democracy, about their rights, and about the ballot.

Hulett knew that most of the young volunteers were in Lowndes County for a short time. They would stay for a few months, perhaps a year, and two years at most. For Stokely Carmichael, Lowndes was a training camp. Hulett knew it and understood.

While Carmichael was learning, Hulett and his people would benefit from their lessons. When a young California law student named Huey Newton came, Hulett was not totally impressed. "As far as I was concerned, Newton was using us. He was using Stokely and Mants and the others. Stokely had come up with the idea of using a black panther as their symbol, and I thought that was ridiculous. Why wave a flag like that in the face of the white people, no matter what you thought of those white people? We had to live with them, which Stokely and Huey Newton and the others did not have to do. They'd go back out West or up North and live their lives there. We were all going to stay here. Here was home."

In 1966, John Hulett, along with a number of other blacks across the state, ran for sheriff. He was defeated. When he examined the ballots, he realized that his people still had a long way to go. A good number had been registered, but that number was not as strong as it should be and would be. Also, he realized, the white landowners were still lording it over many of the black tenants and sharecroppers. Although the blacks had registered, the whites were telling them how to vote. At one polling place on election day, Hulett overheard two blacks talking about how certain whites in the courthouse knew how they voted and would report back to their white bosses. Hulett knew that his people needed more education and should be aware that their votes were private.

The *Southern Courier* covered the campaigns at every rally in every small crossroads in Alabama. Only one black candidate for sheriff won: Lucius Amerson in Macon County. When the thirty-two-year-old Korean War vet was inaugurated in Tuskegee, Meg Gale wrote the headline story for page one in the *Courier*. Jim Peppler shot the four-column photograph. In the same election, Fred Gray fell short by three hundred votes, most from absentee ballots counted after polls were closed, in his attempt to become the state's first black legislator since Reconstruction.

Two years later, Dr. John Cashin, the wealthy black dentist from Huntsville who had introduced Chuck Morgan to Dave McGlathery, founded the National Democratic Party of Alabama. Cashin talked with Hulett about being an NDPA candidate. Hulett agreed. Cashin's people moved into Lowndes County to teach the voters how to mark their ballots for the NDPA. In Greene County, Thomas E. Gilmore, a young black activist, also agreed to run for office. This time around, Gilmore and Hulett won their races for sheriff. Although the *Courier* did not exist by 1968, it didn't hurt that reporters at the paper had written about these two men in their political infancy. Most of their constituents across the Black Belt had gotten to know Hulett and Gilmore in the pages of the weekly newspaper. Now they were the law.

✳

When he had still been considering running for sheriff in 1968, Hulett was walking across the lawn of the courthouse in Hayneville when a lanky white man named Thomas Coleman approached him. Hulett gazed into the face he had always thought sour and disgusted as Coleman smiled and asked Hulett to ride with him to Lowndesboro about twenty miles north on a lonely road across rolling hills where cattle grazed. Considering it, Hulett nodded.

They got into Coleman's pickup and started out. It was not that long ago that Coleman had been charged with the coldblooded afternoon murder of the young Episcopalian Jonathan Daniels. An all-white jury acquitted the man whom the black citizens considered an out-and-out racist.

As they rode north, Coleman asked what Hulett and his people planned.

Without hesitation, Hulett said he planned to run for sheriff. "And I'm going to win," he added.

As quickly, Coleman replied that he would be leaving the county if Hulett was elected.

Riding back south, Hulett told Coleman, "When you were in charge, we didn't leave."

"When we got right outside Hayneville, I told him that our world was changing," Hulett recalled. "'We got some power now. We got the vote. Our folks are learning that they can take care of their own. We're going to change things a whole lot in the courthouses across Alabama.'

"Tom just nodded. His expression didn't change. When I looked back, I saw him driving up the highway toward his house. Before I got into my truck, I looked over toward the store where he'd shot young Daniels. It was dark and lonely in the shadows, the sun going down over the tree tops. It looked kind of eerie to me, remembering."

As he had promised, John Hulett finally became the sheriff of all the people in Lowndes County when he was elected in the fall of 1970. As Hasan Kwame Jeffries points out in his book, *Bloody Lowndes*, the rural county between Montgomery and Dallas "had always been a dangerous place for African Americans, but during Hulett's first term of office he improved conditions considerably. As chief law enforcement officer, he not only ended police brutality, but also stopped random acts of racial violence perpetrated by ordinary white citizens. The key to his success was his willingness to arrest whites for breaking the law, something many people believed a black person would be afraid to do. African Americans were grateful for these reforms, and to preserve them they voted ten to one in favor of Hulett in the 1974 primary."

Several years later, Coleman called Sheriff Hulett in the middle of the night. "I didn't know what to think when I heard his voice. He said he'd heard on the police radio where an eighteen-wheeler had had a wreck down on I-65 near Fort Deposit. 'It's a helluva mess, they say,' he told me. Then he volunteered to go with me down there and help clean up the mess. I told him, 'Let's go,' and I took off, picked him up, and we went down there and worked near-about all night, cleaning up the stuff that had spilled out of that big truck."

Tom Coleman never left Lowndes County.

When Coleman died in June 1997, probate judge John Hulett was one of his pallbearers, laying him to rest in Hayneville soil.

16

SOUTHERN POVERTY LAW CENTER

Since early childhood, Morris Dees had proven time and again that he was what Southern country people called "a real go-getter." And when he decided to plan, organize, and develop the Southern Poverty Law Center, he started with a seed that he knew from the beginning would grow into a mighty tree. After all, he always thought big.

With Joe Levin Jr. at his side, Dees began meticulously planning a nonprofit legal and educational organization. Not only would the lawyer side of his persona be extended, the preacher part of him would be satisfied as well.

In the years ahead, not only would SPLC file lawsuits, it would develop educational programs like Teaching Tolerance, designed to reduce prejudice among the nation's children. Dees said that Levin, who rapidly matured into a fine quick-witted trial lawyer, operated like a brilliant tennis pro, never letting anything get by him. Together, Dees and Levin hired Howard Mandell, a Rhode Island native and Georgetown Law graduate who had clerked for judge Frank Johnson. Mandell heard about Johnson from Chuck Morgan, who had spoken at Georgetown about his experience as a civil rights attorney. At dinner with Morgan, Mandell heard more about the judge. "I started reading some of his decisions and opinions, and I said this is the man I wanted to clerk for if I could get the position," Mandell told Jack Bass, author of *Taming the Storm: The Life and Times of Judge Frank M. Johnson Jr. and the South's Fight over Civil Rights*. Morgan wrote a letter of recommendation, and Mandell was accepted. With Johnson, Mandell had been involved with many major civil rights cases.

From the outset, Dees and Levin let it be known that they would back down from no man or organization. They never seemed to mind being called traitors by the white establishment in their hometown.

To do battle for poverty against well-heeled hate groups and government entities, the Southern Poverty Law Center would need ample funding. To provide it, they hired an expert in direct mail from Doubleday Books, one of the largest publishers in the world.

To make the Law Center instantly viable, they needed a headliner to top the list of names on its blue-ribbon board. The first that came to mind was Julian Bond, the tall, slender, movie-star handsome legislator from Atlanta. In the fall of 1965, he was elected to the Georgia General Assembly. In January 1966, white legislators refused to allow him to take the oath of office because he supported an anti–Vietnam War statement issued by the Student Nonviolent Coordinating Committee, for which he was communications director. Overnight, Julian Bond became a household name in civil rights circles. Soon he was the best-known black political figure in the United States. He was interviewed on *Meet the Press*. Colleges across the country invited him to speak on campus. His soft-spoken, gentle, elegant manner made him instantly popular among liberals.

Five days after the Georgia lawmakers adjourned in the spring of 1966, a special election was held to fill the legislative seat. After Bond received 100 percent of the votes, the legislative body again refused to allow him to take the oath of office. Chuck Morgan took up his cause and filed a lawsuit on his behalf. After the U.S. District Court ruled against Bond, the U.S. Supreme Court unanimously found that "legislators have an obligation to take positions on controversial political questions." By then, Bond was represented by another lawyer, but across the South his name was linked with Morgan's.

Following the court's order, the Georgia General Assembly seated Bond. In the summer of 1968, his name was again splashed across national media when he became the first African American to be nominated as vice president at the Democratic National Convention. Morris Dees was one of millions who were impressed by Bond's "powerful, eloquent speech" declining the honor.

By the time Dees and Levin asked him to take the position of president of the Southern Poverty Law Center, Julian Bond represented strength and integrity as well as quiet brilliance. To serve on the President's Advisory Council, they picked sheriff Lucius Amerson; legal scholar Tony Amsterdam; Greenville, Mississippi, editor Hodding Carter III of the *Delta Democrat-Times*; Charles Evers, brother of slain civil rights activist Medgar Evers; Fannie Lou Hamer of Mississippi; John Lewis of SNCC; and Chuck Morgan.

"It was a great group with a great plan from the beginning," said Morgan. "Morris Dees and Joe Levin were terrific young men who took over the proposition to rid the South of its evil inner self. We needed young people to take over the fight, and they did so with great fervor and virtue. They became great legal warriors, moving the poor, underprivileged minority out of a time of fear into a time of freedom." As far as Dees and Levin were concerned, they had the cream of the crop as SPLC's president and his advisory council. It would be tested in their first mailing to a list of twenty-five thousand prospective contributors.

In the first letter, they outlined the case of a poor black man who had been indicted for murder on circumstantial evidence by an all-white grand jury in Montgomery County. During an initial hearing, when Dees requested bond for his client, Jimmy Lee McCloud, the judge denied bond and indicated that McCloud might get the death penalty. When the judge's statement was published in a local newspaper, Dees and Levin picked it up and used it. The letter asking for funds to defend McCloud and keep him out of the electric chair was enormously successful.

Already known for their fearless audacity, Levin and Dees had filed several lawsuits that challenged the "Southern way of life." With *Nixon v. Brewer*, they attempted to restructure the Alabama Legislature into single-member districts to give poor blacks and whites a stronger voice in the electoral process. The named plaintiff in the case was Edgar Daniel Nixon, already widely known as a civil rights leader. When they filed the suit, Alabama's legislative districts had been drawn into large, white-majority, multimember districts. Basically, the situation resulted in keeping blacks from being elected to the legislature, even though one-fourth of the state's population was African American.

To fight the case, Dees and Levin traveled to Indiana, where an attorney had filed a similar lawsuit and lost. They wanted to find out why.

While visiting the Indiana attorney, they met U.S. senator George McGovern, who was preparing to run for president.

Subsequently, Dees arranged for McGovern to make a contribution to his friend Fred Gray's campaign for the state legislature. When Gray won, he became the first black legislator elected to the Alabama Legislature since Reconstruction.

In the meantime, Dees solidified his relationship with McGovern by writing a seven-page fundraising letter that drew an unheard-of 15 percent response. In Washington, he and his wife, Maureene, rubbed shoulders with the likes of Candice Bergen, Warren Beatty, and other high-profile celebrities who backed McGovern's candidacy. None of these friendships hurt Dees or SPLC. Indeed, it gave him and the organization a national base they did not have previously. Most found Dees to be a good old Southern boy, pleasant and affable but also displaying strong resolve in his actions.

Back in Alabama, after the unsuccessful 1972 presidential election, Dees and Levin took up their defense of Jimmy McCloud. Charged with killing a young white schoolteacher after she found him burglarizing her house, McCloud was uneducated, poor, and facing the death penalty, which both attorneys knew had been unfairly applied to blacks and poor whites. Based on the judge's pretrial comments, they sought and received a change of venue to Birmingham, where they raised enough doubts about the evidence that the jury rendered a verdict of second-degree murder. McCloud was sentenced to ten years in prison.

The McCloud case and *Nixon v. Brewer*, which they also won, became the bedrock on which SPLC's reputation was built. In his autobiography, *A Season for Justice*, written with Steve Fiffer and later published as *A Lawyer's Journey* by the American Bar Association, Dees wrote, "On its face, this was just another criminal case, but like other cases that came into the Center, it turned into much more." He reflected that "gradually more black faces appeared not only in the jury box but in the state legislature.

"Where else was power institutionalized? In the state's police power. A case to integrate the Alabama State Troopers arose when an old friend of mine told me he felt he had been denied the opportunity to join the troopers because he was black. In its thirty-seven years, the agency had never had one black trooper. The all-white force was a symbol of brutal racism that had gripped Alabama for so long. This was the first case where the Center received national attention, and we again won (although the state dragged its feet an unbelievable fifteen years until the U.S. Supreme Court settled the matter in 1987)."

When Dees's friend Eddie Callahan came to SPLC offices and sat down and told Dees about being fined by a justice of the peace, he added that in the State of Alabama justices of the peace received a portion of every fine they levied against a defendant. Researching, Dees discovered his information was correct. Remembering back to his time as a teenager when his father sent him to help their friend and neighbor Clarence Williams, it was no wonder the old JP reacted as he did. As Dees's father had said, the justice kept "two sets of books."

Dees filed *Callahan v. Sanders*, a class action suit that took on the Alabama fine system. As a result, federal judges issued an injunction declaring the system illegal. For his own satisfaction, Dees drove out to Mount Meigs, found Clarence Williams on his front porch, and told him what had happened. Williams smiled and said, "Things are changing."

Early in the 1970s, Dees questioned his beliefs about the death penalty. *Do some people deserve it?* he asked himself. If the death penalty is enforced, the recidivism rate is nonexistent. But then he examined the defendants who were sentenced to death. Across the board, a huge percentage were poor whites and poor blacks. They did not have the money to properly defend themselves. Knowing this, Dees had no problem opposing capital punishment.

Through the early 1970s, SPLC attorneys traveled to North Carolina to defend the Tarboro Three—Jesse L. Walston, Vernon L. Brown, and Bobby R. Hines—who faced the death penalty. They wrote SPLC lawyer Chuck Abernathy, saying they had been convicted and faced death "because of injustice and prejudice."

Dees and Abernathy, who had also been a clerk for Judge Johnson, carried the case to the North Carolina Supreme Court, which ordered a new trial nearly a year after they had begun.

Through an exhaustive investigation, following leads that led them to the roommate of the alleged victim of the Tarboro Three, they found witnesses who showed that the rape case against the trio was not as clear cut as it had seemed. In fact, it became obvious that one major witness had lied. Certainly, legal experts said later, no single attorney in private practice would have the time or the money to spend on such an investigation.

A deal was struck. The men who had been on death row when SPLC took the case would serve ninety more days and then go free. Dees reflected, "If what we did was obvious, the story is even more frightening. It suggests other innocent people sit on death row, the victims of inadequate legal representation. How many have died?"

Also in North Carolina, Dees and SPLC joined flamboyant Durham attorney Jerry Paul in the defense of twenty-year-old Joan Little, a convicted burglar charged with stabbing a sixty-two-year-old jailer, Clarence Alligood, eleven times with an ice pick that he kept in his desk drawer. She had fled, hid out for a week, and finally gave herself up, saying she had killed in self-defense after Alligood had sexually assaulted her.

While incarcerated for three months on the burglary charge, she said, Alligood brought her sandwiches, gave her cigarettes, and talked with her. At 3:30 A.M., he stood outside her cell and "told me he had been nice to me and that it was time that I be nice to him, and that he wanted me to give him some pussy." When she refused, she said, he took off his shoes, unlocked her cell, stepped inside, began feeling her breasts, and put his hand between her legs. While she cried, he took off her nightgown and stepped out of his pants.

With an ice pick pointed at her, she said, the six-foot-tall, two-hundred-pound man forced her to perform oral sex. When he dropped the pick to the floor, she reached for it. They struggled. Then the five-foot-two-inch, one-hundred-pound woman hit him with the pick, and he fell back, she said. She grabbed up some clothes and ran, leaving Alligood bleeding on the floor of the cell. "If I'd known he was going to die," she told her lawyers, "I wouldn't have left him like that."

After Little was captured, district attorney William Griffin Jr. told the grand jury that she had lured Alligood to her cell, seduced him, and stabbed him to death with the ice pick she had earlier stolen from his desk drawer.

Little was a poor black woman raised in a shantytown in rural Beaufort County. The oldest of nine children, she quit school at fifteen. She moved north to live with relatives while seeking a job in the Philadelphia area. She returned, attended school again, but soon left to find a job. It was not long before she was arrested and charged with burglarizing a trailer park. Now she was charged with murder and faced the death penalty.

In *A Season for Justice* Dees wrote, "Joe Levin and I had created the Center to take on cases like this. The trial promised to raise a number of important legal and social issues: the right of a woman to defend herself against a sexual attack; prison conditions for women (evidence was growing that sexual abuse of women inmates was a national epidemic); the discriminatory use of the death penalty against poor people and blacks; selection processes that failed to produce juries of true peers; and the right of a poor person to an adequate defense. But as important as these issues were, one motivation overrode all: we had to save Joan Little's life."

Again, it took time and money. Dees, Levin, and SPLC raised money to pay for expert witnesses and provided a strong and thorough investigation. They interviewed potential witnesses. They combed the Beaufort County jail for any possible evidence. They found Annie Jenkins, who'd been in the jail in 1974 and who said Alligood had tried to feel her breasts and other parts of her body.

The first witness, a sheriff's deputy, testified that Alligood was found dead in Joan Little's cell at about 3:55 A.M. Under cross-examination from Dees, the deputy said Alligood should not have been in a female prisoner's cell. Next, Dr. Harry Carpenter, who had pronounced Alligood dead, testified that the victim was holding an ice pick and that he could "clearly see Alligood's penis." As Dees showed the doctor the medical report that mentioned sperm on Alligood's leg, he asked, "How did it get there?" Carpenter answered, "I assumed it indicated sexual activity."

Earlier, Beverly King, the sheriff's clerk, who doubled as a radio operator, had told Dees that Alligood asked her the location of the other two deputies at 2:55 A.M. "Is that unusual?" Dees had asked her at the time. It was not unusual for him to ask, she said, but it *was* unusual for him "not to request anything." However, when she testified during the trial, King said she "did not remember" making such a statement to Dees.

When Dees questioned King about this assertion, King told the district attorney that Dees had asked her to lie about what had happened, and the trial judge dismissed him from the case. Immediately, Dees was charged with attempted subordination of perjury.

Dees telephoned Levin in Montgomery and informed him of the setup, and Levin called their friend Chuck Morgan, who said he would be in Raleigh the next morning.

When Dees discovered that if convicted of the felony charge he could be sentenced to ten years in prison, he was more than eager to clear his name. He went directly to the sheriff, who had originally been the one to recommend that he talk with Beverly King. Dees asked the sheriff for a sworn statement that Dees had not asked the clerk to lie. The sheriff said he couldn't give him an affidavit. "If I do that, I could never get elected again in this county. But I promise you that I'll testify at your trial."

Dees responded, "Sheriff, think about your own family. If you were in a fix like this, think how it would affect you and your children. I'm sure they love and respect you. I know you're a Christian man. You know what's right and what's wrong. You know this woman has changed her story."

After an hour, the sheriff agreed to sign the affidavit. After Dees read it to him, the sheriff said his clerk had told him more than that. More details were added, making it clear that Dees never asked King to lie. Then the sheriff signed.

In the meantime, Chuck Morgan and two ACLU assistants, Neil Bradley and Norman Siegel, were preparing a federal lawsuit against the trial judge in the Joan Little case. It charged that judge Hamilton H. Hobgood had violated Dees's civil rights. In doing so, the judge had also violated Dees's client's constitutional rights.

Working behind the scenes in his usual manner, Chuck Morgan took copies of Beverly King's testimony and the sheriff's affidavit to his friend Claude Sitton, editor of the *Raleigh News and Observer*. An old friend from days when Sitton was the *New York Times* bureau chief in Atlanta, the newsman listened and read. Responding on Sunday morning, his editorial read: "Judge Hamilton H. Hobgood's actions in summarily excluding one of Joan Little's defense attorneys from the case and then refusing to reconsider that step are regrettable. The appearance of injustice is compounded by the grandstanding of Burley Mitchell Jr., the Wake County district attorney. He raced in with a felony charge of subordination of perjury against Dees. The nation and the world may be pardoned for believing that Dees is the hapless victim of hometown justice."

In the aftermath, Dees visited Burley Mitchell, who agreed to drop the charge if Dees would withdraw his federal suit and withdraw as Joan Little's counsel of record. When Dees agreed, he was allowed to work from an office near the courthouse for the remainder of the trial.

After the defendant's two days of testimony, followed by a pitiful showing from the state, the jury deliberated less than ninety minutes before finding Joan Little not guilty.

Soon after the Little verdict, Joe Levin became chief trial counsel for SPLC while Dees spent time in Atlanta, where he assisted in raising funds for Jimmy Carter's presidential campaign. After Carter won the primaries, Dees returned to Montgomery. Levin moved to Washington, working with the campaign on legal matters. And when Carter won the presidency, Levin was named chief counsel to the National Highway Traffic Safety Administration.

President Carter appointed Maureene Dees to the National Endowment for the Arts and invited the couple to many White House functions. In the meantime, Dees led the SPLC into a new day of progressive litigation, but he knew the Ku Klux Klan was always lurking in the background.

★

Early in 1978, when a severely retarded black man named Tommy Lee Hines was arrested and charged with the rape of a white woman in Decatur, in north Alabama, a court-appointed attorney represented him. Subsequently, an all-white jury convicted Hines after a trial during which white people wearing KKK polo shirts sat in the audience and robed Klansmen stood outside the courthouse. Hines was sentenced to thirty years in prison.

With the trial and verdict fresh on their minds, the KKK flexed its muscles. Imperial wizard Bill Wilkinson stated, "We are providing vigilante law for Decatur." Rallies were held, the verdict was praised, crosses were burned. Known Klansmen surrounded a mixed-race couple in a Decatur diner and threatened them. Later, the Klansmen said they were doing work the police should be doing.

The black community was outraged. Leaders believed it was gross injustice. If Hines had been white, they said, he would have been hospitalized in a mental institution. The cries for a delivery from this evil reached nationwide attention when thousands, led by the Reverend Joseph Lowery of the Southern Christian Leadership Conference, marched on the streets of Decatur.

A year after Hines was arrested, several hundred demonstrators chanting "Free Tommy Lee Hines" marched on the downtown streets. They were met by an equal number of hooded Ku Klux Klansmen led by titan Ray Steele of the Northern Alabama Klan and exalted cyclops David Kelso of the local klavern. Only a meager line of city police separated the two groups when gunfire erupted. Two black marchers and two Klansmen were wounded. Four Klansmen were arrested. Among the demonstrators charged with crimes was forty-nine-year-old city maintenance worker Curtis Robinson, who was arrested for assault with intent to murder Klansman David Kelso.

When a lawyer for Legal Service Corporation called Dees and told him about the defendant, saying Legal Service could not take criminal cases, Dees said he and SPLC were overloaded with work and couldn't give Robinson the time necessary for his defense. Then the attorney put Robinson on the phone. The man made such an impassioned plea for his help, Dees responded that he would go to Decatur and look into the case.

Early in June 1979, Dees, SPLC legal director John Carroll, and legal aide Bill Stanton traveled to Decatur, a hotbed of Klan activity in the early twentieth century after the first resurgence of the Klan and later when the Scottsboro Boys were tried in the Morgan County courthouse.

The SPLC team met with Robinson, a six-foot, trim, outgoing black man who was raised in the area and was known by many people in the town of about twenty thousand. He had worked in city hall for years. He told the story of his innocence. On the Saturday of the demonstrations he planned to take his wife, Eva, and their five children on an outing on the Tennessee River for the long Memorial Day weekend. Although he was relatively poor, he had managed to buy a small second-hand motorboat he dubbed *Red Goose*, his own nickname around town.

After the car was packed, he decided he would check the air-conditioning at city hall before taking off. With Eva and the children, he drove toward downtown. Soon they found themselves surrounded by marchers. By the time they reached the center of town, he could not pull to the side and turn around, he said.

Within minutes, chaos erupted when the KKK met the marchers. The hooded men began hitting his car with clubs. When one tried to open his door, Robinson reached for his pistol and pulled it out. At the same time, several Klansmen jerked him from the car. His pistol fired several times. After he was beaten, he managed to break away. He ran several blocks, fell to the ground, and was found by demonstrators who took him home. When he found his car, it had been dented badly. One of the tires had been shot and a headlight smashed. His family had fled to safety. They were upset but unharmed. The next day he went to city hall to find a policeman he knew, but the man was too busy to see him. On the following Monday, the policeman came to Robinson's house and arrested him.

After hearing his story, Dees shook Robinson's hand. SPLC would represent him. On the drive south from Decatur to Montgomery, Dees talked. His mind worked quickly. Such talk was often his way after he heard the story of a mistreated person. He thought aloud. He wanted aerial photographs of the town. SPLC would conduct an extensive investigation. He wanted names of every marcher, every Klansman, every policeman who was at the site of the clash. He wanted Bill Stanton to find every witness. He wanted newspaper clippings starting with Hines's arrest, ballistics reports from every shot fired that Saturday afternoon, every photograph taken of everyone involved. It was a play-it-for-all-it's-worth modus operandi with which SPLC personnel had become familiar. When it came to preparation, Dees left no stone or leaf unturned. He knew that under there somewhere was the truth.

Several weeks later, Dees returned to Decatur. With Robinson by his side, he visited district attorney Mike Moebes, who called in sergeant Kenneth Collier, the police department's investigator of the incident. Sitting in Moebes's office, Robinson repeated the story he had told Dees. When he finished, Moebes asked if Dees really believed Robinson's story. Dees said he had no reason not to believe his client.

Collier showed photographs: Robinson outside his car surrounded by marchers and Robinson with a gun in his hand about twenty feet from Kelso, who had been shot. Next, Collier took out an incident report from officer Marlon Owens, who had worked with the Decatur Police Department for fourteen years. From the parking lot of an abandoned service station, Owens watched the demonstrators marching toward town. In one of several cars following the marchers, Robinson raised a pistol, waved it, and said, "I'm gonna get me a couple of 'em today." Owens wrote that he called out, "Red Goose, you better get your butt back home. There's gonna be trouble." With that, the DA said he would be seeking a felony conviction for assault with intent to murder.

Still, when they were alone, Robinson insisted that he was innocent. He swore that he had not seen Owens that Saturday and that the conversation never happened.

Back in Montgomery at SPLC headquarters in an old dentist office on South Hull Street, Morris Dees told his people to continue their thorough investigation. In the meantime, the KKK continued to make itself visible in Decatur. In late June, according to the Decatur *Daily*, several hundred Klansmen gathered in a large field and burned a sixty-six-foot-high cross.

As SPLC lawyers and aides worked in Montgomery, Moebes worked against them in Decatur. As they were preparing depositions, he appeared and handed John Carroll a court order barring SPLC from questioning police officers. A frantic Robinson called and said he was being sued for $750,000 by Klansman David Kelso. Dees tried to calm him, saying SPLC would defend him.

In the meantime, the conviction of Tommy Lee Hines was overturned by the Alabama Court of Criminal Appeals in March 1980. It ruled that Hines was mentally incompetent to waive his legal rights. His confession was inadmissible. And he was hospitalized for psychiatric evaluation.

Soon, the FBI issued a report of its investigation into the Saturday clash between demonstrators and the KKK. As in most of the FBI reports, most names were blacked out. However, the FBI did not black out Curtis Robinson's name. Immediately, Carroll asked for a report that had not been blackened. The FBI refused. The SPLC sued in federal court, but before it could be heard, the Robinson case was scheduled to begin. At trial, once again, a black defendant was to be tried by an all-white jury.

At trial, the defense introduced a photograph showing Kelso standing in front of Robinson's car with a raised club like a baseball bat, prior to the time when Robinson fired his gun.

The defense found a video taken by an on-the-scene reporter from WAFF-TV Huntsville. Looking at it frame by frame, they watched as Kelso and other Klansmen rushed the demonstrators and Robinson's car with his wife and children inside.

The first witness for the prosecution was Marlon Owens, who recounted the story he had written on his incident report that he saw Robinson with a gun and told him to go home. During cross-examination, Dees bore in on Owens, asking if he was sure of what he saw and heard that Saturday afternoon. After Owens said yes, he was sure, Dees asked why he hadn't stopped Robinson and arrested him for violating the gun ordinance. "Did you radio ahead to warn your fellow officers?" Dees asked. Owens answered no.

The final witness for the state was Kelso. He was an innocent bystander, he said. He denied hitting anyone. He hadn't even swung a club at anyone. He had never hit a car.

During cross-examination, John Carroll asked Kelso to step down and slip into his KKK robe that he wore as exalted cyclops of the Klan. Standing before the jury, Carroll handed him a club, which he grasped. Kelso said the KKK members acted on their own, stepping out and confronting the unruly demonstrators. Nothing was planned, he said. It was all spur-of-the-moment reactions.

Dees called Collier, the police department's chief investigator. Dees asked if he had ever seen Robinson at any of the protest demonstrations in the past. No, he said, he hadn't. When Dees asked if Kelso and Terry Joe Tucker had been correct that the Klan had not planned a march on the Saturday afternoon in question, Collier said that was "absolutely wrong." Dees asked Collier to identify several photographs; the officer studied them and answered. Then Dees asked: "Do you see a Klansman there with a raised club right in front of Robinson's automobile?" Collier: "Yes, sir." Dees: "Who is that?" Collier: "David Kelso."

In the end, the jury found Robinson guilty and then added, "We also recommend a sentence of probation." The judge sentenced him to five years and immediately suspended the sentence and put him under probation for two years.

To Robinson's family, Dees said, "When the dirty Ku Klux Klan can get by with convicting this man in court, there is no justice. Your daddy is a great man, and they're not going to do anything to him. He's not even going to have a criminal record when we get through." To the press, he added, "This verdict makes history in this state and this nation because it's the first time that a black man has ever been convicted of shooting a robed Klansman who advanced on him with a raised club. This is exactly what we expected would happen by having this case tried in this county. Curtis Robinson would have been acquitted in any other county out of this region and in any other state in the nation."

As the defense team rode south on I-65, Morris Dees was thinking. Somewhere along the way, he said, "Let's sue the Klan."

✳

The last few months of intense investigation told Dees one thing: the KKK was alive and well and thriving in Alabama and the South, if not the nation.

Within days, he let SPLC staffers know about his new idea. Adding to the idea of filing a suit, he would create Klanwatch, an organization to gather information not only about the KKK but all hate groups.

Soon, SPLC hired a former employee who was an energetic and prize-winning journalist with a steel-trap mind and a nose for thorough investigation. Randall Williams, a reporter for newspapers in Birmingham and Montgomery, had worked for SPLC as a legal aide in the mid-1970s. Williams would take control of Klanwatch and write its *Intelligence Report* in which information about the groups would be sent to thousands of SPLC contributors as well as journalists and interested scholars.

One of Williams's first duties was to go to Decatur and dig out all the information he could find about the KKK of north Alabama. He proved himself a skilled investigator. Dees would make sure his words were no idle threat. He would sue the Klansmen on behalf of Curtis Robinson, and he would do everything in his power to keep such planned violence from happening again.

In Decatur and across the Tennessee River Valley of north Alabama, Williams used his reporter's tools and instincts to turn up the details to make a case. Bill Wilkinson was the imperial wizard of the Invisible Empire, Knights of the Ku Klux Klan, which had been the force behind turning a peaceful march into a violent riot that Saturday. A thirty-six-year-old Louisiana native, he had split with David Duke, another Louisiana Klan leader, and come to Alabama, where he had heard about the Hines case. When Wilkinson refused to hand over to SPLC the names and addresses of the members of his organization, citing that it violated Klan members' right to privacy, Dees requested that he be held in contempt of court.

During legal cat-and-mouse games, Wilkinson guarded himself behind a wall of gun-happy ruffians, staying sealed behind locked doors, and made it near impossible to serve him with a subpoena in order to take his deposition. Ultimately, after it became evident through the underground action of the FBI that Wilkinson had been an informant for them, he resigned his position. It was the way of numerous other loud-talking Klan leaders who were actually working undercover for the federal law enforcement agency.

✯

In the meantime a group of Vietnamese fishermen, who had relocated to the Galveston Bay area of east Texas after the war in Southeast Asia, contacted Dees and SPLC, asking for help. Over a period of several years the fishermen had run into a series of setbacks. Their leader, colonel Nguyen Van Nam, did not believe their mounting problems were simple happenstance. Their boats had caught fire and burned, their licenses had been denied, and American fishermen had grown angry over their fishing in the same waters.

In fact, the Americans had gotten so angry, their leader, Gene Fisher, contacted Louis R. Beam Jr., the grand dragon of the Texas Knights of the Ku Klux Klan, who offered the services of his paramilitary group. After all, one of the American fishermen, Jim Stanfield, was a member of Beam's organization. In the following months, after the initial contact, several more of the Vietnamese boats burned.

On a Saturday morning, a group of American fishermen gathered on their shrimp boat. With them were fifteen Kluxers, some in robes, some in black KKK T-shirts, all armed. They boarded with a cannon and a stuffed human figure they hanged by the neck from rigging.

With all aboard, they sailed to the dock on Clear Creek Channel behind Colonel Nam's house. Neither he nor his wife was home. His thirteen-year-old sister-in-law was babysitting her niece. When she saw the boat and the armed men and the person hanging from the boat's stern, she ran from the house with the baby.

Back in Galveston Bay, someone stuffed a blank round into the cannon and fired. The crashing boom echoed across the water. The boat's passengers cheered.

After he read about the incident in the *New York Times*, Morris Dees told cohorts at SPLC that Louis Beam "may look different from some of those old-timers like Bobby Shelton, and he may talk different too, but he smells the same. When it comes right down to it, they're all yellow-bellied sons of bitches." Soon after reading the article, Dees called Colonel Nam. Shortly after their conversation, Dees and his crew from SPLC headed for east Texas.

Dees met with Colonel Nam and his Vietnamese fishermen. Williams and other investigators collected piles of information about Beam and his group. Dees brought together a small but effective team of attorneys from his office in Montgomery. Steve Ellmann was a graduate of Harvard Law School who had clerked with the Eleventh Circuit Court of Appeals. Dees observed, "Steve was not only brilliant but an idealist in his beliefs." John Carroll, SPLC's legal director, was a tough ex-Marine who had finished first in his class at Cumberland Law School in Birmingham. After studying constitutional law at Harvard, where he was awarded a master's degree, he joined SPLC.

Soon, SPLC filed suit in U.S. District Court in Houston on behalf of the Vietnamese Fishermen's Association "to protect the rights of its members from intimidation, harassment, threats, violence, and other illegal actions."

Throughout their time in east Texas, the attorneys, the investigators, and their clients were harassed and threatened by Beam and his people. U.S. district judge Gabrielle McDonald warned Beam that if he continued, "I will find you in contempt."

At a hearing, Dees took the stand. Asked if he felt threatened, he answered, "Yes, I've studied Mr. Beam's statements. I've looked at over five hundred newspaper accounts, what he said to an undercover investigator, and television tapes of his speeches. His attitude is that he is going to kill those people he doesn't believe in. Quite frankly, I think that he is insane."

On the spot, Judge McDonald enjoined Beam and the other defendants from "making threatening and vile remarks, unsolicited hand gestures, and other distracting actions toward the plaintiff's counsel."

Ultimately, after months of investigations, discoveries, depositions, and hearings, Judge McDonald found Beam and his fellow defendants guilty of violations of civil rights statutes, the Sherman Antitrust Act, and Texas's common law tort of interference with contractual relationships. She barred them from engaging in unlawful acts of violence or intimidation against the Vietnamese, including boarding boats armed within view of the refugees, burning crosses near the homes or workplaces of the plaintiffs, gathering of two or more knights of the Ku Klux Klan or other Klan groups within view of the plaintiffs, or engaging in boat-burning, armed boat patrols, assault and battery, or threats of such conduct.

Less than a year later, Dees received a personal letter from Beam. In *A Season for Justice*, Dees quotes from that letter: "It has been brought to my attention that you are still traveling the country practicing perfidy. . . . I personally feel this behavior should no longer be allowed to go unchecked. . . . I therefore challenge you to a dual [*sic*] to the death. You against me. No federal judge, no federal marshals, no F.B.I. agents, not anyone except yourself and I. We go to the woods (your state or mine) and settle once and for all the enmity that exists between us. Two goes in—one comes out. For a White America, Louis R. Beam Jr."

Dees remembered the letter in July 1983 when he received a 4:00 A.M. phone call at his ranch. A spokesman for the Montgomery Fire Department informed him that his offices were on fire.

On his way to town, Dees had a hunch. He believed in hunches. He called his old friend, sheriff Mac Sims Butler, and told him about the fire. Suspecting arson, Dees said he believed it would have been started by Joe Garner and Tommy Downs, who lived in Snowdoun, a community in south Montgomery County. Dees asked the sheriff to send a deputy down to their residence and check if their car engines were still warm. Dees had taken Garner's deposition earlier as part of the Decatur case. SPLC had received a complaint that twenty-year-old Downs had harassed a local white man who had given a black girl rides to school. A witness, they said, had seen Downs putting sugar in the young man's gas tank. Garner was a known Klan operative.

When Dees arrived at his offices, the fire was still smoldering. Inside, Dees was sickened at the sight and the smell. The worst damage was in Randall Williams's office. It was burned black. His briefcase, containing a thick sheath of papers, photographs, and detailed information gathered in their investigation, sat behind the desk. It was charred, but the material inside was in good shape.

During the lengthy investigation into the fire, Bill Stanton found a photograph marked "Birmingham 1980." After it was enlarged, investigators determined that the two figures in Klan robes were Joe Garner and Tommy Downs. Before a grand jury, Downs denied for the second time that he was a member of the Klan. When the district attorney showed him the photo and said that Downs had perjured himself and would spend the next five years in prison, Downs began to weep. He confessed and implicated Garner. Twenty-five years after the KKK had stockpiled explosives to blow up the houses of Martin Luther King Jr., Ralph Abernathy, E. D. Nixon, and others, they were once again storing dynamite to use on civil rights workers.

Garner, Downs, and another KKK cohort, Charles "Dink" Bailey, were arrested. All were indicted by federal and state grand juries. All three pleaded guilty. In state court, Garner was sentenced to a total of fifteen years. Downs and Bailey were sentenced to three years.

By now, Dees and SPLC had put some major chinks in the KKK's armor. But the biggest and most permanent damage would come in the near future.

17

THE PEOPLE'S
ATTORNEY GENERAL

When William Joseph "Bill" Baxley heard about the little girls being killed in the bombing of the Sixteenth Street Baptist Church, he felt sick. A senior at the University of Alabama Law School, Baxley had already begun planning a career in politics and law. When he heard more details about the bombing deaths, he asked himself: *How can a human being do this? How can someone kill little children? Who would do such a thing?* And when he realized in the days and weeks ahead that whoever was responsible for the horrible violence would not be arrested, tried, and made to face the consequences, he grew more determined. "Some day I'm going to do something about this situation," he told a friend.

In the years ahead, that horrendous morning continued to haunt him. He bought a record of his favorite singer, Joan Baez, singing a ballad called "Birmingham Sunday." Every time Baxley heard the lyrics with the refrain, "And the choirs kept singing of freedom," he promised that some day he would do something about it. But he had to finish law school, clerk for an Alabama Supreme Court justice, and complete his apprenticeship as a young lawyer before tackling such a daunting task. "It seethed inside me, knowing the evil was lurking there in Birmingham and my home state," Baxley said. "I knew that I couldn't let the crime go unpunished. I kept thinking that some day I would be a part of solving it and bringing the people who did it to justice."

After graduating, he spent a year in Montgomery as a clerk to a State Supreme Court justice. He lived in an apartment in the Prado, near the intersection of Court Street and Fairview Avenue. His roommate was Walter Turner, who had also recently graduated from the University of Alabama Law School and was a clerk for U.S. district judge Frank Johnson, where he dealt with many of the high-profile civil rights cases filed by Chuck Morgan and others.

Through Turner, Baxley met Johnson, whom he already admired for his courageous, thorough, and unpopular decisions. Baxley believed that Johnson was a great Alabama hero and should be revered for his judicial integrity, not ridiculed as he was by many Alabama politicians on a daily basis, including George Wallace. In their off-hours, Baxley and Turner hung around their apartment, where a pool table dominated their dining room. They sat on the old, overstuffed furniture and talked about what was happening in the world around them. Now and then Baxley mentioned the bombing of the Sixteenth Street Baptist Church, the horrible deaths of the little girls, and how it was a black mark in the history of the state. Another recent graduate and Montgomery native, Jimmy Evans, visited in late evenings and brought his guitar and sang one of his latest compositions, "Stand in the Doorway, George," a satiric account of the governor's unsuccessful attempt to block the young black students from entering the university a year earlier, when they were all students. Often in the wee hours of a Sunday morning, Baxley and others talked about the possibilities of a colorblind future for their state.

After he finished his year's clerkship, Baxley returned to his hometown of Dothan in the heart of the Wiregrass in the southeastern corner of Alabama, where his father was a circuit judge, his mother a librarian, and where his namesake grandfather had been Dothan's mayor. On the shady old residential streets of Dothan he had gone door-to-door while still in elementary school in 1952, campaigning for Adlai Stevenson, the Democratic presidential nominee, and U.S. senator John Sparkman, the vice-presidential nominee.

Less than a year after Baxley returned home, the office of district attorney was vacated, and he was appointed to fill the position. Later, he was elected for a full term. As DA, he did not shirk the headline cases. In fact, he sought them. And it was not long before he was known from the Tennessee River Valley to Mobile Bay as a tough-talking, hard-nosed, no-nonsense law enforcement official. It was written in newspapers across the state that Baxley would take care of the people's business.

In 1970, he ran against incumbent attorney general MacDonald Gallion, letting the public know that he would be "The People's Attorney General." What he meant: I'll be everybody's attorney general, not just for white folks but blacks as well, not just for the well-to-do but for the poor, too. In his mind, he was already planning his first few months in office. He borrowed a page out of his hero's instruction book. Ever since he was a small boy, he had followed the career of James E. "Big Jim" Folsom, whom he considered the finest Alabama politician ever, a big man who would stand up for the little man. Like Folsom, Baxley moved about the state from small town to small town, meeting over coffee with anyone who would listen, telling them he wanted to represent all of them in courtrooms in every county.

During the campaign, Baxley met face-to-face in public with black political leaders, shunning the previous modus operandi of the most liberal of white politicians, sneaking through back corridors or entering through back doors. "Bill Baxley was the first statewide politician to step right through the front door, climb onto the stage, and answer our questions out in the open," said Joe Louis Reed, chairman of the Alabama Democratic Conference. "He broke the ice, and it remained broken. He was a very courageous politician for his time."

Baxley was sworn into office on the same day that George Wallace was taking the oath as governor for his second term, in January 1971. The new attorney general sat in his huge office in the Alabama Administrative Building and talked with one of his first appointees. Pulled up to the edge of Baxley's desk was his chief investigator, Jack Shows, whom he had known and respected for years. Months earlier, Baxley had told his best friends that Shows would be his first appointee. "And he will be one of the most important," Baxley confided.

When his friends frowned, Baxley began talking about Shows and what he had done on the Montgomery Police Department back in the days of the nightly bombings. "When others were looking the other way, Jack Shows was sticking his nose into the dirty business of the bombings of the homes of preachers, firebombings of churches, and the underhanded work of the Ku Klux Klan. He knows every son of a bitch in this state, where they are, and how to get to them. He's going to be my man to uncover some unfinished business," Baxley stated.

On his first day in office, Baxley handed Shows a telephone card. In those days, each new top official was given a card with local telephone numbers. If he was in Mobile, Birmingham, Huntsville, or any other city in the state, he could call the number and a central telephone in Montgomery would answer and forward his call. On the card he had written the names of the little girls killed in the 1963 bombing. "See these names?" he said to Shows. "Every time I use this card, I see these names. It's a reminder to me that this case is my number one priority."

Baxley's office was on the main floor of a building facing the back side of the Alabama capitol. Even on the first day, it was cluttered with dozens of boxes of files he brought from Dothan. When he swiveled 180 degrees in his high-backed chair, he looked across Jackson Street. The back steps led up to the hallway that intersected with a wide hall that led to the governor's office.

In the rotunda of the capitol stood a bust of the late governor Lurleen Wallace, George's first wife, who ran for governor when the state senate would not pass a law allowing Wallace to succeed himself in that office. She won in 1966 but died less than two years later. Now, the new governor was married to his second wife, Cornelia, an attractive young brunette and niece of former governor Folsom, whose portrait would take its place among Baxley's other heroes above a sofa in his new office. Joining Folsom on the wall were Judge Johnson, president Lyndon Baines Johnson, coach Paul "Bear" Bryant, and U.S. congressman Claude Pepper, an Alabama native who was a controversial liberal representative from Florida. Near Baxley's desk were bronze busts of his other heroes: Abraham Lincoln, John F. Kennedy, and Franklin D. Roosevelt. If anyone asked, Baxley would tell him exactly why each was his hero. He had read biographies of each and knew their life stories.

Through the years he had served as district attorney Baxley had become annoyed, irritated, and angered at the numerous lawsuits filed by some of his predecessors in the attorney general's office. Most of the suits, in his estimation, were frivolous pieces of nonsense designed to circumvent civil rights laws, especially pertaining to voting rights and integration of schools. Within days after his inauguration, Baxley called the most mature and seasoned veteran professional into his office. Gordon Madison was a tall, graying, soft-voiced assistant attorney general who had worked under several attorneys general. In his home town of Tuscaloosa he had been a highly respected lawyer and had represented the west Alabama county as a state senator before he moved south to Montgomery to begin his current job. To Baxley, Madison was "the finest and most professional" of all the assistants.

Baxley told Madison to go to the U.S. District Court and dismiss all of the suits that had been filed to circumvent civil rights. On the following afternoon, Madison asked to see Baxley privately. Suspecting that Madison would complain about his assignment, Baxley told his secretary to tell Madison he was busy. In the meantime, Madison sat in a chair in the outer office. Baxley could not leave without passing him. Finally, Baxley asked him to enter. "He stood in front of my desk and said, 'Bill, I want to thank you for giving me the privilege of dismissing those suits. For the first time in many years, when I left federal court yesterday, I was able to hold my head high. I was very proud.'"

Not long after Baxley took office, Jack Shows conferred with retired state investigator Ben Allen, who had been working with the State Department of Public Safety at the time of the Birmingham church bombing. At this time, Allen was working for *Montgomery Advertiser* editor and publisher Harold Martin to uncover shady dealings with the State Department of Corrections. Allen, Shows knew, had been in Birmingham when the church was bombed. Allen had confided to several reporters that "I had an ongoing battle with Al Lingo [Governor Wallace's director of public safety in his first administration]. When we'd report Klan activity in a location, Birmingham, Selma, Montgomery, Tuscaloosa, wherever, he'd shove it under the rug and tell us, 'Come into the office, I want to talk to you.' When we'd walk into his office, he wouldn't have anything to say. He'd lean back in his chair, put his feet up on the desk, and grin like a mule eating briars. As far as I was concerned, he was a no-good son of a bitch. When we stopped a carload of Kluxers on the highway between Birmingham to Tuscaloosa on the night before Wallace's stand in the schoolhouse door, Lingo gave orders to a major to let 'em go. They brought me the six men in the car. I talked to 'em in a campus police office. All the while, Lingo kept calling and saying, 'Don't ask 'em too much and for God's sake don't inform the reporters. You know that damn place is crawling with reporters.'" According to Allen, troopers had found six loaded pistols, two sabers, two bayonets, two nightsticks, and a baling hook in the trunk of the car.

Even in 1963, Allen was a veteran investigator. When Governor Folsom initiated a plan to stop the Klan in 1949, Ben Allen led the charge, uncovering activities across the state and becoming knowledgeable about klaverns from the Tennessee state line to Theodore in south Mobile County. And he became familiar with the personalities, from Bobby Shelton to the lowest of the lows.

Gary Thomas Rowe, an undercover Klansman working for the FBI, later said that Allen was working with the Klan. Once, he claimed, Allen said to Herman Cash, a hardcore Klansman, "Hey, you're not worried about that bombing, are you?" He was referring to the bombing of the Gaston Motel in Birmingham, according to Rowe. And Cash said, "I don't know nothing, I don't know nothing. Please, please, look, I'll get on my knees. Just let me go." Allen made a note of Cash's plea, then let him go. Later, Allen said, "Gary Thomas Rowe was one of the biggest liars in the world. I wouldn't believe him if he swore on a stack of Bibles."

When Jack Shows interviewed him, Allen said his number one suspect in the Sixteenth Street Church bombing was J. B. Stoner, the Georgia Klan leader. Over and over, Allen pointed his finger in Stoner's direction. Baxley sent Shows to Georgia, where the trail soon vanished. However, Shows did discover through a web of witnesses that Stoner was indeed involved in another murder case, which the attorney general's office put aside temporarily.

In the hours after the church bombing, confusion had reigned. FBI agent John McCormick was stricken with a headache as soon as he walked onto the site of the bombing, according to Stephen Currie in his book *The Birmingham Church Bombing*. It was the same symptom he usually experienced when he sniffed out explosives. Within a short time, experts determined that between ten and twenty sticks of dynamite had been used. The explosion ripped through a thirty-inch brick-and-concrete wall and smashed the entire women's restroom, where five little girls had been straightening their dresses before Sunday school. It immediately killed four of them. The fifth, Sarah Collins, Addie Mae Collins's sister, was blinded and severely injured. Nearly ten years later, the cold case was near freezing. The investigation appeared difficult at best.

Soon after they both took office, Baxley walked across the street, sat down with Governor Wallace, and informed him that he was reopening the investigation into the bombing. Wallace offered a ten thousand dollar reward from the state to anyone offering evidence that would lead to the conviction of the murderer or murderers, saying he had always thought it was a horrendous crime.

Several weeks later, Baxley went back to Wallace. "This time, I figured he really didn't want to see me. I sat opposite him and told him I was preparing to file a suit to outlaw the State Sovereignty Commission and the Commission to Preserve the Peace. He looked at me, and I thought he was fixing to tell me not to do it. I was ready to tell him I would do it, no matter what he said. But he never said, 'No.'"

Rather than go against both commissions at once, Baxley made the decision to fight one at a time. He decided that approach was simpler and more direct.

After the suit against the Sovereignty Commission was drawn up, Baxley decided he would file it in the jurisdiction of an old friend, circuit judge Roy Mayhall, who had served on the bench in Walker County until he severely criticized Governor Wallace. As head of the state's Democratic Party, Mayhall felt a strong loyalty to the National Democrats. He did not like the way Wallace was making a mockery out of the party, and he was very vocal in his criticism. As a result, Mayhall was defeated in his bid for reelection. Now, he traveled the state as a supernumerary judge. When he was handling cases in Mobile, Baxley went there and prepared to file his suit. However, when Baxley arrived in the Port City, he discovered that Mayhall had finished his business in Mobile and moved on.

Later, Baxley learned that Mayhall was sitting on the bench in Madison County. "That was even better," Baxley said, "because Martha Witt

Smith, then director of the Sovereignty Commission, lived in Huntsville." Since it was the place of Smith's residency, it would appear natural for the attorney general to file the case in Huntsville. Otherwise, he might be accused of judge-shopping.

Baxley camped out in his old friend Julian D. Butler's law office. Through a court clerk who let him know when Judge Mayhall would be accepting a new suit, he timed his filing exactly right. After Mayhall accepted the case, Baxley feigned ignorance to the local press, saying he had no idea Mayhall was a judge there.

After Mayhall issued a temporary restraining order against the Sovereignty Commission, Butler told Baxley, "You deserve an Academy Award for best actor."

In the Ku Klux Klan's newsletter, *The Southerner,* Asa Carter wrote an editorial criticizing Baxley for his actions against the Sovereignty Commission. On a Birmingham talk show, a right-wing spokesman said, "Baxley is a tool of the communists who are trying to integrate our state."

After the lawsuit was heard, the Sovereignty Commission was declared permanently illegal.

On numerous occasions, the Commission to Preserve the Peace halted black poll workers who attempted to assist numerous voters who could not read or write. The Peace Commission tried to slow down the process of black voting. It ruled that poll workers could assist only one voter on election day, no matter how many presented themselves. In response, Baxley issued an attorney general's opinion saying that poll workers could assist a thousand, if that many voters asked for help. Finally, the legislature stopped funding the Peace Commission, and it ceased to exist.

Little more than a year after he took office, Baxley announced that he was hiring the first black assistant attorney general in Alabama, Myron Thompson, a recent graduate of Yale Law School. A native of Tuskegee, Thompson was a slight young man who walked with a limp as the result of childhood polio. He spoke softly and intelligently with a winning smile.

Once again, Baxley was roundly criticized by spokespersons for the right wing, saying, "Attorney General Baxley is doing everything in his power to bring about race-mixing in our state government." On Birmingham radio, a commentator said, "Bill Baxley is bringing Negroes into state government from Yankee schools like Yale. It's a crying shame."

Years later, after Frank Johnson moved to the U.S. Circuit Court, president Jimmy Carter appointed Thompson to the U.S. District Court in Alabama.

Even in the early days of the investigation into the Sixteenth Street Church bombing, Baxley knew that it would be a long and arduous process. At times it would be terribly frustrating. However, as attorney general, he knew he had to be the chief cheerleader and the head coach. He had to keep the process going, even when his team hit brick walls, even when potential witnesses lied to them. Baxley was determined to find the true killers and bring them to justice, even if it took every minute of two full terms of his administration. "At times, it really got rough," Shows remembered. "At times Bill got phone calls from leaders in the Ku Klux Klan, threatening him and his family. Sometimes when we'd be traveling through Birmingham and stop at one of his favorite restaurants, a stranger would step up to the table and say, 'You'd better get off this bombing case, Baxley, if you know what's good for you.' He'd look up at the person and smile and say, 'I'm glad I have your support.' That's the way he handled the pressure. He was cool as a cucumber."

As the investigation continued, Shows was joined in the day-to-day work by deputy attorney general George Beck and assistant attorneys general George Royer and John Yung, whom Baxley assigned to the case. They questioned numerous people mentioned in the bombing case. They examined evidence collected by Ben Allen and other investigators with the Alabama Department of Public Safety, the Birmingham Police Department, and the Jefferson County Sheriff's Department. "All of it was pretty fruitless," Baxley recalled.

While J. Edgar Hoover was still director of the FBI, Baxley made numerous trips to Washington, D.C., asking to see the files concerning the agency's original investigation at the scene in Birmingham. He told the director his intention: he wanted to bring the suspects to trial. Each time, Hoover turned him down. After Hoover died, Baxley visited with several interim directors. Each proved just as stubborn and unhelpful as Hoover. When Clarence Kelley, a Birmingham native, became FBI director, Baxley tried again.

In 1975, after Kelley refused to allow him access to the files, Baxley called another Alabama native who worked in the nation's capital. Pulitzer Prize–winning reporter Jack Nelson, Washington bureau chief of the *Los Angeles Times*, had been interested in the bombing since the morning it happened. A relentless investigative reporter, Nelson had gotten his hands on some files through the Freedom of Information Act. Nelson had always been persistent as a journalist and had written critical accounts of the FBI in his books as well as the pages of the newspaper. Over dinner, Nelson told Baxley what he had and gave him clippings of several articles he had written. Baxley told him, "I'm going to get the bastards who killed those kids. But I really do need the information that the FBI has. They've been stonewalling me for years."

On the following morning, Nelson telephoned Baxley at his room in the Madison Hotel. "Were you serious?" Nelson asked. "Do you really want the FBI's investigation?"

Baxley assured him, "I was dead serious."

Within days, Nelson visited U.S. attorney general Edward M. Levi and told him he had learned that the FBI was withholding information that would help Baxley's investigation and prosecution. In his quiet, bulldog manner, Nelson promised Levi that if the Justice Department did not act soon and turn over the records, he would write about the stonewalling in the *Los Angeles Times*. Furthermore, Baxley would bring the families of the four victims to Washington, where they would hold a press conference on the steps of the Justice Department. It would get national attention, Nelson promised. Several days later Nelson received a call from a Justice Department spokesperson saying the agency would turn over files to Baxley's office.

For Baxley and his investigative team, this was a major breakthrough. Although many of the names were blacked out, they could decipher who had said what to whom.

"When we insisted on more, the FBI invited us to use an office in the building in Birmingham where they were located," Baxley said. "As it turned out, the FBI's idea of cooperation was 180 degrees opposite of my idea. If we didn't ask the right questions, they would not give us the right answer."

In 1976, halfway through his second term as attorney general, Baxley hired an extra investigator, forty-three-year-old Bob Eddy, who moved into the office with Shows and began poring over the piles of information with a fresh set of eyes.

Soon Baxley sent Eddy to Birmingham to talk with anybody he could find about the case that was now almost fifteen years old. "I put him on it full-time," Baxley said. "Like Shows, Eddy leaves no stone unturned." There, Eddy moved from person to person, tying tiny tales together, slowly and thoroughly weaving a case with Birmingham police captain Jack LeGrand and sergeant Ernest Cantrell, who had been assigned by mayor David Vann to assist.

Throughout the investigation, Baxley received a number of threats via phone calls or letters, and a few in person. He was accused publicly of playing politics with the church bombing. When a known Klansman friend of J. B. Stoner wrote and accused Baxley of playing for the black bloc vote, Baxley wrote back: "My response to your letter of February 19, 1976, is—kiss my ass. Sincerely, Bill Baxley." After he named Vanzetta Penn Durant as the first black female assistant attorney general, several Klansmen threatened to hurt or kill him. In speeches across Alabama, Bobby Shelton and other KKK leaders said the young attorney general was "a nigger-lover who deserves to be lynched" and "the worst excuse for public office we've ever experienced in this state." J. B. Stoner said, "Baxley is a dirty rotten turncoat and a traitor to the South."

Over and over again, the name of Robert Edward Chambliss rose to the surface. He was the same Dynamite Bob who had made dozens of deliveries to Montgomery in the mid-1950s and after the bus boycott. Fifty-nine years old in 1963 at the time of the bombing, he had worked for the city and had driven a truck for a dealer in auto parts. By 1977, he was retired.

In mid-September 1936, a black woman from Detroit named Gertrude Glenn was visiting Birmingham. According to an FBI document found by Baxley's investigators, she became suspicious of a white-and-turquoise Chevrolet she saw parked outside the Sixteenth Street Baptist Church early on Sunday morning, September 15, 1963, at 2:00 A.M. Three white men were sitting inside. When she was shown thirty-four photographs of Klansmen, she pointed to three. All three were of Robert Chambliss in different poses.

Back in Detroit the following month, Glenn called the local FBI and said she recognized a white man whose photo was in *Jet* magazine. He was the man, she said, that she had seen sitting in the Chevrolet. The man in the photo was Robert Chambliss.

Shows and Yung went to Detroit to question Glenn. Once again she told them what she had seen, and again she identified Chambliss from their photos. But she said she did not want to return to Alabama to testify. She was afraid.

Stymied, Baxley thought of several scenarios. According to reporter Frank Sikora in *Until Justice Rolls Down: The Birmingham Church Bombing Case*, Baxley decided to ask Rosa Parks to talk to Glenn. Then he thought of his friend, black attorney Fred Gray. They had tried several cases together. Baxley and Gray had expressed mutual respect for each other. "I have always found Fred Gray to be cooperative," Baxley said in a subsequent interview. "He is an upstanding man and an outstanding attorney." When Baxley called and asked for help, Gray said, "When do we go?"

After hearing Gray, Glenn said she would return to Birmingham and testify. Shows promised he would meet her plane and would stay in the motel room next to her.

"It is very difficult to keep together all of the pieces of a major, complex investigation like this," Shows said years later. "There is an intensity that grows more and more in the beginning. If it goes on for years, like this one, there's times when you want to walk away and throw all the files in a dumpster. But Baxley wouldn't let us do that. He kept the fire burning inside all of us. He would pace the floor in his office and go over the facts that we gathered. He put the pieces together like a huge jigsaw puzzle."

Finally, at 9:00 A.M. on November 14, 1977, thirty-five-year-old Bill Baxley stood before the bench of circuit judge Wallace Gibson as the trial of the *State of Alabama v. Robert Edward Chambliss* began in the Jefferson County courtroom. A jury of nine whites and three blacks was selected.

The defendant was a slender, sallow-faced, seventy-three-year-old with sparse gray hair and thin, colorless lips. When he looked toward Baxley, his light gray eyes glared with hatred. By now, Baxley was accustomed to the words of hate, the telephone calls warning him to be careful and telling him that he might get hurt, and even a threat from a north Alabama federal inmate who contracted from his jail cell for a hit man to kill the attorney general. When the Department of Public Safety caught wind of the plot—to shoot Baxley from a school overpass on the South Bypass while he was driving to work—an investigator called Jack Shows, who arranged for Baxley to begin using a plainclothes state trooper to drive him and act as his bodyguard.

Surrounded by his team, Baxley began with an overview of that Sunday morning in September more than fourteen years earlier when a bomb ended the lives of four little girls and wrecked the lives of many more.

John Yung questioned the pastor of the Sixteenth Street Church, Reverend John Haywood Cross, who said the explosion "sounded like the whole world was shaking." Afterward, when he looked around, there "was so much dust and soot—and glass had fallen, and plaster—it was so smoky in there, and some of the people could not be identified three feet from me."

Outside the church, someone handed him a loudspeaker. "I told the people to remember the lesson. I said the lesson for the day was love and that we should be forgiving, as Christ was forgiving. 'Father, forgive them, for they know not what they do.' And then we started digging, some civil defense workers and myself. We must have gone down one or two feet and someone said, 'I feel something soft.' It was a body, and we pulled that one out and dug a little deeper, and there was a second one and a third one and finally a fourth one. They were all found on top of one another."

Then Sarah Collins Riley, who was now twenty-seven, described how she and the other four girls were in the restroom adjusting their dresses when the explosion occurred.

Yung said, "Tell the jury what you remember happened after the explosion."

Riley answered, "Right after the explosion, I called my sister."

"What did you say?"

"I called about three times. I said, 'Addie! Addie! Addie!'"

After a moment, Yung asked, "Did Addie answer you?"

"No, she didn't."

"What happened after that?"

"Then I heard somebody calling out. They said that somebody had bombed the church. Then somebody came and brought me outside."

"Were you taken to the hospital?"

"Yes."

"Could you see?"

"No."

"How long was it before you could see?"

"About a month."

"Out of both eyes?"

"No, just the left."

"Do you still have your right eye?"

"No, they had to take it out."

Preparing for the trial, Baxley was eager to present testimony from James Lay, a civil defense captain who told the FBI in 1963 that he had seen two white men near the church prior to the explosion. He told Bob Eddy that the men were Robert Chambliss and Tommy Blanton Jr. However, now Lay would not testify, saying he couldn't remember and suffered from amnesia. Baxley went to him, sat with him, pleaded with him, but Lay refused. The FBI refused to listen to him at the time, he said, so he wouldn't talk now. Baxley said, "I'm listening. I've been working on this thing for six years. But I need your help." But Lay only shook his head.

Baxley told writer Frank Sikora that he called Chris McNair, the father of Denise McNair, and asked if he would prepare a breakfast for the Sunday morning before the trial. He would invite Lay and Baxley. Listening to him and McNair talk, Baxley thought, perhaps Lay would change his mind. Still, Lay refused. If he took time off from work, he said, he would be fired from his job.

Angry, Baxley ordered his people to subpoena Lay. He couldn't make him testify. "If he won't help us, then we'll keep the son of a bitch tied down at the courthouse while the trial goes on."

When the trial started, a second witness, a black disc jockey named Tall Paul White, did not appear. He too said that he had seen two white men near the church. They resembled Chambliss and Blanton, he told Eddy. But he still did not show.

On Wednesday, Baxley asked the judge to seal the courtroom for security purposes. Defense attorney Arthur Hanes Jr. objected. Baxley told the judge that he was about to call his star witness and he was afraid for her.

The judge agreed.

John Yung, who had interviewed Elizabeth Cobbs earlier, began to examine the witness. She identified herself as pastor of Denman Memorial Methodist Church.

Yung: "Mrs. Cobbs, I will ask you whether or not you are in any way related to this defendant, Robert E. 'Bob' Chambliss."

Cobbs: "He is married to my mother's sister."

She explained that she had been visiting the Chambliss family on the Saturday before the church explosion. Mrs. Chambliss had been sick. Mr. Chambliss was mad because he had read in the newspaper about a white girl who had been stabbed in the arm by a black girl. She said he had used "vile language."

Judge Gibson leaned toward the witness and said, "I'm not trying to embarrass the witness, but I think the language. . . . Sometimes we can't deal in niceties, and I think this is one of those times."

Moments later, she continued, "He said that if anyone had backed him up, that they would have had the g.d. niggers in their place by now. He always used the term 'nigger' when referring to blacks."

Yung asked, "Did he often use profanity?"

"Often."

"Did he say 'g.d.'?"

"No."

"Did he say what the words 'g.d.' stand for?"

"Yes, sir."

"Can you describe his demeanor or his tone of voice?"

"He was very agitated, very angry. He said he had been fighting a one-man war."

"What else did he say?"

"He said George Wallace was a coward or he could have stopped all this."

Chambliss, she said, left the house and returned shortly with a newspaper and sat down at the kitchen table. After he read for a while, she said, "He started again, very loudly and angrily, cursing, swearing. He said if he had been there that that nigger wouldn't have gotten away."

"Those were his words?"

"Yes, sir."

"What else was said?"

"He said he'd gotten the address of the, quote, nigger girl that was going to integrate the school. I cautioned him against doing anything foolish and he said, 'Don't worry,' that if he did anything, it would be something he could get away in."

"Something he could get away in?"

"Yes, sir."

"He said that on the morning of the fourteenth?"

"Yes, sir."

"Was anything else said that you recall?"

"He told me that he had enough stuff put away to flatten half of Birmingham."

Yung pointed. "This defendant, Robert Chambliss . . ."

"Yes, sir."

". . . said that he had enough stuff put away to flatten half of Birmingham?"

Hanes said, "Say it one more time."

"Yes, sir."

"And this was the day before the explosion at the Sixteenth Street Baptist Church?"

"Yes, sir."

"Did he say anything else, Mrs. Cobbs?"

"He told me that the FBI or police could pick him up and search all they wanted to, but they wouldn't find it unless he pointed it out to them."

"Find what?"

"The stuff."

"Is that his words?"

"Yes, sir."

"The stuff that would flatten half of Birmingham?"

"Yes, sir."

"Did you make any reply or say anything after he made that statement?"

"I asked him what good he thought any of that would do."

"Did he say anything?"

"At that point he placed his hand upon the newspaper in front of him. He looked me in the face and said, 'You just wait until after Sunday morning. And they will beg us to let them segregate.'"

"You just wait until after Sunday morning and they will beg us to let them segregate?"

"Yes, sir."

"Mrs. Cobbs, what if anything else was said?"

"I asked him what he meant, and all he would say was, 'Just wait. You'll see.'"

"Just wait, you will see?"

"Yes."

Yung asked, "Did you see?"

Hanes jumped to his feet. "Judge, wait. Just a minute. I move to exclude that."

Judge: "Sustained."

Hanes: "I ask for a mistrial on that point, Judge."

Judge, to the jury: "Ladies and gentlemen, don't consider that question or that answer."

Yung: "Did the defendant make any further statements after the explosion at the church?"

"Yes, he did. To the best of my recollection, it was the following Saturday evening. He was seated on the sofa in the living room. He was watching television. A news broadcast came on concerning the investigation of the church explosion."

"Did he make a statement during that news broadcast?"

"The announcer said there was the possibility of murder charges being made."

"What, if anything, did he say?"

"He said it wasn't meant to hurt anybody. It didn't go off when it was supposed to."

"To whom did he make that statement, Mrs. Cobbs?"

"To the television announcer, I assume."

"Did he say anything to you?"

"No."

"Did you say anything to him?"

"No, sir."

"Did he say what he was attempting to do?"

"To preserve white supremacy and keep the niggers in their place."

"Did he say whether or not he was in, or part of, any organization in this connection?"

"He was a member of the Ku Klux Klan."

"Did he tell you why he was a member of or what the Ku Klux Klan was planning to do?"

"In order to fight to maintain segregation and keep niggers in their place."

"Did he state to you how that was to be done by him through the Ku Klux Klan?"

"Many times he said he would do anything possible."

"Anything possible?"

"Yes, sir."

"That's all."

Defense attorney Art Hanes Jr. began his cross-examination. He and his father were well-known lawyers for KKK defendants. Art Hanes Sr. was the former mayor of Birmingham who, with Bull Connor, had shut down all of the parks in the city. Art Jr. had defended James Earl Ray after he was accused of assassinating Martin Luther King Jr. He and his father had represented the three Klansmen accused of killing Viola Liuzzo at trial in Lowndes County.

Hanes asked, "You have heard George Wallace say that he was fighting to help save segregation, haven't you?"

Cobbs: "Yes, sir."

Hanes: "And you have heard many people in Jefferson County say that, have you not?"

"Yes, sir."

"And at that time, your uncle was—what?—sixty years old?"

"Approximately."

"You were talking about 'stuff.' Did you ever see any 'stuff,' please, ma'am?"

"That is his words, Mr. Hanes."

"I am asking you: did you ever see any?"

"That's a question I cannot answer, Mr. Hanes, unless you define what you're asking me."

"Ma'am?"

"You asked me what he said?"

"So, you don't even know what 'stuff' is, is that correct?"

"He did not tell me."

"How old are—I hate to ask you—how old you are now, please, ma'am?"

"I am thirty-seven."

"That would have made you twenty-three then, is that correct? Did you make any notes on alleged conversations at the time they were had?"

"Mental notes only, sir."

"Oh, I see. Did you write down any of these things?"

"No, sir."

As Hanes persisted, Cobbs said that she told FBI agents about the conversation soon after the church bombing.

Bob Eddy was able to track down Yvonne Fike Young, a former girlfriend of Klansman Ross Keith. When she did not show up to testify, Eddy told her he would return with a court order. Reluctantly, she said she would appear.

As George Beck questioned her, she said she and Keith visited the Chambliss house about two weeks before the bombing. While Keith and Chambliss talked, she said, she visited with Mrs. Chambliss in the kitchen.

When Young asked to use the restroom, she said, Mrs. Chambliss pointed the way. "I started to the restroom, and I went in the wrong door."

Beck: "You say you went to the wrong door?"

Young: "Yes, sir."

"Who told you it was the wrong door?"

"Ross Keith."

"Did you open that door?"

"Yes, sir."

"What did you do? What happened when you opened the door?"

Chambliss, she said, started cussing. "He scolded me as though I was a child that had done something real bad."

When she opened the door, she said, "There were three or four bundles on the floor. They were tied with a cord like you would fix a package to mail with."

Beck: "Could you be more specific about the bundles? What did they look like?"

Young: "They looked like oversized firecrackers."

"Can you tell us what color they were?"

"They were between a beige and a brown."

Under cross-examination, she said she told the FBI in 1963.

Hanes: "Have you filed for any reward? Did you know of any reward?"

Young: "I read about it in the newspaper, but that's blood money, and I want no part of it."

When the defense started its case, Hanes rose and stated, "Your honor, we call the defendant Robert Chambliss to the stand." The defendant shook his head. When Hanes persisted, he muttered, "I ain't goin'. No, sir, I ain't goin'."

After a brief recess, during which Chambliss and Hanes met in a nearby conference room, the trial was delayed until the next day.

On Wednesday morning, November 17, the defense rested.

After George Beck summarized the evidence, Baxley stood. He strode before the jury, looking into the face and eyes of each. He lifted the photographs of the little girls who were killed fourteen years ago. When he held up one image, he said, "Today is Denise McNair's birthday."

He let the words sink in. Then he said in a solemn tone: "If she had lived, she would have been twenty-six."

Baxley turned to face the defendant. "If you feel sympathy with him because of his age, look at these pictures." He placed each picture faceup in front of the jury.

"When that blast went off, it was truly a bomb heard around the world. The crime was against all of us, against the people of Birmingham and the state of Alabama.

"Give Denise McNair a birthday present."

After the closing, Baxley excused himself, telling his team he needed some fresh air. He walked five blocks to the Sixteenth Street Baptist Church. In the empty church, he felt alone but proud. He stopped at the plaque commemorating the lives of the four girls. He said a quick silent prayer of thanks. At last, he had fulfilled the promise he had made to himself back when he was a student. In the last year of his two terms as state attorney general, Baxley knew that the trial would be his legacy to the people of Alabama. He felt proud that he had at least brought one of the culprits to justice.

On Friday morning, the jury found Chambliss guilty of murder.

Asked if he had anything to say, Chambliss said, "Judge, I swear to God I didn't bomb that church. I never bombed nothing. I never hurt nobody. I have never been near that church."

Judge Gibson said, "The sentence is life in prison."

Years later, Baxley told filmmaker Spike Lee, "I think Bob Chambliss is responsible for more evil than any other human being in the history of this county and maybe this state." In Lee's documentary *4 Little Girls*, Baxley continued, "I'm not saying he is the most evil man. Who am I to judge? But he was responsible for nearly all the bombings in Birmingham in the forties, fifties, sixties. He was called Dynamite Bob. Instead of being scared, concerned, or worried, he was proud of it. He didn't care about being tried for the crime, he wore it like a badge of honor. He was Dynamite Bob."

As it turned out, Chambliss's conviction was only the beginning. Other prosecutions would follow.

After Baxley lost the governor's race in 1978, he filled out his term as attorney general with most of the staff he had put together nearly eight years earlier. When he left office, John Yung stayed behind to prosecute the old Klansman J. B. Stoner, who had traveled in and out of Montgomery and Birmingham throughout the years since the late 1950s. Bob Eddy assisted Yung in his investigation, putting together information the office had gathered earlier when they had been misled that Stoner was the bomber of the Sixteenth Street Church. Both Yung and Eddy knew the newly elected attorney general, Charles Graddick, did not wish to vigorously continue the work Baxley had started.

Still, Yung presented his case, indicting Stoner in Birmingham on the charge that he set an explosive at the Bethel Baptist Church in 1958. In May 1980, as Yung prepared to go to trial, Graddick fired Bob Eddy. As soon as Yung convicted Stoner and the old Klansman was sentenced to ten years, Yung held a press conference on the steps of the Jefferson County Courthouse. He announced that he was resigning as assistant attorney general and criticized Graddick for his action against Eddy.

In 1977, G. Douglas Jones, a student at the Cumberland School of Law at Samford University south of Birmingham, traveled daily back and forth to the courtroom in downtown Birmingham to watch the Chambliss trial. While he skipped his classes at Cumberland, Jones felt that he was learning much more in the courtroom than he would gain in the classes. "It was great lawyering, magnificent drama, and, for me, the trial of the century," he told me years later. Watching it, Jones became as motivated as Baxley had been years earlier. When he saw Chambliss and the other members of the Ku Klux Klan joking with one another in the halls of the courthouse, he was sickened.

At the time of the bombing in September 1963, Doug Jones was a nine-year-old child living with his parents in the blue-collar community of Fairfield, about ten miles northwest of downtown Birmingham. For Jones, it might as well have been a thousand miles away. It was not until years later that the tragedy hit him as a terrible happening in his world.

In the tenth grade his high school was integrated by the federal court, first given the freedom of choice and then ruled a paired school, requiring blacks to go to the white school and whites to the formerly black school. Still, as a white senior, Jones was elected president of his class. At the end of that year, the superintendent of schools wrote a letter of commendation, stating that Jones had shown extraordinary leadership when racial problems came up. As president of his class, he talked to people on both sides of the issue and reached a compromise.

While an undergraduate at the University of Alabama, Jones met and became friends with Chris McNair, the father of one of the victims of the bombing. As their friendship grew, Jones became aware of the agony the tragedy had caused Mr. and Mrs. McNair through the years. He knew that the same feelings would be multiplied by four, for each family that had lost a loved one in the bombing.

After he was accepted into Cumberland Law School, he followed the trial as Attorney General Baxley and his team began putting together their case.

While still a student at Cumberland, Jones worked in Alabama chief justice Howell Heflin's campaign for the U.S. Senate. "Right out of law school in 1979," Jones said, "I went to work for Senator Heflin in Washington." Soon he became staff counsel to Heflin on the Senate Judiciary Committee.

Back in Alabama, Jones served four years as an assistant U.S. attorney in Birmingham. In Heflin's last days as a senator, he sent Jones's name to president Bill Clinton, who was beginning his second term. As a result, Jones was appointed U.S. attorney for the Northern District.

Twenty-four years after he witnessed the Chambliss trial as a student, Doug Jones took over the bombing case. He sought indictments against Klansmen Thomas Edwin Blanton Jr. and Bobby Frank Cherry. After presenting FBI evidence, the grand jury indicted them on May 16, 2000. Nearly a year later, a jury found Blanton guilty of multiple counts of murder. He was sentenced immediately to life in prison. For Doug Jones, "It was a return to the scene of my early witnessing great moments in a courtroom. We tried Blanton in the same courtroom where I had seen Bill Baxley and his team so masterfully try and convict Bob Chambliss. It was courtroom magic."

Following months of intricate and complex psychological testing, Bobby Frank Cherry stood trial on the same charges. His lawyer claimed repeatedly that Cherry was suffering from dementia and could not assist in his defense. Just as vigorously, Jones and his staff argued that Cherry was faking his psychological problems. For this trial, judge James Garrett moved the trial to a basement courtroom he considered more secure. Once again, Jones presented the evidence collected by the FBI. Cherry's ex-wife, Willadeen Brogdon, and his granddaughter, Teresa Stacy, testified that Cherry had often talked about his involvement. The defendant was found guilty and sentenced to life in prison.

After Jones completed his successful prosecutions, Baxley wrote a scathing piece for the op-ed page of the *New York Times*. He criticized the FBI and its bureaucratic leadership, especially Director Hoover, who had stonewalled access to the information of its investigation for years. "If the FBI had truly cooperated with the attorney general's office, the criminals would have been brought to justice years before they were finally found guilty and put in prison," Baxley said.

Nowadays, Jones, a successful trial lawyer, is called upon frequently to speak on the subject, "Justice Delayed, Not Denied: The Sixteenth Street Baptist Church Bombing Prosecutions." For Jones, "The Birmingham community has embraced our case. To this day, people stop me on the street and thank me and tell me how much the prosecution means to so many."

18

BREAKING THE KLAN

When Morris Dees talked about the dozens of lawsuits filed by the SPLC through the years, he spoke with determination. He had a winning smile and a twinkle in his eyes. However, when his personality was explored, I found in Dees a remarkable depth and a sincere feeling for his fellow man. When he was approached by Beulah Mae Donald, a Mobile black woman who told him in simple but halting words about the death of her son, Dees knew that he would do whatever he could to help the woman find justice and escape her misery.

"Although it took me a while to come to terms with my deep feelings about the segregated society in which I was raised, my thoughts about my fellow man have always been strong," Dees said. "My parents gave me a strong feeling of honor and respect for all people. We were raised as Christians. We believed in the Golden Rule."

On Friday night, March 20, 1981, two self-proclaimed good-old-boy members of the United Klans of America, the organization that Bobby Shelton had founded and had been overseeing and promoting for decades, decided they were going to do something for their white community in south Alabama. They were members of a klavern called Unit 900, operating out of an old frame building in a rural area near Theodore in Mobile County. Twenty-seven-year-old Henry Hays was raised in a KKK family. His father, Bennie, was grand titan of the south Alabama klavern, making him the area's highest-ranking officer in the United Klans of America. In 1981, Bennie was in his midsixties. Henry enjoyed his status as the top guy's son. He had been raised to believe that the Klan was the American way. African Americans were the enemy. To Bennie and Henry, blacks were trying to destroy America. Bennie preached that his son and his friends should fight against such destruction.

With Henry on this Friday night was seventeen-year-old James "Tiger" Knowles. The two had seen an early television newscast about a trial that was taking place in downtown Mobile. A jury of eleven blacks and one white was deliberating after hearing a case against a black man named Josephus Anderson who was charged with killing a white policeman. In the early evening, the jury announced it could not reach a verdict. It was deadlocked.

Later, Bennie Hays told Morris Dees that Red Betancourt read a clipping about the Anderson trial to a meeting of Unit 900. When Betancourt finished, Bennie said, another Klansman, Bill O'Connor, told the group, "There ought to be a damned nigger hung if this guy is turned loose."

At a party at 117 Herndon Avenue, with several other Klan members, including Henry Hays's brother-in-law, Frank Cox, the exalted cyclops of Unit 900, they heard more about the trial. When they left the party with Cox, all three were still drinking beer. Their conversation drifted to the idea of lynching a black man, just to make sure that justice was done—an eye for an eye. That way, they said later, they would be sure to have payback, even before a verdict was rendered in the Anderson trial.

At Cox's mother's house in Theodore, they borrowed a rope. At a nearby trailer park, they borrowed a gun from another member of Unit 900. On the way back to Mobile, Knowles tied a hangman's noose with thirteen knots. Passing it around, they commented about how it was a perfect KKK knot. They would use the knot, Knowles said, to rid Mobile of "another sorry nigger."

In Mobile, the grand dame of Alabama's cities, huge live oaks lined Government Street, which ran from the state docks on Mobile Bay to the western suburbs of Theodore. Alabama's oldest city, Mobile was founded in 1702 and had once been the capital of colonial French Louisiana. In 1763, following the Seven Years (or French and Indian) War, it fell into the hands of Britain. And nearly twenty years later the town was controlled by Spain. In 1813 it became a part of the Mississippi Territory and then the Alabama Territory. In December 1819, the state of Alabama was created.

By 1850, Mobile was the second-largest exporter of cotton in the United States after New Orleans. Massachusetts journalist Hiram Fuller described his mid-nineteenth-century visit to the place known as the Cotton City: "People live in cotton houses and ride in cotton carriages. They buy cotton, they sell cotton, think cotton, eat cotton, drink cotton, and dream cotton. They marry cotton wives, and unto them are born cotton children. In enumerating the charms of a fair widow, they begin by saying she makes so many bales of cotton. It is the great staple—the sum and substance of Alabama. It has made Mobile, and all its citizens."

In 1819, when it became part of the state, Mobile's city population was 809. By 1860, its white population was 29,258. At the time, 1,195 blacks lived in its city limits. In Mobile County, 1,785 slaveowners held 11,376 blacks. The county's total population was 41,130.

From 1817 until the beginning of the Civil War in 1861, more than thirteen million bales of cotton shipped out of the port of Mobile. Most of it came from the river ports of Montgomery and Selma.

Like the members of the Ku Klux Klan throughout Alabama, those in Mobile and its suburbs were determined that integration would not succeed. They would stop integration at any cost.

Henry Hays and James Knowles returned to the party on Herndon Avenue, where they heard that the trial of Josephus Anderson had ended with a hung jury. "A nigger trial," someone commented. Angry at what the Klansmen considered an acquittal of the defendant, Hays and Knowles left again, talking angrily to each other. They drove through Mobile, talking and wishing that they lived back in the days when "niggers would hop and jump when a white man told him to." The more they drove, the angrier they got. Soon they began looking for a black to kill. When they saw Michael Donald, the nineteen-year-old walking alone down the sidewalk was seen immediately as the perfect victim.

He was on his way home after going to the store to buy his sister a pack of cigarettes. The two white men pulled alongside him and asked for directions.

As he began speaking, he leaned toward the window on the passenger side. Knowles pulled the revolver they had borrowed.

Knowles got out of the car and pushed Donald into the backseat. Knowles followed, holding the gun while Hays drove through the tunnel under Mobile Bay, across the parkway, and into Baldwin County.

In a secluded wooded area, Knowles ordered Donald out. In the dark, Knowles later told a crowded courtroom, Donald pleaded, "Please don't kill me."

Nervous and frightened, Donald knocked the gun from Knowles's hand. When it hit the ground, a shot was fired.

Donald ran.

The two white men ran after him, tackled him, pushed his head into the ground, and began beating him with tree limbs.

According to Knowles's testimony, Donald acted "like a crazed madman all of a sudden."

As the two Klansmen beat Donald senseless, he collapsed.

With his head pushed back, the two whites slipped the noose around his head and pulled it tight around his neck. According to Knowles, Hays pressed the sole of his boot against Donald's forehead and pulled the rope tighter and tighter.

Still not sure if their victim was dead, Knowles said, Hays pulled his knife and reached down and cut Donald's throat three times. Blood, he said, spurted from the wound.

At the time Tiger Knowles was nineteen, the same age as the victim. For two years, he remembered each detail of the night he and Henry Hays killed Michael Donald, loaded his ripped and tattered body into the trunk of Hays's car, and carried the body back to Herndon Avenue, where the party was still going strong.

At the house, Frank Cox came out and viewed the body. Then he and his Klansman buddy Teddy Kyzar took off downtown to the Mobile County Courthouse, where the jury had announced earlier that it could not reach a verdict in the Anderson case, and they burned a cross in front of it.

In the meantime, Hays and Knowles lifted the body to the lowest limb of a nearby tree and tied the rope around the limb. Donald's body was found hanging from the tree the next morning by passersby.

At first, the Mobile Police Department thought Donald was the victim of a drug deal gone bad, but Beulah Mae Donald, Michael's mother, insisted that her son had never been involved with drugs. Not in any way, she stated. And his sister told investigators that he was running an errand for her, purchasing cigarettes.

As the investigation proceeded, police became convinced that the Donalds were telling the truth. When the investigators began probing into Hays and Knowles and discovered their Klan membership, the case began to take shape.

At the murder trial, Dees sat and watched. When the defense attorney asked Knowles why he and Hays chose Donald, the witness answered that they killed him because he was black "and to show the strength of the Klan . . . to show that they were still in Alabama."

After Kyzar, a fat, slow-witted Klansman, indicated on the stand that he was afraid of Bennie and Henry Hays, circuit judge Braxton L. Kittrell Jr. asked Kyzar if Bennie Hays had intimidated him. "He told me if I took the fall for murder and went to jail, he'd take care of me," Kyzar said.

Bill O'Connor testified that six months after the murder, Henry Hays told him, "We hung that nigger," then explained just how it was done.

Henry Hays was convicted of first-degree murder and sentenced to die in the electric chair. He proclaimed his innocence until a few days before his execution, when he confessed to the Reverend Bob Smith, president of Mobile's NAACP. He died on June 6, 1997. It was the first time in Alabama since 1913 that an execution was carried out for a white-on-black murder.

James Knowles was allowed to plead guilty to a federal charge for giving state's evidence in the murder trial. He was sentenced to life.

Bennie Hays was tried years later. The judge declared a mistrial. Before Hays could be tried again, he died of a heart attack.

★

As Morris Dees listened to the story of Michael Donald's brutal death unfold, he knew exactly what he and SPLC would do. On behalf of Michael's mother, a lawsuit was filed in U.S. District Court in the Southern District of Alabama. Named defendants were United Klans of America Inc., Knights of the Ku Klux Klan, Bennie Jack Hays, Henry F. Hays, James Llewellyn Knowles Jr., Frank Cox, Thaddeus O. Betancourt, and William O'Connor. Dees wrote later, "This was a classic Klan murder down to the thirteen knots on the hangman's noose."

As Dees wrote years later: "Members of the UKA had beaten the Freedom Riders in Birmingham and Montgomery in 1961, had bombed the Sixteenth Street Baptist Church in 1963, and had killed Viola Liuzzo as she drove Selma marchers in 1965. All three events had been crucial to my personal education. The Freedom Riders case brought me into contact with the young man who questioned my values; the Birmingham church bombing led to my split with my old church and neighbors; the Selma march marked my first involvement in the civil rights movement."

As with all of the other cases he and SPLC tackled during the years, Dees did not let up on the investigation simply because he thought he had it won on the surface. If anything, he tightened the bolts and increased the intensity of delving and questioning. As they did later in North Carolina to a Klan group that killed a young black, and the KKK in Texas, and white paramilitary outfits in the Pacific Northwest, the SPLC investigators turned over every page in every file they discovered on the way to the courtroom.

By trial time, the members of the KKK hierarchy were turning on one another. Bennie Hays accused Bobby Shelton of wrongdoing. Shelton pointed an accusing finger at his underlings.

After a jury heard the facts of the case, it found for the plaintiff, Michael Donald's mother, and fixed damages at seven million dollars. On February 12, 1987, U.S. district judge Alex T. Howard Jr. signed a final judgment, ordering all of the defendants to pay Beulah Mae Donald the full damages.

After their only asset was sold and the money was collected, it did not amount to seven million dollars. But the final amount, about fifty thousand dollars from the sale of a warehouse the Klan used as a meeting hall, was enough to pay for Mrs. Donald's first house. The United Klans of America and its officers were broke and would remain broke.

In the meantime, according to the *Montgomery Advertiser*, the SPLC took in more than nine million dollars from its solicitations in which the death was not only described in detail but also illustrated with a photograph of Michael Donald's body hanging from the tree.

Dees and the SPLC did not stop after the Donald verdict. They moved from case to case, bringing the Klan to trial in state after state. "Sometimes," he said, "you begin to realize that hate truly has no borders. It has no start and stop times." Masking his face in an agonizing gesture, he continued, "It seems as though it goes on and on throughout time, growing meaner and meaner. On farms in Alabama when I was growing up, I'd see some farmers who would not treat their animals with care. I would wonder, what is wrong with these people? 'They're just mean,' my daddy told me. Some people are the same way with other people: they can't see that all folks are human beings, just wanting to be treated like human beings."

As he suspected would happen throughout his long, interesting, and controversial career, Dees has been criticized from the right and the left. Not only have blogs called him names from "poverty pimp" to "hate crime king," *Harper's* magazine quoted a former associate saying, "He's the Jim and Tammy Faye Bakker of the civil rights movement." Wherever he traveled, Dees faced harsh criticism from those who disagreed with him. Through it all, Dees continued his fight, citing success after success in his fight against injustice.

"Ever since I read Clarence Darrow's autobiography, I have thought strongly about what I do." He smiled as he recalled "thinking about being a preacher when I was a boy. I thought of the Bible as a living, breathing work that actually lives through people who read it and try to follow its teaching. As a boy, I was taught to believe in those loving words. I still try to live my life from those teachings when I was a boy. It's truly a simple thing, when you think about it."

19

"FORGIVE ME, FOR I HAVE SINNED"

In January 1971, while George Wallace was being sworn in as governor for the second time, his former speechwriter, Asa Earl Carter, who had run against his old boss and had finished fourth in a four-man race, picketed the inauguration. With a group of fellow Klansmen from northeast Alabama, he demonstrated, waving his sign, WALLACE SOLD OUT. Others read: WALLACE THE TURNCOAT and SEGREGATION FOREVER!

Covering the event for the *Alabama Journal*, I called in my main story from the capitol pressroom. Then I caught up with Carter and sat with him on the back steps, where he lamented the way things had turned out. "Wallace is a no-account liar," he told me in an emotional outpouring. "I believed in him. I sat with him. I held his hand. I nurtured him. I believed deeply that he was the great man we had been waiting for. And now . . ." Tears streamed down his puffy cheeks.

"God! The office of governor has a *nothing* filling the chair where greatness is supposed to sit. There is a void. It is pitiful, absolutely pitiful.

"If we keep on the way we're going, with the mixing of the races, destroying God's plan, there won't be an Earth on which to live in five years."

Indeed, Asa Earl "Ace" Carter was right. His old boss and mentor had only moments earlier finished his second inaugural address. It was not written by Carter. It stated: "Alabama belongs to us all—black and white, young and old, rich and poor alike." For the first time, black people marched in an inaugural parade. The uniformed bands strutted past the reviewing stand and received the new governor's salute.

Still crying, Asa Carter rose and walked to the car where his friends were waiting.

Several years later, I read a novel sent to the newspaper for review. It was called *Gone to Texas*, about a Confederate veteran named Josey Wales who returned to his home to find it destroyed. He headed to Texas, seeking revenge. It was filled with colorful characters and plenty of action. I reviewed the book, written by an author named Forrest Carter, for the Sunday *Advertiser*, saying it was a good, fast, enjoyable read. At lunch on Monday, I ran into a friend from the Alabama legislature at the Sahara restaurant. "Ol' Asa fooled you too," said Ray Andrews, assistant to the secretary of the House of Representatives.

After that encounter, I began to poke around. I reread the novel and found some interesting rhetoric that sounded similar to Asa's speech-writing for Wallace, and later I discovered an advertisement in *Publishers Weekly* for "a true story" entitled *The Education of Little Tree* by Forrest Carter about "Cherokee wisdom imparted by his grandparents to the orphaned Little Tree." I pulled out an old file that I had been saving about Asa Carter and his shenanigans. In it was a brochure for Asa Carter's campaign for governor with a photograph showing him with his parents who were very much alive in 1970. He did not grow up as an orphan.

Forrest Carter had been interviewed by Barbara Walters on the *Today Show* and claimed to be "storyteller to the Cherokee nation." To me and his book editor at Delacorte Press, he denied being Wallace's old speechwriter. However, Andrews and several others chuckled when I asked about his identity. Oscar Harper showed me an autographed copy of the privately published edition of *Gone to Texas* entitled *The Outlaw Josey Wales*, which was also the name of the Clint Eastwood movie made from the novel. I wrote about the bestselling author's true identity in the pages of the *Alabama Journal* and the *New York Times*.

Finally, soon after Carter died of asphyxiation while eating a steak dinner in Wichita Falls, Texas, his widow confessed that he was indeed the founder of the Original Ku Klux Klan of the Confederacy and George Wallace's former speechwriter.

In the meantime, as Carter had suspected, George Wallace changed. An assassin's bullet wedged in his spine while he was campaigning for the 1972 Democratic nomination for president, paralyzing him from the waist down. After surgery in a Maryland hospital, he flew back to Alabama. With Wallace out of state, the lieutenant governor had been made acting governor until his return. Upon Wallace's touchdown, he was immediately reinstated as governor. Then he flew on to Miami to speak to the Democratic National Convention. Even as he spoke on nationwide television, doctors said he was on the verge of death from complications. Later, he recuperated for months in a Birmingham hospital.

In 1976, two years after he won a third term as Alabama governor, he once again prepared to run for the Democratic nomination for president. In the basement of the governor's mansion in Montgomery, he worked for hour after hour to strengthen himself. He lifted his paralyzed body on parallel bars, walked hand-over-hand down the bars, shifting his body until he could balance himself behind a podium and speak without noticeable assistance. The strength in his upper body and in his arms and hands was remarkable. He enjoyed grabbing the hand of a visitor and squeezing it until it hurt. When he did, he chuckled with delight. His young wife, Cornelia, who had fallen atop his prone body as he lay bleeding on the asphalt of the shopping center parking lot, worked with him daily. At night, she read *Sunrise at Campobello*, the inspirational story of Franklin Delano Roosevelt's recovery after being stricken by polio. If Roosevelt could do it, Cornelia said, Wallace could do it. They watched the movie in which the candidate, played by actor Ralph Bellamy, lifted himself from the wheelchair and walked on aluminum crutches to the podium, where the excited and breathless crowd greeted him with great applause. Wallace pictured himself in a similar situation.

By the time the primary season started, Wallace had perfected pulling himself up from his wheelchair and leaning forward into the podium. He would not do it in public until exactly the right moment. It had to be on national television. He wanted the people of America to see that he was just as healthy and ready for the presidency as anyone. He would snap a wide strap that would hold the lower part his body in place, freeing his arms and hands with which he would gesture.

He had already begun to moderate his tone on the racial question. No longer did he snarl and snap like an angry dog at reporters who asked him pointed questions. He even carried several black reporters in his entourage. He enjoyed the company of Norman Lumpkin, who now reported news for the NBC affiliate in Montgomery.

During the Florida primary, where Georgia governor Jimmy Carter was nipping at Wallace's heels, he was moving from speaking engagements to outdoor rallies to fundraising benefits, being flown around the state in a private jet. At one of the stops in the panhandle, his men inadvertently dropped him as he was being placed aboard the plane. A week later someone noticed a swelling in his thigh. Wallace himself, because he was paralyzed, had not felt the pain. But now, aides discovered that his leg had turned purple and he was suffering with a high fever. Suddenly, he was very weak. After he was rushed to a hospital, it was discovered that he had broken a bone in his leg and an infection had spread. By the time it finally subsided, Wallace knew he would never lift himself to a standing position again. According to Mickey Griffin, who had been a close campaign aide since 1968, "When they dropped him down there in the panhandle, it was all over for us. That was the day the campaign should have folded up."

Week after week during the primaries, Jimmy Carter was counting victories. Wallace fell further and further behind. In mid-June, he invited Carter to Montgomery, where the two met in a private conference at the governor's mansion. When they faced the press, Wallace threw his support to Carter.

In his final years, confined to a bed or wheelchair, Wallace told me again and again, "I'm not a racist. I've never been a racist. I came out publicly for Jimmy Carter, didn't I?"

Asked about his declaration, "Segregation forever!" Wallace shook his head vehemently and stated, "Those were just words."

And what about the stand in the schoolhouse door? "As I said then, I repeat today," he said to his audience of one, as though he were making a speech to thousands, "it was a symbolic stand for the rights of the individual and the states against a mighty federal government that was overpowering all of us. I was standing there for the little people."

What about those two people—James Hood and Vivian Malone—who were simply trying to register to enter the University of Alabama? His eyes grew large. He sat up on his bank of pillows. "You think they weren't making a symbolic statement for their people?"

What about Dave McGlathery? "Who?" he asked. The young man who entered the University of Alabama at Huntsville two days after Hood and Malone. "Oh, well, he's another case altogether."

Throughout his second and third terms as governor, from 1971 to 1979, George Wallace leaned more and more toward a new racially progressive philosophy.

In the late 1970s, John Lewis, the former SNCC field worker who had been beaten in downtown Montgomery by the KKK when the Freedom Riders rolled into the bus station, and who had been arrested several times in Selma, received a telephone call from Wallace. At the time, Lewis was serving on the city council in Atlanta. Wallace knew that Lewis's mother lived in Troy. On Lewis's next visit with her, Wallace asked, "Could I drop by to say hello?" Lewis was stunned. He wasn't sure about such a request. Did the man simply want publicity, perhaps because Lewis had become a well-known black leader?

Yet Wallace sounded sincere. Lewis finally told him to come on down to Troy. They met in Lewis's mother's living room. They shook hands. Wallace was very cordial. At first Wallace used his old-time excuse. "It was all just states' rights talk," he said, trying to explain his stand for segregation. Then he leaned forward and stared into Lewis's eyes. "I've come to ask your forgiveness," he said. "I want to ask your forgiveness for anything I've done to wrong you." Later, Lewis said, "It was like a confession." The two men clasped hands and bowed their heads in prayer.

Soon Wallace, the candidate, appeared on statewide television and said, "I was wrong about segregation." It was a simple statement, but it resonated like a riptide rolling up through the coastal plain into the Piedmont, across the Black Belt, into the hill country, and over the Tennessee River Valley. According to Stephan Lesher in his biography, *George Wallace: American Populist*, "eventually, Wallace recognized that he was selling a myth, and that what he had intended as dignified resistance had become, for the most part, obstreperous pandering. So, in the twilight of his career, he went to Alabama's blacks and, by extension, the blacks of America, to ask their forgiveness. There were three reasons—two self-serving, but one epiphany. First, with the unabashed brass of which politicians are capable, he needed and wanted black votes in his last run for governor. Second, as he approached the end of his life, he hoped to present his past racism from obscuring his messages of social conservatism and economic populism. But his third reason revealed a humanity so often lacking in his actions: alone and crippled, forced to introspection for the first time in his life, he realized that though he had purported to be the champion of the poor and the helpless, he had trampled on the poorest and the most helpless of all his constituents—the blacks."

For several months in 1978, the last full year of his third term as governor, Wallace mulled over the idea of running for the U.S. Senate. From his bed in the governor's mansion he called hundreds of old friends and told them his thoughts. He even called former newspaper reporters who had covered his administrations and campaigns. But in the final analysis, the immensely popular chief justice of the Alabama Supreme Court, Howell Heflin of Tuscumbia, threw his hat into the ring, and Wallace decided against running.

In the next four years, Wallace had little to do but think. Few friends from his statehouse days visited. Several newspaper reporters who had sat and listened to his tales of running in nationwide races came by and listened to his remembrances. And one day he began to look ahead and think aloud that he had one more chance. He would run for a fourth term as governor. If he were elected, he told me and others, he would be able to mend fences with people he had hurt back in the early 1960s.

As the days passed and the time neared for him to announce his candidacy in 1982, he told an old observer, "I don't just want to tell them I was wrong, I want to prove to them that I will do more for them than any politician they've ever seen in the state of Alabama. I want to make a difference. You know, the Ku Klux Klan were mean sons of bitches. They did some awful things back in the old days. Looking back on it, I guess I made it easy for them, and I'm truly sorry about that. They were a cowardly bunch."

When my friend Howell Raines, executive editor of the *New York Times*, called and asked if I could arrange for him to interview Wallace, I asked when he wanted to come. Raines sent a letter for Wallace and a copy of his book, *My Soul Is Rested*, autographed to Wallace. At his home, I handed Wallace the letter. He slipped on his glasses and read, and then I handed him the book, which he examined. A moment later, he pointed at the letter and said, "I'm not too interested in this," then he pointed to the title of Raines's book. "I am interested in *that*." Still, he said he would be glad to meet with Raines and wondered aloud, "You think he can help me with my soul?"

By early 1982, Wallace had spoken several times at the Dexter Avenue King Memorial Baptist Church, where Dr. King had been minister in 1955 at the outset of the bus boycott. In 1974, Wallace spoke to the Alabama Progressive Baptist State Convention at the invitation of Dr. Robert M. Dickerson, the pastor there, and Dickerson remembered the occasion as "a time of healing." However, in 1982, he was rolled into the packed sanctuary in his wheelchair by his constant companion and physical therapist, Eddie Holsey, who had been with him for ten years. Wallace's appearance was unannounced. Few in the audience knew that he would speak. As he was rolled in, the congregation hushed. From a position on the pulpit, next to the preacher's podium, Wallace spoke. "I know what it means to suffer," he said in a ringing, high-pitched voice.

A woman said, "Amen!"

His head cocked sideways. His face twisted as if in pain. "I know that I have hurt y'all, but I didn't mean to do it."

Several others said, "Amen!"

In conclusion, he said, "I was wrong. I'm sorry. I want to ask for your forgiveness."

Someone shouted, "Praise the Lord!"

As he sat there, a man alone, tears rolling down his cheeks, someone began to sing, "Amazing grace, how sweet the sound . . ." Others joined. The sounds of their voices rose into the rafters.

In the words of Stephan Lesher, "Wallace said he had been wrong. He apologized. The injustices he perpetuated in the name of segregation need not be dismissed nor forgotten to be forgiven. But because Wallace admitted his guilt and sought to atone for it, many forgave. Coretta Scott King forgave him. Fred Gray forgave him. E. D. Nixon forgave him. Jesse Jackson forgave him."

In the 1982 Democratic primary for governor, he led the ticket, defeating Speaker of the House Joe McCorquodale. In a runoff with George McMillan of Birmingham, Wallace won 51 percent to 49 percent, with the majority of the black vote.

In the general election, he faced the strongest Republican opposition of the century. Montgomery mayor Emory Folmar, an outspoken, tough-talking, pistol-toting opponent of every social and economic program proposed by Democrats, ran a well-funded campaign. However, Wallace was backed by his former Democratic opponents as well as every black organization in the state. Wallace won by a landslide.

In the next four years, he did more for the black citizens of his state than any other governor. He appointed a black journalist as his press secretary. As though listening once again to president Lyndon Johnson's admonitions of twenty years earlier, he supported legislation that doubled the number of black voting registrars. He named almost two hundred blacks to governing committees throughout the state. A black leader from Birmingham was appointed to head up an important transportation commission. Wallace established an oil and gas fund to provide money to pay for unpopular programs to improve prisons and mental health facilities. According to E. D. Nixon, former state president of the NAACP, "George Wallace was the most important friend that black people could have in the early 1980s. As governor he provided a lot of jobs for blacks. He elevated public housing to a new high. He never backed down once when me or some other black leader went to see him and asked him to help out."

20

"LIKE A MIGHTY STREAM"

"We are not satisfied and we will not be satisfied until justice rolls down like waters and righteousness like a mighty stream," said Dr. Martin Luther King Jr. in his "I Have a Dream" speech in Washington, D.C., in the summer of 1963.

Those words are now emblazoned on the granite wall on the south side of Washington Avenue in Montgomery, Alabama, five blocks from the state capitol and near the Dexter Avenue King Memorial Baptist Church. It sits opposite the ultramodern office of the Southern Poverty Law Center, which reflects sunlight or moonlight in brilliant streams of glitter from its stainless-steel facade.

In 1989, a crowd gathered in front of the Civil Rights Memorial designed by Maya Lin, famed for her Vietnam War Memorial in Washington, D.C. With the waters streaming down to enhance King's words and bubbling up over the round granite memorial where names of fallen warriors in the struggle for civil rights are etched, SPLC's first president, Julian Bond, spoke.

"We are gathered in the Cradle of the Confederacy," Bond said, "to dedicate a monument to those who died so all might be free. As we do so, let us rededicate ourselves to freedom's fight. Let us gather not in recrimination but in reconciliation, remembrance, and renewed resolve."

In eloquent tones, the tall and slender man who had served the cause for many years spoke of the history of the civil rights movement. As the Cradle once "rocked with the violence of our opponents, today it is soothed by the waters of this monument. A monument which, like the movement it honors, is majestic in its simplicity, overwhelming in its power. It bears the names of forty men, women, and children who gave their lives for freedom. It recalls their individual sacrifice. And it summons us to continue their collective cause."

Recalling the fight that resonated through the years since *Brown v. Board* and the Montgomery bus boycott, the long, hard, sad years after, and the fight to overcome the evil of Jim Crow and the Ku Klux Klan, Julian Bond stated, "Most of those who made the movement weren't the famous; they were the faceless. They weren't the noted; they were the nameless.

"We honor all of them today."

Among the names of the Freedom Forty etched on the never-ending circle of granite was Willie Edwards Jr. for everyone to see and to remember. Etched nearby beneath the thin film of water that spilled over the precipice were the names of Jimmie Lee Jackson, Jonathan Daniels, and Sammy Younge.

In the midst of silence on a bright November afternoon, Julian Bond concluded: "May the waters of this monument create ripples of hope—now and forevermore."

ACKNOWLEDGMENTS

So many people have given me so much for this book. This one has been a long time in the making, beginning back in the 1960s when I was a reporter for the *Alabama Journal*.

My original editor on the *Journal*, Ray Jenkins, hired me and instantly became my mentor. Ray and his lovely wife, Bettina, became friends and guided me through numerous personal and professional minefields.

I have always been blessed with the greatest friends. My fellow journalists at the *Journal* and the *Montgomery Advertiser* shared their vast knowledge and expertise when I was still wet behind the ears. Not least of these were Tom Cork, Betty Cork, Claude Duncan, Judith Helms, Joe McFadden, and many others. Through the years I have had the good fortune to know and learn from wonderful journalists like Jack Nelson of the *Los Angeles Times*; Gene Roberts, Roy Reed, Jim Wooten, and Howell Raines with the *New York Times*; Brandt Ayers, the inimitable editor and publisher of the *Anniston Star*; and so many more I can hardly count them all.

At the *New York Times* in the 1970s, Charlotte Curtis was the editor of the op-ed page who liked my folksy pieces about Alabama and encouraged me, publishing fourteen in a decade, including several about the Ku Klux Klan and governor George Wallace.

The former editors and staff members of the *Southern Courier*, a wonderful and unique weekly newspaper that covered civil rights from May 1965 until December 1968 in Alabama and parts of Mississippi, were more than generous with their time and their remembrances. Watching the DVD of their fortieth reunion, held in the spring of 2006 in Montgomery at Auburn University, was like visiting with them in person. Their e-mails and phone conversations furnished full details of much of their work—this was especially true of photographer Jim Peppler, whose generosity is overwhelming. He is a person whose work I have admired for years.

A few years ago I met Donnie Williams, a young grocer who pursued me diligently until I finally sat down with him and let him show me his boxes filled with material about the bus boycott of the mid-1950s. As a result, Donnie and I wrote *The Thunder of Angels: The Montgomery Bus Boycott and the People Who Broke the Back of Jim Crow*. It was a wonderfully rewarding experience. And now I miss Donnie, who died early in 2009 after suffering from cancer. Working on that project gave me the idea to go back into my own life and experiences and my research as a reporter when I was covering civil rights demonstrations every day.

My friend Penny Weaver with the Southern Poverty Law Center shared some of her fabulous photographs and found others in the SPLC archives. Her husband, Kendal, is a great friend and an inspiration as a journalist with the Associated Press in Alabama.

All of the drum majors for justice, Charles Morgan Jr., Morris Dees, Bill Baxley, Doug Jones, Orzell Billingsley Jr., J. L. Chestnut Jr., and Solomon Seay Jr. opened their thoughts about their vast experiences through the years as attorneys for people across the South and the nation. Others who assisted them were equally open with their professional lives.

I appreciate greatly the enormous assistance of Dr. Edwin C. Bridges, director of the Alabama Department of Archives and History, and his staff, particularly Linda Overman, Norwood Kerr, and Cynthia Luckie.

My editor at Lawrence Hill Books, Yuval Taylor, once again offered thoughtful professional advice in a timely fashion. I also appreciate the work of other Chicago Review Press editors, including Jerome Pohlen and Lisa Reardon.

And finally, my wife, Sally, has once again nurtured me and my work with her love and her intellectual understanding.

SOURCES

1. Willie's First Day

Author Interviews: Willie Edwards Sr., C. D. Jones, Jack D. Shows, Tom Ward, Gene Hudson, and Ralph Graves.

Montgomery Police Department records, incident reports, and interviews by Jack D. Shows and Tom Ward with Edna and Henry Alexander, William "Sonny Kyle" Livingston, Raymond C. Britt, and James D. "Jimmy" York.

Greenhaw, Wayne. *Montgomery: The River City*. Montgomery, AL: River City Publishing, 2003.

Cold Case Files, Episode 34. The History Channel, December 23, 2004.

Nossiter, Adam. "Murder, Memory and the Klan: A Special Report." *New York Times*, September 4, 1993.

2. The Legacy of Willie Edwards

Author Interviews: Jack D. Shows, Tom Ward, Willie Edwards Sr., Ella Edwards, Sergeant George Malloy of the Montgomery Police Department, Louis Kushner, and Sam Rainey of the Alabama Department of Public Safety's Bureau of Investigation.

Parks, Rosa. *Rosa Parks: My Story*. With Jim Haskins. New York: Dial Books, 1992.

Sims, Patsy. *The Klan*. New York: Stein & Day, 1978.

Greenhaw, Wayne. "Remembering Bobby Shelton and the Ku Klux Klan." *New York Times*, July 8, 1978.

Lights, Camera, Alabama Presents: The Rebirth of the Klan. University of Alabama Make-A-Movie. http://video.google.com/videoplay?docid=6340152737523525980#.

3. Klan on Trial

Author Interviews: Leila Ann Ramsey, Roscoe Williams, Jack Shows, Tom Ward, Joe Pilcher, Frank Long, Jo Ann Flirt, and Joe Azbell.

Unpublished notebooks of Tom Ward.

Montgomery Police Department records, transcripts of interviews conducted by Jack Shows and Tom Ward with William "Sonny Kyle" Livingston and Raymond C. Britt and unnamed witnesses.

Reporter's notes: *State v. Britt and Livingston.*

Newspaper accounts in the *Montgomery Advertiser*, including Joe Azbell's column, City Limits.

Abernathy, Ralph David. *And the Walls Came Tumbling Down.* New York: Harper & Row, 1989.

Graetz, Robert S. *A White Preacher's Story: The Montgomery Bus Boycott.* Montgomery, AL: Black Belt Press, 1998.

King, Martin Luther, Jr. *The Autobiography of Martin Luther King Jr.* Edited by Clayborne Carson. New York: Grand Central Publishing, 1998.

4. Hound-Dog Determined

Author Interviews: Jack Shows, Tom Ward, Gene Hudson, Leland McRae, Allen Rankin, and Neil Andrews.

Sims, Patsy. *The Klan.* New York: Stein & Day, 1978.

Ward, Gladys. "The Life of Ryland Randolph." Master's thesis, University of Alabama, 1932.

Wiggins, Sarah Woolfolk. "The Life of Ryland Randolph as Seen Through His Letter to John W. Dubose." *Alabama Historical Quarterly*, Volume 30, Numbers 3–4, Fall and Winter, 1968.

Logue, Calvin M., and Howard Dorgan. *The Oratory of Southern Demagogues.* Baton Rouge: Louisiana State University Press, 1981.

5. "Fight Everything Segregated"

Author Interviews: E. D. Nixon, Johnnie Rebecca Carr, Fred D. Gray, Orzell Billingsley Jr., and Sue Ellen Clifford.

Montgomery Advertiser June 12, 1957; August 21, 1958; and November 15, 1960.

Gray, Fred D. *Bus Ride to Justice.* Montgomery, AL: Black Belt Press, 1995.

Chestnut, J. L., Jr. *Black in Selma: The Uncommon Life of J. L. Chestnut Jr.* With Julia Cass. Tuscaloosa: University of Alabama Press, 1990.

MLK Online. http://www.mlkonline.net/nation.html. "The Birth of a New Nation." Sermon at Dexter Avenue Baptist Church, April 7, 1957.

Griggs, Lee. "Attack on the Conscience." *Time*, February 18, 1957.

King, Coretta Scott. *My Life with Martin Luther King Jr.* New York: Holt, Rinehart, and Winston, 1969.

Seay, Solomon S., Jr. *Jim Crow and Me: Stories from My Life as a Civil Rights Lawyer.* With Delores Boyd. Montgomery, AL: NewSouth Books, 2009.

"Folsom Commutes Death Sentence." Associated Press, September 30, 1958.

6. The Making of a Segregationist

Author Interviews: George C. Wallace, Oscar Harper, Frank Long, Jack Shows, Rex Thomas, Frank M. Johnson Jr., Ruth Johnson, Seymore Trammell, and Gerald Wallace.

Trammell, Seymore. "My Life with George Wallace." Unpublished manuscript.

Bass, Jack. *Taming the Storm: The Life and Times of Judge Frank M. Johnson Jr. and the South's Fight Over Civil Rights.* New York: Doubleday, 1993.

Greenhaw, Wayne. *Watch Out for George Wallace.* Englewood Cliffs, NJ: Prentice-Hall, 1976.

7. The Pair from Howard

Author Interviews: J. L. Chestnut Jr., Orzell Billingsley Jr., and Carlton Simmons.

Chestnut, J. L., Jr. *Black in Selma: The Uncommon Life of J. L. Chestnut Jr.* With Julia Cass. Tuscaloosa: University of Alabama Press, 1990.

Seay, Solomon S., Jr. *Jim Crow and Me: Stories from My Life as a Civil Rights Lawyer.* With Delores Boyd. Montgomery, AL: NewSouth Books, 2009.

8. "Segregation Forever!"

Author Interviews: Michael B. Sullivan, Asa Earl Carter, George C. Wallace, John Peter Kohn, Grover Cleveland Hall Jr., Tom Johnson, Bill Jones, Seymore Trammell, Carl "Bear" Statum, and Earl Pippin.

McWhorter, Diane. *Carry Me Home: Birmingham, Alabama: The Climactic Battle of the Civil Rights Revolution.* New York: Simon & Schuster, 2001.

Lesher, Stephan. *George Wallace: American Populist.* New York: Addison-Wesley Publishing Company, 1994.

Bernard, William D. *Dixiecrats and Democrats: 1942–1950.* Tuscaloosa: University of Alabama Press, 1974.

Carter, Dan T. *The Politics of Rage: George Wallace, the Origins of the New Conservatism, and the Transformation of American Politics*. New York: Simon & Schuster, 1995.

Greenhaw, Wayne. *Watch Out for George Wallace*. Englewood Cliffs, NJ: Prentice-Hall, 1976.

9. Education of a Liberal

Author Interviews: Charles Morgan Jr., George W. Dean Jr., U.S. senator Howell Heflin, Marc Ray Clement, Jay W. Murphy, and Janeece Langham.

Greenhaw, Wayne. *Alabama on My Mind*. Montgomery, AL: Sycamore Press, 1987.

Morgan, Charles, Jr. *A Time to Speak*. New York: Harper & Row, 1964.

Morgan, Charles, Jr. *One Man, One Voice*. New York: Holt Rinehart Winston, 1979.

New York Times. Obituary of Jay Murphy. December 21, 1992.

Shelby, Richard. "Remembering Professor Jay Murphy." *Congressional Record*, December 21, 1992.

Wendt, Simon. "God, Gandhi, and Guns: The African-American Freedom Struggle in Tuscaloosa, Alabama, 1964–1965." *Journal of African-American History*, Volume 89, 2004.

Unpublished letters by Charles Morgan Jr. to the author.

Charles Morgan Papers at the Alabama Department of Archives and History.

"Birmingham: An Alabaman's Great Speech Lays the Blame." *Life*, September 27, 1963.

Morgan, Charles, Jr. "I Watched a City Die." *Look*, October 1963.

King, Dr. Martin Luther, Jr. "I Have a Dream." http://www.americanrhetoric.com/speeches/mlkihaveadream.html.

Holt, Len. "Eyewitness: The Police Terror at Birmingham." *National Guardian*, May 16, 1963.

Life. "Birmingham: An Alabaman's Great Speech Lays the Blame." September 27, 1963.

Morgan, Charles, Jr. "I Watched a City Die." *Look*, October 1963.

10. Country-Boy Lawyer

Author Interviews: Morris Dees, Joe Levin Jr., Charles Morgan Jr., Millard Fuller, and Earl Pippin.

Dees, Morris. *A Lawyer's Journey: The Morris Dees Story*. With Steve Fiffer. Chicago: American Bar Association, 2001.

Greenhaw, Wayne. "Morris Dees: Pro Bono." *American Lawyer*, May 1988.

Greenhaw, Wayne. "The King of Desegregation: Morris Dees." *Southern Voices*, October 1978.

11. The Alabama Story

Author Interviews: George C. Wallace, Oscar Harper, John Peter Kohn, Bill Jones, Bob Ingram, Dave Silverman, and Grover Cleveland Hall Jr.

Jones, Bill. *The Wallace Story*. Northport, AL: American Southern Publishing Company, 1966.

Carter, Dan T. *The Politics of Rage: George Wallace, The Origins of the New Conservatism, and the Transformation of American Politics*. New York: Simon & Schuster, 1995.

Greenhaw, Wayne. *Watch Out for George Wallace*. Englewood Cliffs, NJ: Prentice-Hall, 1976.

Lesher, Stephan. *George Wallace: American Populist*. New York: Addison-Wesley Publishing Company, 1994.

Brill, Steven. "The Real Governor of Alabama." *New York*, April 26, 1976.

12. Requiem for Jimmie Lee Jackson

Author Interviews: J. L. Chestnut Jr., Lawton Hughes, and Walter Givhan.

Chestnut, J. L., Jr. *Black in Selma: The Uncommon Life of J. L. Chestnut Jr.* With Julia Cass. Tuscaloosa: University of Alabama Press, 1990.

Gaillard, Frye. *Cradle of Freedom: Alabama and the Movement that Changed America*. Tuscaloosa: University of Alabama Press, 2004.

Lewis, John. *Walking with the Wind: A Memoir of the Movement*. New York: Simon & Schuster, 1998.

Webb, Sheyann, and Rachel West Nelson. *Selma, Lord, Selma: Girlhood Memories of the Civil Rights Days*. As told to Frank Sikora. Tuscaloosa: University of Alabama Press, 1980.

Sikora, Frank. *The Judge: The Life & Opinions of Alabama's Frank M. Johnson Jr.* Montgomery, AL: Black Belt Press, 1992.

Herbers, John. "A Death in the Black Belt." *New York Times*, February 27, 1965.

Reed, Roy. "Attack on the Bridge." *New York Times*, March 8, 1965.

Goodwin, Richard. *Remembering America: A Voice from the Sixties*. Boston: Little, Brown & Company, 1995.

13. Don Quixote of the South

Author Interviews: Charles Morgan Jr., George W. Dean Jr., and Reber F. Boult Jr.

Belfrage, Sally. *Freedom Summer*. Charlottesville: University Press of Virginia, 1965.

Greenhaw, Wayne. *Alabama on My Mind*. Montgomery, AL: Sycamore Press, 1987.

Morgan, Charles, Jr. *A Time to Speak*. New York: Harper & Row, 1964.

Morgan, Charles, Jr. *One Man, One Voice*. New York: Holt Rinehart Winston, 1979.

Bayless, Les. "Remembering the Martyrs of Mississippi Freedom Summer, 1964." *People's Weekly World*, May 25, 1996.

Unpublished letters by Charles Morgan Jr. to the author.

Charles Morgan Papers at the Alabama Department of Archives and History.

14. The *Southern Courier*

Author Interviews: Michael Lottman, Robert Ellis Smith, Jim Peppler, Stephen E. Cotton, Joan Clark Tornow, Geoffrey Cowan, and Mary Ellen Gale.

Transcript and DVD of fortieth reunion of the *Southern Courier* staff, Auburn University at Montgomery, April 1, 2006.

Web site: http://www.southerncourier.com.

Cotton, Stephen E. *"The Southern Courier." Harvard Crimson*, Summer Edition, July 21, 1967.

Pippins, Erica. "The Courage of *The Courier." Montgomery Advertiser*, March 27, 2006.

Tornow, Joan, PhD. "Memory's Jagged Edge: Reflections on Birmingham, 1967." Sermon delivered to Saltwater Unitarian Universalist Church, Des Moines, Washington, August 14, 2005.

Smith, Robert Ellis. "Reporting the Civil Rights Movement." Paper given to the seventy-third meeting of the Southern Historical Association, Richmond, VA, November 2, 2007.

Southern Courier files at the Alabama Department of Archives and History.

15. The Rise of John Hulett

Author Interview: John Hulett, Knox McLaney, and Harrell Hammond.

Gaillard, Frye. *Cradle of Freedom: Alabama and the Movement that Changed America*. Tuscaloosa: University of Alabama Press, 2004.

Jeffries, Hasan Kwame. *Bloody Lowndes: Civil Rights and Black Power in Alabama's Black Belt*. New York: New York University Press, 2009.

Southern Courier files at the Alabama Department of Archives and History.

16. Southern Poverty Law Center

Author Interviews: Morris Dees, Joe Levin, and Charles Morgan Jr.

Bass, Jack. *Taming the Storm: The Life and Times of Judge Frank M. Johnson Jr. and the South's Fight Over Civil Rights*. New York: Doubleday, 1993.

Dees, Morris. *A Lawyer's Journey: The Morris Dees Story*. With Steve Fiffer. Chicago: American Bar Association, 2001.

Stanton, Bill. *Klanwatch: Bringing the Ku Klux Klan to Justice*. New York: Grove Weidenfeld, 1991.

"Advocates for Justice and Equality," "Morris Dees: Center founder and chief trial counsel," "Joseph J. Levin Jr.: Center founder and president emeritus," "Julian Bond: First Center president and member of the board," http://www.splcenter.org.

Goldman, Ari. "Oldest Rabbinical Student." *New York Daily News*, May 11, 2008.

Greenhaw, Wayne. "Remembering Bobby Shelton and the Ku Klux Klan." *New York Times*, April 18, 1968.

Greenhaw, Wayne. "Remembering and Believing: Morris Dees." *Alabama Journal*, February 27, 1974.

Greenhaw, Wayne. "Morris Dees: Pro Bono." *American Lawyer*, May 1988.

Greenhaw, Wayne. "The King of Desegregation: Morris Dees." *Southern Voices*, October 1978.

17. The People's Attorney General

Author Interviews: Bill Baxley, John Yung, Jack Shows, and G. Douglas Jones.

Cobbs, Elizabeth. *Long Time Coming*. With Petric J. Smith. Birmingham, AL: Crane Hill, 1994.

Currie, Stephen. *The Birmingham Church Bombing: Crime Scene Investigations*. Farmington Hills, MI: Lucent Books, 2006.

Hemphill, Paul. *Leaving Birmingham*. New York: Viking Press, 1993.

McWhorter, Diane. *Carry Me Home: Birmingham, Alabama: The Climactic Battle of the Civil Rights Revolution*. New York: Simon & Schuster, 2001.

Sikora, Frank. *Until Justice Rolls Down: The Birmingham Bombing Case*. Tuscaloosa: University of Alabama Press, 1991.

Baxley, Bill. "Why Did the FBI Hold Back Evidence?" *New York Times*, May 3, 2001.

Bragg, Rick. "Survivor of '63 Bombing Recalls Glass Shards and a Sister Lost." *New York Times*, May 18, 2002.

Yellin, Emily. "A Changing South Revisits Its Unsolved Racial Killings." *New York Times*, November 8, 1999.

Trial transcript, *State of Alabama v. Robert Chambliss*.

4 Little Girls. Directed by Spike Lee. 40 Acres and a Mule Filmworks, June 25, 1997.

18. Breaking the Klan

Author Interview: Morris Dees.

Beulah Mae Donald v. United Klans of America, Final Judgment, United States District Court, Southern District of Alabama, Southern Division, U.S. district judge Alex T. Howard Jr., February 12, 1987.

Silverstein, Ken. "The Church of Morris Dees." *Harper's Magazine*, November 2000.

Tucker, James P., Jr. "Victim of Smear Campaign Gets Even With Morris Dees." http://www.AmericanFreePress.net, March 26, 2006.

19. "Forgive Me, for I Have Sinned"

Author Interviews: Asa Earl Carter, George Wallace, and Oscar Harper.

Greenhaw, Wayne. *My Heart Is in the Earth: True Stories of Alabama and Mexico.* Montgomery, AL: River City Publishing, 2001.

Lesher, Stephan. *George Wallace: American Populist.* New York: Addison-Wesley Publishing, 1994.

20. Like a Mighty Stream

Bond, Julian. "Civil Rights Memorial Dedication Speech." http://www.splcenter.org. November 5, 1989.

"Civil Rights Memorial Dedicated." *Art in America*, December 1989.

Grogan, David, and Linda Kramer. "Maya Lin Lets Healing Waters Flow over Her Civil Rights Memorial." *People Weekly*, November 20, 1989.

BIBLIOGRAPHY

Books

Abernathy, Ralph David. *And the Walls Came Tumbling Down: An Autobiography.* New York: Harper & Row, 1989.

Ali, Muhammad. *The Greatest.* New York: Random House, 1975.

Applebone, Peter. *Dixie Rising: How the South Is Shaping American Values, Politics, and Culture.* New York: Harcourt Brace, 1997.

Ashby, Warren. *Frank Porter Graham: A Southern Liberal.* Winston-Salem, N.C.: Blair, 1980.

Ashmore, Harry. *An Epitaph for Dixie.* New York: Norton, 1958.

———. *Civil Rights and Wrongs: A Memoir of Race and Politics: 1944–1996.* Columbia: University of South Carolina Press, 1997.

———. *Hearts and Minds: The Anatomy of Racism from Roosevelt to Reagan.* New York: McGraw-Hill, 1982.

Baez, Joan. *And a Voice to Sing With.* New York: Summit, 1987.

Bailey, D'Army. *Mine Eyes Have Seen: Dr. Martin Luther King Jr.'s Final Journey.* Memphis: Towery, 1993.

Baldwin, Lewis V. *Freedom Is Never Free: Biographical Portrait of Edgar Daniel Nixon.* Atlanta: A. Woodson, 1992.

Barrett, Paul M. *The Good Black: A True Story of Race in America.* New York: Dutton, 1999.

Barry, Jason. *Amazing Grace.* New York: Saturday Review Press, 1978.

Bass, Jack. *Ol' Strom: An Unauthorized Biography of Strom Thurmond.* Atlanta: Longstreet, 1998.

————. *Taming the Storm: The Life and Times of Frank M. Johnson Jr. and the South's Fight Over Civil Rights.* New York: Doubleday, 1993.

————. *Unlikely Heroes: The Dramatic Story of the Southern Judges of the Fifth Circuit who Translated the Supreme Court's Brown Decision into a Revolution for Equality.* New York: Simon & Schuster, 1981.

Bass, Jack, and Walter De Vries. *The Transformation of Southern Politics: Social Change and Political Consequences Since 1945.* New York: Basic Books, 1976.

Bass, Patrik Henry. *Like a Mighty Stream: The March on Washington.* Philadelphia: Running Press, 2002.

Bass, S. Jonathan. *Blessed are the Peacemakers: Martin Luther King Jr., Eight White Religious Leaders, and the "Letter from the Birmingham Jail."* Baton Rouge: Louisiana State University Press, 2001.

Beasley, Maurine Hoffman, and Richard R. Harlow. *Voices of Change: Southern Pulitzer Winners.* Washington, DC: University Press of America, 1979.

Belfrage, Sally. *Freedom Summer.* New York: Viking Press, 1965.

Bell, Derrick A. *And We Are Not Saved: The Elusive Quest for Racial Justice.* New York: Basic Books, 1987.

Bernard, William D. *Dixiecrats and Democrats, 1942–1950.* Tuscaloosa: University of Alabama Press, 1974.

Blasi, Anthony J. *Segregationist Violence and Civil Rights Movements in Tuscaloosa.* Washington, DC: University Press of America, 1980.

Blue, Matthew. *The Works of Matthew Blue.* Edited and annotated by Mary Ann Neeley with a foreword by Edwin C. Bridges. Montgomery, AL: NewSouth Books, 2010.

Blumberg, Rhoda Goldstein. *Civil Rights: The 1960s Freedom Struggle.* Boston: Twayne Publishers, 1984.

Bond, Horace Mann. *Negro Education in Alabama: A Study in Cotton and Steel.* New York: Atheneum, 1969.

Branch, Taylor. *Parting the Water: America in the King Years, 1954–63.* New York: Simon & Schuster, 1988.

Brinkley, Douglas. *Rosa Parks.* New York: Viking Penguin, 2000.

Bullard, Sara, and Julian Bond. *Free At Last: A History of the Civil Rights Movement and Those Who Died in the Struggle.* Montgomery, AL: Southern Poverty Law Center's Civil Rights Education Project, 1989.

Campbell, Will D. *Forty Acres and a Goat.* Atlanta: Peachtree Publishers, 1986.

Carlson, Jody. *George C. Wallace and the Politics of Powerlessness: The Wallace Campaigns for the Presidency, 1964–1976.* New Brunswick, NJ: Transaction Inc., 1981.

Carmer, Carl. *Stars Fell on Alabama.* New York: Farrar & Rinehart, 1934.

Carr, Charles E., Jr. *On The Road to Freedom: A Guided Tour of the Civil Rights Movement.* Chapel Hill, NC: Algonquin Books, 2008.

Carson, Clayborne et al., comps. *Reporting Civil Rights, Part One: American Journalism 1941–1963.* New York: Library of America, 2003.

———. *Reporting Civil Rights, Part Two: American Journalism 1963–1973.* New York: Library of America, 2003.

Carter, Dan T. *The Politics of Rage: George Wallace, the Origins of the New Conservatism, and the Transformation of American Politics.* New York: Simon & Schuster, 1995.

Carter, Hodding, III. *The South Strikes Back.* Garden City, NY: Doubleday, 1959.

Cash, W. J. *The Mind of the South.* New York: Alfred J. Knopf, 1941.

Cashin, Sheryll. *Agitator's Daughter: A Memoir of Four Generations of One Extraordinary African-American Family.* New York: Public Affairs, 2008.

Chalmers, David M. *Hooded Americanism: The History of the Ku Klux Klan.* Raleigh, NC: Duke University Press, 1987.

Chestnut, J. L., Jr., and Julia Cass. *Black in Selma: The Uncommon Life of J. L. Chestnut Jr.* New York: Farrar, Straus, and Giroux, 1990.

Clark, E. Culpepper. *The Schoolhouse Door: Segregation's Last Stand at the University of Alabama.* New York: Oxford University Press, 1993.

Cobbs, Elizabeth H. *Long Time Coming: An Insider's Story of the Church Bombing That Rocked the World.* With Petric J. Smith. Birmingham, AL: Crane Hill, 1994.

Cook, James Graham. *The Segregationists.* New York: Appleton-Century-Crofts, 1962.

Cox, Archibald. *The Court and the Constitution.* Boston: Houghton Mifflin Company, 1987.

Crass, Philip. *The Wallace Factor.* New York: Mason / Charter, 1976.

Currie, Stephen. *The Birmingham Church Bombings.* Farmington Hills, MI: Lucent Books, 2006.

Daniels, Jonathan. *A Southerner Discovers the South.* New York: Macmillan, 1938.

Dees, Morris. *A Lawyer's Journey: The Morris Dees Story.* With Steve Fiffer. Chicago: American Bar Association, 2001.

Diouf, Sylviane A. *Dreams of Africa in Alabama: The Slave Ship Clotilda and the Story of the Last Africans Brought to America.* New York: Oxford University Press, 2007.

Dittmer, John et al. *Essays on the American Civil Rights Movement.* College Station: Texas A&M Press, 1993.

Dixon, Thomas, Jr. *The Clansman: An Historical Romance of the Ku Klux Klan.* With an introduction by Thomas D. Clark. Lexington: University Press of Kentucky, 1970.

Dorman, Michael. *We Shall Overcome.* New York: Delacorte, 1964.

Durr, Virginia Foster. *Freedom Writer: Letters from the Civil Rights Years.* With Patricia Sullivan. Nashville, TN: Routledge, 2003.

————. *Outside the Magic Circle.* Tuscaloosa: University of Alabama Press, 1985.

Eagles, Charles W. *Outside Agitator: Jon Daniels and the Civil Rights Movement in Alabama.* Tuscaloosa: University of Alabama Press, 2000.

Egerton, John. *Speak Now Against the Day: The Generation Before the Civil Rights Movement in the South.* New York: Knopf, 1994.

Eskew, Glenn T. *But for Birmingham: The Local and National Movements in the Civil Rights Struggle.* Chapel Hill: University of North Carolina Press, 1997.

Farmer, James. *Freedom—When?* New York: Random House, 1965.

————. *Lay Bare the Heart: An Autobiography of the Civil Rights Movement.* New York: Arbor House, 1985.

Feldman, Glenn. *Politics, Society and the Klan in Alabama, 1915–1949.* Tuscaloosa: University of Alabama Press, 1999.

————. *The Disenfranchisement Myth: Poor Whites and Suffrage Restriction in Alabama.* Athens: University of Georgia Press, 2004.

Fitts, Alston, III. *Selma: Queen City of the Black Belt.* Selma, AL: Clairmont Press, 1989.

Flynt, Wayne. *Alabama in the Twentieth Century.* Tuscaloosa: University of Alabama Press, 2004.

————. *Montgomery: An Illustrated History.* Woodland Hills, CA: Windsor Publications, Inc., 1980.

Forman, James. *The Making of Black Revolutionaries.* New York: Macmillan, 1972.

Frady, Marshall. *Wallace.* New York: World, 1968.

Gaither, Gerald. *Blacks and the Populist Revolt: Ballots and Bigotry in the "New South."* Tuscaloosa: University of Alabama Press, 1977.

Gaillard, Frye. *Cradle of Freedom: Alabama and the Movement that Changed America.* Tuscaloosa: University of Alabama Press, 2004.

Garrow, David J. *Bearing the Cross: Martin Luther King Jr. and the Southern Christian Leadership Conference.* New York: Morrow, 1986.

Gaston, A.G. *Green Power.* Birmingham: Birmingham Publishing Company, 1968.

Goodwin, Richard. *Remembering America: A Voice from the Sixties.* Boston: Little Brown Company, 1995.

Graetz, Robert S. *A White Preacher's Story: The Montgomery Bus Boycott.* Montgomery, AL: Black Belt Press, 1998.

Grafton, Carl, and Anne Permaloff. *Big Mules and Branchheads: James E. Folsom and Political Power in Alabama.* Athens: University of Georgia Press, 1985.

Grantham, Dewey. *Southern Progressivism.* Knoxville: University of Tennessee Press, 1983.

Gray, Fred D. *Bus Ride to Freedom.* Montgomery, AL: Black Belt Press, 1995.

Greenhaw, Wayne. *Alabama on my Mind.* Montgomery, AL: Sycamore Press, 1987.

————. *My Heart Is in the Earth: True Stories of Alabama and Mexico.* Montgomery, AL: River City Publishing, 2001.

———. *Montgomery: The River City.* Montgomery, AL: River City Publishing, 2002.

———. *Watch Out for George Wallace.* Englewood Cliffs, NJ: Prentice-Hall, 1976.

Hackney, Sheldon. *Populism to Progressivism in Alabama.* Princeton, NJ: Princeton University Press, 1969.

Halberstam, David. *The Children.* New York: Random House, 1998.

———. *The Fifties.* New York: Fawcett Columbine, 1993.

Hamilton, Virginia Van der Veer. *Alabama: A History.* New York: Norton, 1977.

Hampton, Henry, and Steve Fayer. *Voices of Freedom: An Oral History of the Civil Rights Movement from the 1950s Through the 1980s.* New York: Bantam, 1990.

Hemphill, Paul. *Leaving Birmingham: Notes of a Native Son.* New York: Viking, 1993.

Horn, Stanley F. *Invisible Empire: The Story of the Ku Klux Klan 1866–1871.* New York: Haskell House Publishers, 1973.

Horton, Myles. *The Long Haul.* With Judith Kohl and Herbert Kohl. Garden City, NY: Doubleday, 1990.

Houck, Davis W., and David E. Dixon. *Rhetoric, Religion and the Civil Rights Movement, 1954–1965.* Waco, TX: Baylor University Press, 2006.

Huie, William Bradford. *He Slew the Dreamer.* Foreword by Wayne Greenhaw. Montgomery: Black Belt Press, 1997.

———. *Three Lives for Mississippi.* New York: WCC Books, 1965.

Jackson, Harvey H., III. *Inside Alabama: A Personal View of My State.* Tuscaloosa: University of Alabama Press, 2004.

Jeffries, Hasan Kwame. *Bloody Lowndes: Civil Rights and Black Power in Alabama's Black Belt.* New York: New York University Press, 2009.

Jones, William G. *The Wallace Story.* Northport, AL: American Southern Publishing, 1966.

Kennedy, Robert Francis, Jr. *Judge Frank M. Johnson.* New York: G. P. Putnam's Sons, 1978.

Kennedy, Stetson. *The Klan Unmasked.* Gainesville: University Press of Florida, 1990.

Key, V. O. *Southern Politics in State and Nation.* New York: Knopf, 1949.

King, Coretta Scott. *My Life with Martin Luther King Jr.* New York: Holt, Rinehart and Winston, 1969.

King, Martin Luther, Jr. *The Autobiography of Martin Luther King Jr.* Edited by Clayborne Carson. New York: Warner Books, Inc., 1998.

———. *Stride Toward Freedom: A Leader of His People Tells the Montgomery Story.* New York: Harper & Brothers, 1958.

———. *Strength to Love.* New York: Harper & Row, 1964.

———. *Why We Can't Wait.* New York: Harper & Row, 1963.

King, Richard H. *Civil Rights and the Idea of Freedom.* New York: Oxford University Press, 1992.

Kohn, John Peter. *The Cradle: Anatomy of a Town—Fact and Fiction*. New York: Vantage Press, 1969.

Lesher, Stephan. *George Wallace: American Populist*. New York: Addison-Wesley, 1994.

Levy, Peter B. *Let Freedom Ring: A Documentary History of the Modern Civil Rights Movement*. New York: Praeger, 1992.

———. *The Civil Rights Movement*. New York: Greenwood Press, 1998.

Lewis, John. *Walking with the Wind: A Memoir of the Movement*. With Michael D'Orso. New York: Harcourt Brace, 1998.

Loevy, Robert D., et al. *The Civil Rights Act of 1964: The Passage of the Law That Ended Racial Segregation*. New York: State University of New York Press, 1997.

Logue, Calvin M., and Howard Dorgan. *The Oratory of Southern Demagogues*. Baton Rouge: Louisiana State University Press, 1981.

Lowery, Charles D., and John F. Marszalek. *Encyclopedia of African-American Civil Rights: From Emancipation to the Present*. New York: Greenwood Press, 1992.

Manis, Andrew M. *A Fire You Can't Put Out: The Civil Rights Life of Birmingham's Reverend Fred Shuttlesworth*. Tuscaloosa: University of Alabama Press, 1999.

May, Gary. *The Informant: The FBI, the Ku Klux Klan, and the Murder of Viola Liuzzo*. New Haven: Yale University Press, 2005.

McIlhanany, William H., II. *Klandestine: The Untold Story of Delmar Dennis and His Role in the FBI's War Against the Ku Klux Klan*. New Rochelle, NY: Arlington House Publishers, 1975.

McMillan, Malcolm C. *Yesterday's Birmingham*. Miami: E. A. Seemann Publishing Inc., 1975.

McWhorter, Diane. *Carry Me Home: Birmingham, Alabama: The Climactic Battle of the Civil Rights Revolution*. New York: Simon & Schuster, 2001.

Morgan, Charles. *A Time to Speak*. New York: Harper & Row, 1963.

———. *One Man, One Voice*. New York: Holt, Rinehart and Winston, 1979.

Morris, Willie. *North Toward Home*. Boston: Houghton Mifflin, 1967.

———. *The South Today, 100 Years after Appomattox*. New York: Harper & Row, 1965.

Neeley, Mary Ann. *Montgomery Capital City Corners*. Dover, NH: Arcadia Publishing, 1997.

Nelson, Jack. *Terror in the Night: The Klan's Campaign Against the Jews*. New York: Simon & Schuster, 1993.

Norrell, Robert J. *Reaping the Whirlwind: The Civil Rights Movement in Tuskegee*. Chapel Hill: University of North Carolina Press, 1985.

Nunnelly, William. *Bull Connor*. Tuscaloosa: University of Alabama Press, 1991.

Oates, Stephen B. *Let the Trumpet Sound: The Life of Martin Luther King Jr.* New York: Harper & Row, 1982.

Owen, Thomas McAdory. *History of Alabama and Dictionary of Alabama Biography*. 4 vols. Chicago: S. J. Clarke, 1921.

Parks, Rosa. *Rosa Parks: My Story*. With Jim Haskins. New York: Dial Books, 1992.

Powledge, Fred. *Free At Last: The Civil Rights Movement and the People Who Made It*. New York: Harper Perennial, 1991.

Raines, Howell. *My Soul Is Rested*. New York: G. P. Putnam's Sons, 1977.

Roberts, Gene, and Hank Klibanoff. *The Race Beat: The Press, the Civil Rights Struggle, and the Awakening of a Nation*. New York: Alfred A. Knopf, 2006.

Rogers, William Warren, et al. *Alabama: The History of a Deep South State*. Tuscaloosa: University of Alabama Press, 1994.

Rowe, Gary Thomas, Jr. *My Undercover Years with the Ku Klux Klan*. New York: Bantam Books, 1976.

Seay, Solomon S., Jr. *Jim Crow and Me: Stories from My Life as a Civil Rights Lawyer*. With Delores R. Boyd. Montgomery, AL: NewSouth Books, 2009.

Sherrill, Robert. *Gothic Politics in the Deep South: Stars of the New Confederacy*. New York: Ballantine, 1968.

Sikora, Frank. *The Judge: The Life and Opinions of Alabama's Frank M. Johnson Jr.* Montgomery, AL: Black Belt Press, 1992.

———. *Until Justice Rolls Down: The Birmingham Church Bombing Case*. Tuscaloosa: University of Alabama Press, 1991.

Sims, George E. *The Little Man's Big Friend: James E. Folsom in Alabama Politics, 1946–1958*. Tuscaloosa: University of Alabama Press, 1958.

Sims, Patsy. *The Klan*. New York: Stein and Day, 1978.

Stampp, Kenneth M. *The Peculiar Institution: Slavery in the Ante-Bellum South*. New York: Random House, 1956.

Stanton, Bill. *Klanwatch: Bringing the Ku Klux Klan to Justice*. New York: Grove Weidenfeld, 1991.

Stanton, Mary. *From Selma to Sorrow: The Life and Death of Viola Liuzzo*. Athens: University of Georgia Press, 1998.

Taylor, Sandra Baxley. *Me 'n' George: A Story of George Corley Wallace and His Number One Crony, Oscar Harper*. Mobile, AL: Greenberry Publishing, 1988.

Terkel, Studs. *Race: How Blacks and Whites Think and Feel About the American Obsession*. New York: Doubleday, Anchor Books, 1992.

Thompson, Jerry. *My Life in the Klan: A True Story by the First Investigative Reporter to Infiltrate the Ku Klux Klan*. New York: G. P. Putnam's Sons, 1982.

Thomson, Bailey, ed. *A Century of Controversy: Constitutional Reform in Alabama*. Tuscaloosa: University of Alabama Press, 2002.

Thornton, J. Mills. *Dividing Lines: Municipal Politics and the Struggle for Civil Rights in Montgomery, Birmingham, and Selma*. Tuscaloosa: University of Alabama Press, 2002.

Wakefield, Dan. *Revolt in the South*. New York: Grove Press, 1960.

Webb, Samuel L., and Margaret E. Armbrester, eds. *Alabama Governors*. Tuscaloosa: University of Alabama Press, 2001.

Webb, Sheyann, and Rachel West Nelson. *Selma, Lord, Selma*. With Frank Sikora. Tuscaloosa: University of Alabama Press, 1997.

Weisbrot, Robert. *Freedom Bound: A History of America's Civil Rights Movement*. New York: W. W. Norton, 1990.

Williams, Donnie, and Wayne Greenhaw. *The Thunder of Angels: The Montgomery Bus Boycott and the People Who Broke the Back of Jim Crow*. Chicago: Lawrence Hill Books, 2006.

Williams, Juan. *Eyes on the Prize: America's Civil Rights Years, 1954–1965*. New York: Penguin Books, 1987.

Woodward, C. Vann. *Origins of the New South*. Baton Rouge: Louisiana State University Press, 1951.

Yarbrough, Tinsley E. *Frank Johnson and Human Rights in Alabama*. Tuscaloosa: University of Alabama Press, 1981.

Newspapers and Magazines

Ashmore, Harry S. "Black Power & White Inertia." *Center Magazine*, January 1968.

Baxley, Bill. "Why Did the FBI Hold Back Evidence?" *New York Times*, May 3, 2001.

Bayless, Les. "Three Who Gave Lives: Remembering the Martyrs of Mississippi Freedom Summer." *People's Weekly World*, May 25, 1996.

Bragg, Rick. "Survivor of '63 Bombing Recalls Glass Shards and a Sister Lost." *New York Times*, May 18, 2002.

Brill, Steven. "The Real Governor of Alabama." *New York*, April 26, 1976.

Cashin, Sheryll. "Family Inheritance: From Reconstruction to Post Civil Rights." *Vanderbilt Magazine*, Fall 2008.

Cotton, Stephen E. "Working on the Southern Courier." *Harvard Crimson*, July 21, 1967.

Cox, Major W. "Justice Still Absent in Bridge Death." *Montgomery Advertiser*, March 2, 1999.

Fee, Stephen M. "Hope Alongside Hatred: The Staff of a Civil Rights Newspaper, Started by Two Harvard Juniors, Returns to Alabama." *Harvard Crimson*, April 12, 2006.

Greenhaw, Wayne. "The King of Desegregation: Morris Dees." *Southern Voices*, October 1978.

———. "Morris Dees: Pro Bono." *American Lawyer*, May 1988.

———. "Remembering Bobby Shelton and the Ku Klux Klan." *New York Times*, July 8, 1978.

———. "Sir Galahad of the South: Charles Morgan Jr." *Southern Voices*, April 1977.

Griggs, Lee. "Attack on the Conscience." *Time*, February 18, 1957.

Holt, Len. "Eyewitness: The Police Terror at Birmingham." *The National Guardian*, May 16, 1963.

Huie, William Bradford. "Alabamians Against Wallace." *Look*, April 30, 1968.

————. "Humanity's Case Against George Wallace." *Genesis*, March 1976.

————. "The Truth About the Lie That Made George Wallace Famous." *Village Voice*, January 12, 1976.

————. "The U.S. *Must* Say No to George Wallace." *True: The Men's Magazine*, July 1968.

Jenkins, Ray. "George Wallace." *New York Times Magazine*, April 7, 1968.

————. "Mr. and Mrs. George Wallace Run for Governor of Alabama." *New York Times Magazine*, April 24, 1966.

————. "The Queen of Alabama and the Prince Consort." *New York Times Magazine*, May 21, 1967.

Montgomery Advertiser. "Suspects Bound in 1957 Slaying." February 27, 1976.

Moore, Deborah Hayes. "*Southern Courier* Staffers Enjoy Garden Party." *Montgomery Advertiser*, April 6, 2006.

Nossiter, Adam. "Murder, Memory and the Klan: A Special Report; Widow Inherits a Confession to a 36-Year-Old Hate Crime." *New York Times*, September 4, 1993.

Southern Courier, May 1965–December 1968

Wendt, Simon. "God, Gandhi, and Guns: The African-American Freedom Struggle in Tuscaloosa, Alabama, 1964–1965." *Journal of African-American History*, Volume 89, 2004.

Wiggins, Sarah Woolfolk. "The Life of Ryland Randolph as Seen Through His Letter to John W. Dubose." *Alabama Historical Quarterly*, Volume 30, Numbers 3–4, Fall and Winter, 1968.

Wooten, James. "George Wallace: The Island of his Exile," *Washington Post Magazine*, April 1, 1984.

Yellin, Emily. "A Changing South Revisits Its Unsolved Racial Killings." *New York Times*, November 8, 1999.

Unpublished Printed Sources

Ward, Gladys. "The Life of Ryland Randolph." Master's thesis, University of Alabama, 1932.

Tornow, Joan Clark. "Covering Birmingham for the *Southern Courier*." Essay read at the reunion of the *Southern Courier* staff in Montgomery, 2006.

Transcript of the *Southern Courier* reunion. Auburn University, Alabama, April 1, 2006.

Trial transcript: *State of Alabama v Robert Chambliss*.

Hearings before the Committee on Un-American Activities, House of Representatives, Eighty-Ninth Congress, Second Session, January 4–7, 11–14, and 28, 1966; Parts 1, 2, and 3.

Television and Film

4 Little Girls. Directed by Spike Lee. 40 Acres and a Mule Filmworks, June 25, 1997.

Cold Case Files, Episode 34. The History Channel, December 23, 2004.

Eyes on the Prize: America's Civil Rights Years. PBS Home Video, Blackside, 1986–87.

George Wallace: Settin' the Woods on Fire. Big House and Midnight Films Production for *The American Experience*, PBS/WBGH Boston, 2000.

The Lowndes County Freedom Organization, produced by the University of Alabama Center for Public Television and Radio.

Reunion of the *Southern Courier* staff. DVD. Auburn University, AL, April 1, 2006.

Online Resources

Encyclopedia of Alabama, Alabama Humanities Foundation and Auburn University, http://www.encyclopediaofalabama.org.

Lights, Camera, Alabama Presents: The Rebirth of the Klan. University of Alabama Make-A-Movie. http://video.google.com/videoplay?docid=6340152737523525980#

U.S. Supreme Court Ruling, *Lee v Washington*. March 11, 1968. http://supreme_justia.com/390/333/case.html

"Advocates for Justice and Equality," "Morris Dees: Center founder and chief trial counsel," "Joseph J. Levin Jr.: Center founder and president emeritus," "Julian Bond: First Center president and member of the board," http://www.splcenter.org.

INDEX